Environmental Policy in Europe

Environmental Policy in Europe

Industry, Competition and the Policy Process

Edited by
François Lévêque
*Professor of Economics, CERNA,
Ecole Nationale Supérieure des Mines de Paris*

Edward Elgar
Cheltenham, UK • Brookfield, US

© François Lévêque, 1996

All rights reserved. No part of this publication may be reproduced, stored in a retrieval system, or transmitted in any form or by any means, electronic, mechanical, photocopying, recording, or otherwise without the prior permission of the publisher.

Published by
Edward Elgar Publishing Limited
8 Lansdown Place
Cheltenham
Glos GL50 2HU
UK

Edward Elgar Publishing Company
Old Post Road
Brookfield
Vermont 05036
US

British Library Cataloguing in Publication Data
Environmental policy in Europe : industry, competition and
   the policy process
   1. Environmental policy – Europe 2. Environmental protection
   – Europe
   I. Lévêque, François
   363.7'07'094

Library of Congress Cataloguing in Publication Data
Environmental policy in Europe : industry, competition, and the policy
   process / edited by François Lévêque.
      Includes index.
      1. Environmental policy—European Union countries. 2. Industrial
   policy—European Union countries. I. Lévêque, François.
   HC240.9.E5E624   1996
   363.7'0094—dc20   96–600
                                                                    CIP

ISBN 185898 466 1

Printed and bound in Great Britain by
Biddles Ltd, Guildford and King's Lynn

Contents

List of figures		vii
List of tables		ix
Foreword		xi
A.I. Sors		
Acknowledgements		xiii

1. Introduction   1
   François Lévêque

2. The European fabric of environmental regulations   9
   François Lévêque

3. The regulatory game   31
   François Lévêque

4. From environment to competition — the EU regulatory process in pesticide registration   53
   Alain Nadaï

5. The energy sector response to European combustion emission regulations   75
   Antony Ikwue and Jim Skea

6. Playing on two chessboards — the European waste management industry: strategic behaviour in the market and in the policy debate   113
   Sebastiano Brusco, Paolo Bertossi and Alberto Cottica

7. Voluntary agreements between industry and government — the case of recycling regulations   143
   Thomas Whiston and Matthieu Glachant

8. Voluntary initiatives and public intervention — the regulation of eco-auditing   175
   Jürgen F. Franke and Frank Wätzold

9. Conclusion   201
   François Lévêque

Index   209

Figures

2.1	EU environmental legislation adopted each year	10
2.2	Article 130R §1 and §2 of the Treaty on Political Union	15
4.1	The life-cycle of a pesticide	56
4.2	The distribution of task-forces for the review process in 1994	67
4.3	The three periods of the EU pesticide regulatory process	69
4.4	The dynamic of the EU pesticide regulatory process	70
6.1	Choosing a compliance level	124
6.2	Relating to a fragmented market	128
6.3	Relating to planning units	129
6.4	Relating to a segmented market	129
6.5	Playing in the policy arenas	136
7.1	Simplified materials flowchart for vehicles industry	148
7.2	Current disposal process	149
7.3	Strategic options: variation of materials value added against degree of dismantling	150
7.4	Projections of shredder margins and costs	151
7.5	The packaging and packaging waste chain	163
7.6	General organization of the Duales System	168

Tables

1.1	List of studied regulatory process	6
3.1	The factors which determine a firm's involvement and their effects	42
4.1	Sales of the 12 leading agrochemical companies	55
4.2	Profile of a modern plant protection product	58
5.1	SO_2 emission reduction requirements for existing plant under the LCP directive	91
6.1	Overall recycling rate, 1990	120
6.2	Laws and regulations: administrative levels involved	122
7.1	Production of domestic waste in Germany and France	162
7.2	Prices of different secondary materials	164

Foreword

During the last few years, environmental policies at the global, regional, national and local levels have undergone profound changes. There are many reasons for this. First of all, there is a clear shift of concern away from local, acute pollution problems towards broad, long-term issues such as climate change, loss of biodiversity, depletion of freshwater resources, and so on; these issues are characterised by complexity and uncertainty. The basic assumptions which underlie environment policies are also changing; the application of the polluter pays principle, the internalisation of external costs of environmental damage and the principle of precaution are all of growing importance. At the same time, environmental protection is being seen not only as a necessity but as an opportunity. For example, the global market for environmental technologies is estimated to be worth more than 300 billion ECU per year and is continuing to expand rapidly.

The European Union (EU) is responding to these challenges through an ambitious and innovative approach to environmental policy, entitled 'Towards sustainability'. This Action Programme is focused on the integration of environmental consideration into economic and sectoral policies and on the broadening of the range of environmental instruments, in order to improve both the effectiveness and efficiency of environmental management. These are crucial objectives, especially in view of the need simultaneously to protect Europe's environment and to maximise the competitiveness of European industry in the face of new challenges.

Environment policy can only be effective and efficient if there is an adequate and proper interaction and dialogue between the 'regulators' and the 'regulated'. In order to improve these interactions it is important to develop a clear view and analysis of the process of environmental regulation in practice. This is the subject of this important book.

The European Union's Environment and Climate Research Programme contains work on a broad range of issues including global environmental change, environmental technologies, earth observation from space and sustainable development. The last of these involves interdisciplinary research on the societal and economic aspects of the environment with projects on environmental and ecological economics, social perception and behaviour, sustainable development in the context of technological change and integrated environmental assessment.

This book arises out of a project which was implemented within the framework of the above Programme, in the research area focused on sustainable development. The project was co-ordinated by François Lévêque of CERNA (Centre of Industrial Economics at the Ecole Nationale Supérieure des Mines de Paris). This is a comprehensive piece of work including comparative studies covering four European countries and a number of important industrial sectors from agro-chemicals to packaging waste and taking into account eco-audit regulations. The book contains articles by a number of the project participants as well as synthetic chapters. It is an example of high quality research in a policy relevant sector. The Directorate-General for Science, Research and Development is very pleased to be associated with this work.

A.I. Sors
Head of Unit
Research on economic and social
aspects of the Environment
Directorate-Generale for Science,
Research and Development
European Commission
Brussels

Acknowledgements

The research support of the Directorate-General for Science, Research and Development and the Ecole Nationale Supérieure des Mines de Paris, was indispensable, and it is gratefully acknowledged.

The editor wishes especially to thank Scott Barrett, Landis Gabel and Pierre-Noël Giraud for their scientific advice, William Watts for his administrative support, Véronique Dubarry for her technical assistance, and Godefroy de Commarque for his hospitality.

1. Introduction

François Lévêque[1]

Customarily, the economic analysis of environmental policy is centred on its effects. The intervention of economists consists in studying and modelling the impact of environmental regulations on technological change, economic growth, international trade, competitiveness of firms, employment, and so forth. Their normative implications are primarily focused on the choice of policy instruments. Most of them call for the development of economic instruments such as taxes and tradeable permits.

The focus of this book is very different. It deals with the genesis of new environmental regulations. Environmental policy is not considered as a given and exogenous parameter to which economic agents respond. It is viewed as the outcome of a process — the regulatory process — involving several concerned parties, in particular industrial interest groups.

This shift of focus is motivated by both empiric and theoretic considerations.

Environmental policies do not come out of the blue. Environmental policies are preceded by a phase of consultation and negotiation between interested parties and public authorities. The European Commission in its programme of policy and action in relation to the environment places a great emphasis on the involvement of interested parties and the creating of a new interplay between the main groups of actors (government, enterprise, public). It intends to secure as much support as possible for a measure before making a formal proposal. As elsewhere, EU countries endorse the use of stakeholder consultation in the development of new environmental policy. Coordination among government departments, dialogue with business, and public consultation are the rule. The building of close relations between all the interested parties is viewed as essential for the successful implementation of environmental policies.

Institutions and regulatory methods are changing. The Act of Political Union signed in 1992 in Maastricht has marked an important change in environmental rule-making within the European Union. Qualified majority between Member States, instead of unanimity as before, is introduced for most environmental measures. The role of the European Parliament is enhanced. The principle of subsidiarity is adopted. Moreover, like in other OECD countries, a trend in the use of new policy instruments is noticeable in the European Union. Currently, the emphasis is put on economic incentives rather than on the traditional regulatory instruments such as command-and-control. Environmental taxation is progressing in several Member States and the use of voluntary agreements between government and industry is growing. Similar to the regulation of public utilities in the energy, telecommunication, or transportation sector, a regulatory reform is taking place in regulating pollution.

Firms are de facto involved in the regulatory process. A firm's participation is the result of encouragement from policy makers or pro-active strategy. Pride of place is given to consultation with industry. Most of the information concerning the amount of pollution, abatement costs and technology is only known by firms. As a consequence, the regulator cannot fix the pollution reduction objective (for example, a threshold for an emission standard) before collecting data from industry. Moreover, it is commonly observed that companies undertake intense lobbying activities before any proposals are drafted by government. The civil servants of DG-XI, the General Directorate of the European Commission in charge of the environment, are under daily pressure from industrial lobbies. The rule of thumb is that industrialists must intervene early in the European policy process. Once a directive is published, it is too late for firms to defend their interests. Like Washington, Brussels has become a prime forum in the world for industrial lobbyists and lobbying consultancy firms.

Adopted regulations do not look like those prescribed in textbooks. Environmental policies significantly differ from the recommended solutions made by scholarships. A good example is provided by the eco-tax project proposed by the Commission. The final version of the proposal is a strange animal. The tax is aimed at reducing carbon dioxide emission, but it applies also to energy in general (e.g., electricity generated by nuclear power). It contains several exemptions, in particular for the largest emitters. In general, the main function of adopted 'green taxes' is to raise revenues for implementing policy measures elsewhere instead of stimulating polluters to change their behaviour towards the environment. Charge or fee levels are generally too low to provide incentives for economic agents. One also observes that the use of voluntary agreements and the mixture of different instruments is largely made by policy-makers whereas the environment economics literature is quasi mute on this topic.

Regulatory failures also exist. How to regulate pollution is not only a matter of valuating externalities and selecting a policy instrument. Environmental economics has made sound progress on these aspects, especially over the past few years on the techniques related to the valuation of environmental goods. However, the discipline has not integrated the new building blocks provided by other branches of micro-economics, in particular the economics of regulation. Environmental economics is very marked with Pigou's concept of externality. Externality is a major cause of market failure. This leads most of environmental economists to call for public intervention: a regulation is required to remedy the misallocation of resource. But, as argued by the economics of regulation, the market failure is a necessary but not a sufficient condition to regulate. Like the market, the regulator may also fail in allocating resources. The regulator may be self-interested. He may pursue his own specific objectives such as power and office rather than benevolent objectives. The regulator may lack information. The access to, and the interpretation of, information is critical to devise an efficient regulation. It is rarely independent of the regulated. In consequence, its provision provides opportunities for industry interest groups to manipulate it to gain favourable outcomes. Another source of regulatory failure is the lack of power of the regulator to precommit to future policy. The temptation exists for the regulator to behave opportunistically after the regulation is adopted. For instance, he may tighten the emission standard or increase an eco-tax just a few years after the new policy is passed. Public intervention to remedy externalities is only worthwhile when market failures exceed regulatory failures.

Market structure does matter. The regulation of pollution is primarily oriented to industry since the latter is the largest contributor to pollution as a user of environmental resources, or as an emitter of polluting gases and waste. In the literature of environmental economics, the commonly considered market structure is the model of pure and perfect competition. The introduction of a new environmental regulation cannot increase competitive advantages or competitive losses for firms. Such a restrictive hypothesis is obviously not helpful in explaining the fierce inter-firm competition within the regulatory arena which is observed in the real world. But above all, the hypothesis prevents sideways vision on two major theoretical concerns. The first relates to the access of the regulator to the information. Whether the regulator is confronted with a monopoly of information for the industry, is reduced to one firm, or may use rivalry between firms to collect information, is critical. The second concern deals with the nexus between competition and environmental regulations. Environmental policies may change the market structure of an industry; in particular, they may introduce distortions of competition at the detriment of firms whose interests are not represented within the devising process of regulation or whose bargaining power is weak.

The goal of the book is to enlarge the traditional perspective of environmental economics on public policy. It integrates the recent advances of both economics of regulation and industrial economics.

1. ISSUES

The focus of the book on the genesis of environmental policy responds to positive and normative issues.

The positive perspective is to explain the development of the regulatory process and its outcome. The addressed question is 'how is new environmental legislation formed and what is the influence of industry?'. The purpose is not to reflect on what environmental regulations should be but to examine what forces and factors make regulations what they are. Several issues are examined in depth such as: How do firms compete in the regulatory arena? How do they organize their lobbying activity and interest grouping? Which firms obstruct the process and which support it, and why? What are the main changes between the initial and final contents of regulatory proposals? How do these changes relate to the influence of industry interest groups? Is there a collusion between public authorities and interest groups? What are the channels and tactics of regulators to gain access to the information? What is the divergence of interests between the various public authorities involved in the regulatory process? Are environmental regulations used as a source of competitive advantage for firms and countries?

The normative perspective which motivates the study of the genesis of regulations is rooted in the question of public policy effectiveness. The modern debate in public policy is not about *laissez-faire versus* public planning. Given that both markets and regulators fail, and given the prevalence of environmental externalities a degree of pragmatism is required. The major concern is how to regulate — how to intervene to minimize costs — rather than whether to intervene at all. One response provided by environmental economics, deals with the choice of instruments. Techniques for valuating environmental goods, like the contingent analysis, and incentive instruments to abate pollution are quite useful to the policy maker. Another aspect, as critical as the choice of instruments, concerns the regulatory institutions. The procedures to design regulations (for instance, according to whether they facilitate the access of the regulator to information, whether they encourage the presence of all interested parties, and so on) may limit the potential for regulatory failures. In short, the effectiveness of public policy is not only a matter of instrument; it depends also on the regulatory process.

The purpose of this book is descriptive and positive rather than normative. The analysis is focused on the actual behaviour of firms and public authorities and not on the designing of optimal institutional schemes. However, the analysis attempts to cast light on two normative issues. The first relates to a firm's involvement within the regulation devising process. As pointed out throughout the book, the policy that is finally adopted prescribes less stringent abatement objectives than those indicated in the initial regulatory project; and industry lobbying plays an important role in this decrease. Does a firm's involvement distort public interest? Are environmental regulations captured by industry? The second issue concerns the nexus between environmental and competition policies. The book documents that the strategic use of the regulatory process by firms is a pervasive phenomenon. They attempt to counter balance their loss due to abatement costs with a gain on their competitors. Does the environmental policy result in restrictions of competition?

2. METHODOLOGY

The case of the European Union provides a rich variety of regulatory levels and contexts. One encounters local, national and community processes and different institutional features depending on the Member States. The European Union has operated an explicit environmental policy since 1973, when it developed the first of its Action Programmes following the 1972 Stockholm Conference on the Human Environment. The European Union is a very appropriate case to study the connection between the different levels of government and the application of the subsidiarity principle. Member states differ in several aspects such as industrial organization, legal system, green groups pressure and enforcement effectiveness. These aspects induce strong variations related to national regulatory processes and vested interests. The Brussels arena offers a relevant point of observation to scrutinize the economic rivalry between Member States associated with the setting of environmental policy. Rivalry and regulatory differences between Member States are studied throughout the book through the analysis of four European countries: France, Germany, Italy, and the United Kingdom.

As case studies, eleven environmental pieces of EU legislation have been traced and are reported in the book (cf. Table 1.1). They are mostly directives. Directives are the main legal instrument of EU policy. Directives are proposed by the European Commission and have to be approved by the Council of Ministers. They are binding as to the result to be achieved, but leave the method of implementation to individual Member States. The range of case studies covers a wide spectrum of policy instruments, industries and environmental concerns. It deals with the major environmental policies which have taken place in the European Union over the past five years. A new environmental directive belongs to a train of legislative measures. It is a new piece of legislation which takes place in a more general framework and story — a *regulatory cycle*. It has been preceded by other regulations on the same concern or it marks the beginning of a new train of regulations. The regulatory cycle of each directive is detailed and explained. A new directive also has its own story from the moment the initial version is drafted to the moment it is adopted — the *regulation devising process*. The contents of the initial and final versions of the examined directives are described in terms of: principle (polluter pays principle, liability rules); environmental and non-environmental objectives (e.g., employment creation); conditions of compliance and enforcement; and policy instruments. This description is aimed at documenting the changes of the proposal and how the changes relate to the actions of concerned parties.

On the whole, two concerned parties are scrutinized in the book: firms and public authorities. Firms are described according to their competitive position in the market and their interest grouping, and public authorities according to their geographical field of competence (European, national, local) and their sectoral competencies (environment, trade, energy, etc.).

The economic analysis of the regulatory process is carried out in reference to strategic game. A small number of participants are involved. No more than a dozen public authorities and industry interest groups can be circumscribed as exerting a key influence. These players are mutually interdependent. The payoff of each participant depends upon the action of the others. Each participant is aware and takes into consideration the interests and reactions of the others. He elaborates and makes his decision according to his anticipation and expectations of the others.

Table 1.1   List of studied regulatory process

Regulatory process	Final draft or adopted legislation
Registration of pesticides	European Directives 91/414 and 94/43
Eco-tax	Commission Proposal COM (92) 226
NO_x and SO_2 emissions controls	Air quality Directives (80/779 and 85/203) Large Combustion Plant Directive (88/609)
Packaging waste	Directive 94/62
End of life motor-vehicles	Proposal of ELV End-of Life Vehicle strategy, Feb. 1994
Municipal waste facilities	Directive 89/369 and 89/429
Eco-management and audit scheme	Council Regulation 93/1836

3.   PLAN OF THE BOOK

Apart from the introduction and the conclusion, the book is divided into seven chapters. Each may be read separately depending on the specific interest of the reader. The book is, however, structured according to a general progression.

The first two chapters are introductory. Chapter 2 is centred on the hows: How does the regulatory game work in European Union? How are interest groups, in particular from industry, involved in, and how do they influence, the regulatory process? This chapter includes a presentation of the institutions and the legal framework. It also includes a synthesis of the main patterns observed through the case studies. Chapter 3 presents the analytical framework which is used in this economic analysis of the environmental regulatory process. It briefly surveys theories in economics of regulation and presents a stylization of a firm's involvement in the regulation devising process and of different modes of regulation.

The following five chapters are case study chapters. Chapter 4 deals with the registration of pesticides. It is a very relevant case study to start with for it is a good *condensé* of the evolution of the EU environmental fabric. The regulatory process started during the mid-seventies with the first steps of the Community in the field of the environment. Moreover, it is a simple case of conflict between two industry interest groups. Chapter 5 is dedicated to environmental policy in the energy sector where firms are equipped with a formidable lobbying machine. It focuses on the control of SO_2 and NO_x emissions and on the project of Carbon/Energy taxation. It soundly documents the bargaining and conflicts between public authorities, in particular between the Directorates General of the Commission. Chapter 6 deals with waste disposal regulations. They create winners: waste management firms whose demand is boosted by environmental regulation and whose local monopoly power is enhanced. However, the gain mainly benefits large firms which possess an advantage over small and medium-sized enterprises in both the market and regulatory arenas. Chapter 7 concerns the very innovative environmental policy related to specific waste regulations. The genesis of European directives in car recycling and packaging waste is studied in depth. It shows how industry has been very active in the regulation devising phase, in particular in the choice of the measures to achieve the policy set objectives of recycling. Chapter 8 also analyses an innovative instrument, the environmental management and audit scheme. Interestingly, it appears as an alternative to self-regulation arrangements undertaken by industry and for industry which suffer in the lack of credibility in the eye of public opinion.

The conclusion ends the book with a discussion of the two normative issues mentioned above: does a firm's involvement in the regulatory process distort the environmental policy and does environmental policy result in restrictions of competition?

4. TERMINOLOGY NOTE

The terms regulation and environmental regulations have different meanings depending on the chosen border. In Europe, regulation is often associated with a broad meaning. It covers the whole realm of legislation and public intervention. By contrast, in the United States of America regulation has a more specific meaning. It concerns the control exercised by public agencies like the Environmental Protection Agency or the Federal Communications Commission over certain social activities and public utilities. In environmental economics, regulation has a more specific meaning. It defines a particular kind of policy instrument like emission standards which specify allowable input or output quantities of pollution. This category of instrument, named also command-and-control or regulatory approach, is opposed to market-based instruments like tax or tradeable permits. Throughout the book the term regulation is used with a broad meaning and consequently the terms environmental regulation and environmental policy are indifferently used.

The term regulatory process designates the dynamic game defined by the set of players in the regulatory arena, their preferences and strategies and the set of rules and their evolution. Its outcome determines what regulations are and their changes. It does not refer to a particular phase of the regulation dynamics. On the contrary, the terms regulation devising process and regulatory cycle refer to a particular period: the phase of negotiation between stakeholders between the first draft of a regulatory proposal and the enactment of the proposal that is finally adopted, the long period of movement which characterizes specific waves of regulation (or deregulation) associated with historical patterns of regulatory institutions and modes of action, respectively.

NOTES

1. François Lévêque, Professor of economics, Deputy Director of CERNA, Centre of Industrial Economics, Ecole Nationale Supérieure des Mines de Paris, 60, bld St Michel, 75272 Paris Cedex 06, France, tel: 33140519091/9071; fax: 33144071046.

2. The European fabric of environmental regulations

François Lévêque[1]

This chapter is aimed at introducing the main features of the European fabric of environmental policy. How are environmental policy fabricated in the European Union? How are interest groups, in particular from industry, involved in, and how do they influence, the devising process of regulation? How does the regulatory game work in the environment?

It is divided into two parts. The first presents the institutional features of the European environmental policy and briefly traces its history. It is argued that a new regime is taking place in the regulation of the environment. The second part surveys the patterns and discusses the regularities as they appear in the genesis of recent environmental directives. This part provides a synthesis of the case studies which are detailed in the following five chapters.

1. A NEW REGULATORY REGIME

In the European Union, the regulation of the environment is growing tremendously (cf. Figure 2.1). At first glance, it contrasts with the regulating of the utilities where deregulation is taking place. But those familiar with privatization and liberalization know that deregulation is a regulatory reform, or a re-regulation, rather than the withdrawal of regulation. We will see that the current trend in environmental regulation is not only a growth in the legislation; it also relates to a new approach in regulating pollution.

As an introduction, it is worth briefly reminding the reader of the three main European legal instruments. The *directives* are the most used instruments in the field of the environment. They are proposed by the Commission and approved by the Council of Ministers. Directives are binding as to the result to be achieved, but leave the method of implementation to individual Member States. They must be transposed to the national legislation. As an indirect act of legislation, they contribute to the two-tier legal system which characterizes the European Union. On the contrary the *regulatory act* must be directly implemented by Member

States. It has been used for instance in regulating environmental management and eco-audit (regulatory act 93/1836) and traffic of waste (regulatory act 93/259). Finally, there is the *recommendation* which can be proposed by the Commission or the Council. It is the weakest form of policy instrument for it is a non-binding decision. It has been used, for instance, to promote paper recycling (recommendation 81/972).

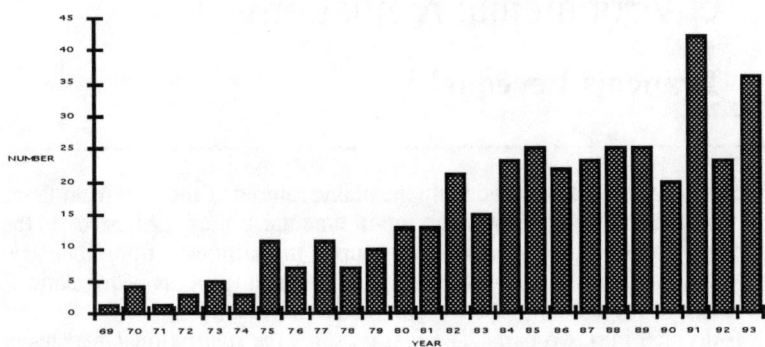

Source: I.E.E.P., 1994

Figure 2.1   EU environmental legislation adopted each year

1.1   The ante-Maastricht European fabric

The Act of Political Union signed in 1992 marks a new era in the building of Europe. It also entails a very important step in regulating the environment. Qualified majority between Member States was introduced for most environmental measures and the principle of subsidiarity was enacted. The same year, a new *Programme of Action,* the fifth, was adopted. It signalled a largely more environmental ambition and a breach with the past in terms of both policy articulation and modes of action.

The European Union has operated an explicit environmental policy since 1973, when it developed the first of its action programmes following the 1972 Stockholm Conference on the Human Environment. The initial programme lasted four years (1973—1976) and was followed by three progressively more ambitious and effective ones.

The first two programmes took place in the absence of a specific reference to environmental matters in the 1957 Treaty of Rome. The legal foundation of European environmental policy dates only from the Single European Act (1986). The lack of specific legislation was overcome by using two provisions of the Treaty: article 100 related to the Common market and the catch-all article 235. Article 100 permits actions that 'directly affect the establishment or functioning of the common market'. Article 235 applies if 'action by the Community should prove necessary ... and this treaty has not provided the necessary powers'.

For instance, the directive 85/339 aimed at promoting the re-using and recycling of beverage packaging was based on article 235. No mention of harmonization between national legislation in reference to the internal market was made. On the contrary, improving the functioning of the internal market has been indicated by the Commission as the single rationale to regulate at the European level the registration of pesticides. In some cases, both articles might be referred to. The first directive dealing with waste (directive 75/442) was founded by the Council of Ministers by arguing that, on the one hand, the diversity in Member States' legislation might rise to unfair competitive advantage, and that, on the other hand, European waste regulation contributes to the protection of the environment and human health — an essential objective of the Community despite the lack of necessary powers provided by the founding fathers of Europe.

The Single Act establishes environmental protection as an explicit action of the Community and provides the necessary powers to implement it in article 130. Emphasis is put on the priority of prevention and source reduction, on the polluter-pays principle, and on integration of environmental concerns into other Community policies. Co-decision with the European Parliament has been introduced, and the use of qualified majority vote has been extended to several policy areas, including that of article 100. When decisions on internal market are concerned, the Council of Ministers must work in co-operation with the Parliament instead of simply consult it, and the unanimity requirement of Member States is no longer obligatory. These new rules do not apply for regulating the environment with article 130. Besides, article 100 is more restrictive than article 130 on the possibility for a member state to adopt a higher environmental standard.

The difference in procedures between articles 100 and 130 raised several conflicts between European institutions. The choice of the legal basis to regulate when there is both an environmental and internal market dimension became subject to strategic use (Hannequart, 1993). The case of the second directive (91/156) related to waste provides a sound illustration. Directive 91/156 modifies and deepens directive 75/442. The proposal was set by the Commission as based on article 100. It was expected to be supported by the Parliament which tends towards a green position due to the success of Green parties in the 1989 election. The Parliament agreed on the choice of this legal basis, whereas the Council opposed it. Finally, the Council adopted the directive by arguing on article 130, and it was later approved by the European Court of Justice. As a rule, one observes that Commission proposals emphasize the argument of free trade whereas the final decisions of the Council retain the environmental argument as the primary one. One third of waste directive proposals from the Commission were legally based on article 130 and two thirds on article 100. When one looks at the decisions of the Council, the proportions are inversed: two thirds of the final directives were based on article 130.

From the first action programme to the signature of the Maastricht Treaty, the European fabric of environmental policy is characterized with three major features.

Firstly, environmental policy was intertwined with the European economic policy. The then adopted environmental regulations were conceived as a contribution to building the single market as well as a contribution to protecting the environment. The economic consideration to remove trade barriers and harmonize legislation must not be viewed as simply a disguise to pass environmental policies at the Brussels level and to strengthen the power of the Commission in a new area. Although, tactical and bureau considerations were not absent. For instance, when the proposal was made in 1975 to regulate waste, the waste concern was very local. It did not raise economic distortion between individual Member States, nor sensitive trans-boundary externalities (the public outcry related to the Seveso dioxin release occured in 1976). To refer to article 100, the Commission was obliged to argue that the local dimension would no longer be the 'relevant one in the future for waste technology would push forward a consolidation and an internationalization of the industrial activities' (COM (74)1297).

Secondly, the ante-Maastricht European fabric specialized in producing technical standards. It concerned both product standards with the economic purpose of removing barriers to trade and process standards on the grounds that differing standards across the Community give rise to unfair competitive advantage. At the beginning, the harmonization of product standards was welcomed and even supported by large international enterprises, such as oil or chemical companies. The existence of different requirements in Member States was viewed by business as generating significant additional costs. At the beginning of the seventies, the oil industry complained about the difficulties caused by national differences in oil product specifications. Moreover, some Member States, in particular Germany, were planning additional legislation. This led the Commission to take swift action. A directive on the sulfur content of gas oil was agreed in 1975 (directive 75/716). Although primarily a trade measure, it was acknowledged to have important environmental benefits. The subsequent revision of the gas oil directive in 1987 (directive 87/219) was not so popular with industry. The tightening of sulfur limits was strong and had more to do with environmental concerns. In relation to the acid rain concern, the Commission set a proposal in 1983 aimed at regulating combustion plants rated at greater than 50 MWt. It established limits for SO_2, NO_x and dust from new power stations, refineries and larger industrial sources and established national quotas for emissions from existing plants. The reduction targets are 60 per cent for SO_2, 40 per cent each for NO_x and dust by 1995. It took five years to find a compromise between Member States on this proposal. The Large Combustion Plant directive (directive

88/609) was adopted in 1988. To briefly illustrate the emphasis on the use of technical standards over the considered period, we referred above to the regulating of atmospheric emissions. We could have had similarly developed the case of waste policy. Several standards related to landfilling and incinerating were set during the period (cf. Chapter 5).

Thirdly, Member States *mènent la danse*. During this period the European policy in the field of the environment followed national legislative initiatives rather than taking the lead in legislating first, or proposing regulatory innovations. The European ante-Maastricht fabric of environmental policy was marked with the unanimity requirement.[2] This requirement means that environmental regulations faced a very high political hurdle and had to be broadly acceptable to Member States. The Large Combustion Plant directive mentioned above is a sound example. When the proposal was released in 1983, it was highly criticized by some Member States, in particular the United Kingdom. Negotiations were characterized by strong support for the proposal from Germany, the Netherlands and Denmark and opposition from the UK, Ireland, Italy and later Spain and Portugal. UK, the largest SO_2 emitter, led opposition to the proposal. Early negotiations were fruitless. It was not until the initiative in negotiations passed from the Commission to the Member States holding the Council Presidency (from 1986) that significant progress was made. Successive Dutch, Belgian and German Presidencies introduced the elements that eventually led to agreement in 1988. Major concessions included: reducing the reduction targets for some countries; modifying the emission limits proposed for new plants and existing plants; and extending the deadline of compliance to 2003. Considerable pressure was exerted on the UK to accept these revisions. Conscious of the need to remove uncertainty about clean-up costs prior to the privatization of the British electricity industry, the UK fell in line and the directive was agreed at the Environment Council in June 1988.

Another way for individual countries to block or delay the European policy consisted in postponing the implementation of the directive in the national legislation. For instance, Italy approved its main waste disposal law in accordance to the waste directive (75/442) seven years after the publication of the directive. To remain in the waste area, another example is noteworthy. The already mentioned directive 85/339 required the Member States to set programmes aimed at re-using and recycling beverage packaging. These programmes were due to be implemented before January 1987 and to be periodically reviewed and updated every four years. Only a few Member States proposed a programme before the deadline, and three years later 5 countries had not have submitted any programme.

1.2 The post-Maastricht European fabric

Following the Single European Act by only six years, the Treaty on Political Union has pursued the trend in moving power away from Member

States, as represented by the Council of Ministers, towards the Community's own institutions, in particular the European parliament. However, to counter-balance their greater power, the Treaty of Maastricht specifically invokes the principle of subsidiarity. As stated in article 3b, the Community will take action 'only if and insofar as the objectives of the proposed action cannot be sufficiently achieved by the Member States and can therefore, by reason of the scale or effects of proposed action, be better achieved by the Community'. The subsidiarity principle applies for most policy areas, including the environment.

The Maastricht Treaty extends the co-decision procedures, previously reserved for measures relating to the internal market, and the qualified majority vote to environmental concerns. There are three major exceptions mentioned in article 130, however:

- provisions primarily of a fiscal nature;
- measures concerning town and country planning, land use and management of water resources;
- measures significantly affecting a member state's choice between different energy sources and the general structure of its general supply.

These exceptions relate to areas where several Member States jealously guard their sovereignty and the application of the subsidiarity principle is particularly pertinent. Measures falling into any of these categories continue to require unanimous agreement in the Council of Ministers and although the Council must consult the European Parliament over these exceptional matters, it need not act in co-operation with it. It is interesting to note that the proposed carbon/energy tax (cf. Chapter 4) impinges on two policy domains — taxation and energy — that have been of particular sensitivity in the debate on the respective roles of the Community and its Member States.

The Maastricht Treaty gives a large place to the environment which is explicitly mentioned in the *princeps* articles. The promotion of sustainable growth respecting the environment is introduced in article 2 as a mission of the Community. The policy in the sphere of the environment is included in the list of activities of the Community (article 3). The new article 130 (see Figure 2.2) differs from the previous version in the Single European Act by advancing a more ambitious environmental policy. A high level of protection is explicitly mentioned and the scope of the policy is enlarged to international concerns. One may also notice that the term of action has been substituted with the term of policy in the new article 130.

The Fifth Programme of Action and Policy in relation to the environment (1993—2000) entitled 'Towards Sustainability' is largely more ambitious than the previous ones. It explicitly refers to the notion of sustainable development. It stresses that the actions over the past twenty years have been insufficient to stop environmental degradation and calls for a reversion of the trend. The programme contains the definition of a new regulatory approach. It is observed that past environmental action has largely been based on top-down approach and the use of command-and-control instruments exercised by government over manufacturing industry. In future, the Commission intends to secure as much as possible for a measure before making a formal proposal. The programme places a greater emphasis on involvement and creating 'a new interplay between the main groups of actors (government, enterprise, public) and the principal economic sector (industry, energy, transportation and tourism)'. There is a recommendation to use a wider range of instruments, notably market incentives and voluntary approaches.

---

§1. Community policy on the environment shall contribute to pursuit of the following objectives:

- preserving, protecting and improving the quality of the environment;
- protecting human health;
- prudent and rational utilization of natural resources;
- promoting measures at international level to deal with regional or worldwide environmental problems.

§2. Community policy on the environment shall aim at a high level of protection taking into account the diversity of situations in the various regions of the Community. It shall be based on the precautionary principle and on the principles that preventive action should be taken, that environmental damage should as a priority be rectified at source and that the polluter should pay. Environmental protection requirements must be integrated into the definition and implementation of other Community policies.

Figure 2.2   Article 130 R §1 and §2 of the Treaty on Political Union

Further elaboration of what a move towards sustainable development in the EU would entail was contained in the Commission's White Paper 'Growth, Competitiveness and Employment' published in December 1993. The Commission argues that the twin challenges currently facing the Community of environmental pollution and high unemployment are the result of a fundamental inefficiency in the economic system in which there is an over-use of natural resources combined with an under-use of the quality and the quantity of the labour force. A new economic development model is required in which *inter alia* the burden of taxation is shifted from employment towards resource use in order to secure both jobs and environmental protection.

1.3 A new regulatory regime

The European fabric of environmental policy has changed between the end of the eighties and the beginning of the nineties in two ways. The first is specific to the European Union. It is linked with the reform of the Community institutions and rule-making. The second corresponds with a new way of regulating the environment. Interestingly, the latter is common to all industrialized countries.

The Treaty on European Union has vigorously enhanced the involvement of Community in the field of the environment and has modified environmental rule-making. Undoubtedly, this would entail consequences on the nature of future environmental directives. However, as is always true when a new era is beginning, the consequences are difficult to assess (Skea, 1995). One expected outcome is that regulations will be passed more quickly. The move to the qualified majority vote should make it harder for a minority of countries to form an effective blocking coalition that leads to environmental measures being abandoned or delayed *sine die*. On the other hand, it is possible that the complexity of the post-Maastricht co-operation procedures could act as a brake on the adoption of environmental measures. Once the Commission has presented a formal proposal to Parliament and the Council of Ministers, the number of potential obstacles to agreement rises considerably under the new procedure. Problems can arise in the Council itself, in Parliament and its committees, and through differences of views between Council and parliament. The issue whether the new rule-making would lead to 'greener' EU policy is also debatable. Parliament tends towards ambitious environmental objectives, partly because of the weight of green parties, partly because environmental issues have proved a useful lever for enhancing the status of weak institution. It is likely to take advantage of its new role to continue its promotion of environmental issues. On the other hand, the Parliament is attracting the attention of more ambitious politicians and a wider range of interest groups, including business associations.

The environmental directives and regulatory acts examined in this book started to be discussed as proposals before the Maastricht Treaty. They have one foot in the old policy articulation where the game was mainly played between the Council and the Commission. It is too early yet to assess the general effect of the Maastricht procedures on environmental policy.

Besides the change in institutions, a change in regulatory methods and modes of action is noticeable in regulating the environment. It concerns the target, the instrument, and the devising phase of environmental regulations. The classical target that regulation addressed during the previous regime was that of local externalities, causing obvious adverse effects on human beings and the environment, between clearly identified polluters and pollutees in a small number. The stereotypic case is the regulating of sulfur emissions caused by large industrial sites which affect human health of the surrounding population. Chimneys are installed and pollution is dispersed.

Environmental policy mandates certain add-on technologies ('end-of-pipe') and bans others. Today, the stereotypic case is the green house effect: a global concern whose long term consequences have not been ascertained, whose interested parties are numerous and disseminated all around the planet; attempts have been made to solve it using market incentives. More accurately, the current context is illustrated by two typical cases — the macro one referred to above, and the micro one where regulations specific to products such as button-batteries or beverage glass packaging are set to promote systems of collecting and recycling schemes. The target moves away from correcting to preventing environmental damages. Conduct regulations tend to prevail on structure regulation and economic incentives tend to replace classical emission standards.

Conduct regulation refers to measures concerned with how firms behave in their activities while structure regulation refers to measures concerned with the determination of which firms are allowed to engage. As pointed out by Kay and Vickers (1990), the former aims to create a situation in which the incentives or opportunities for undesirable behaviour are removed, while the latter addresses not the undesirable underlying incentives, but the behaviour that they would otherwise induce. Structural regulations directly influence the environmental performances of polluters by regulating processes or products used, by mandating the use of specific environmental or pollution control technologies, by forbidding or limiting the discharge of certain pollutants, by restricting activities to certain areas, etc. Their main feature is that there is no other choice left to the polluter. Examples of conduct regulations are the economic instruments and voluntary agreements. Economic instruments are measures that use market-based incentives to channel economic activity in environmentally desirable directions. They include tradable permits, fees, taxes, deposit — refund system, etc. They affect costs and benefits of alternative action open to firm with the effect of influencing decision-making. They leave actors free to respond to certain stimuli in a way they themselves think most beneficial. Voluntary approaches internalize environmental awareness and responsibility into decision-making by applying pressure or persuasion. They group self-regulation arrangements (e.g., green industrial charts) and covenants between government and business (e.g., voluntary agreements in relation to car and packaging recycling).

The change in the choice of policy instruments is a world-wide trend. Eco-taxes, tradable permits and voluntary approaches have been growing in number in industrialized countries since the beginning of the nineties. As far as the European Union is concerned, we pointed out above that the broadening of the set to policy instruments beyond command and control regulation is one of the key orientations of the new EU approach as defined in the fifth action programme 'Towards Sustainability'.

Another key orientation of the new EU approach is the dialogue and consultation with concerned parties. This change in the devising of environmental policy is also a general trend in the regulating of the environment. Nowadays, all countries endorse the use of stakeholder consultation in the development of new regulation in the field of the environment (Lévêque *et al.*, 1992). In most industrialized countries, green plans have been set with an impressive participation of concerned parties. In Australia, the so-called Ecologically Sustainable Plan prompted comments and suggestions from industry, unions, academics, conservation organizations, and State and Territory Governments. Collectively, some 400 recommendations were made. In the Netherlands, interested parties, in particular industrialists, were involved in the setting of the National Environmental Policy Plan. This Plan published in 1989 states very detailed objectives of pollution abatement according to economic sectors. Industry has been committed to achieving them in co-operation with public authorities.

It is clearly documented that a regulatory reform is taking place in regulating pollution, especially in Europe where this trend is accompanied by important institutional change. The current trend is not simply an increase in the number of environmental regulations. To this respect, as we announced in the introduction of this chapter, the regulation of pollution is not dissimilar to the regulation of utilities where, in addition to privatization, new regulatory methods are being implemented.

The environmental regulatory reform is rooted in the recognition of some limitations of the command and control regulation and of failures of implementation and enforcement. By its nature, command and control tends to focus on pollution from readily identifiable sources such as manufacturing industry or products, rather than on more diffuse sources or activities. It leads to the adoption of end of pipe rather than preventive approaches to pollution control. Furthermore, command and control regulation reflects a top-down approach. The lack of consultation with concerned parties increases the likelihood of implementation and enforcement failures. Failure to put the requirements of EU environmental directives into effect was a serious problem of the ante-Maastricht European fabric. At the beginning of the nineties the number of suspected infringements of environmental directives came second only to those relating to the internal market (IEEP, 1994). Many environmental directives include varying requirements that government must report regularly to the Commission on how they are implementing the legislation. However, these reports have often been compiled only infrequently, incompletely, or not at all.

The EU environmental regulatory reform is a recent, on-going process. Whether it would succeed in overcoming the limitations of the old regulatory regime and in implementing more efficient environmental regulations is an open question. A historical perspective to assess the result of the new approach is lacking. Environmental policies marked with the seal of regulatory reform, such as those related to packaging and car waste recycling, environmental management scheme and eco-auditing or CO_2 taxation are just entering the implementation phase or are blocked in the pipe-line (e.g., the eco-tax proposal). It is too early to make an assessment of their effectiveness. However, one may look at one of the dimension of the regulatory reform, namely the consultation with interested parties which has taken place during the devising processes related to the new environmental regulations. This is the purpose of the following section.

2. THE GENESIS OF EUROPEAN ENVIRONMENTAL POLICIES

This section surveys the general patterns which have been observed in studying the genesis of the environmental policies detailed in Chapters 4 to 8. It shows how environmental policy is devised and how the bargaining between the actors involved in the process influences its outcome, in particular by limiting the stringency of the initial proposal. It details the players of the game and those who are not represented, and the strategic use of the process by Member States and industry interest groups.

2.1 The players of the European regulatory game and those off the stage

It is sound to start with those who are off the stage or whose performance is limited to a small tirade. Because their voice is inaudible, their interest is less likely to be taken into account. Paradoxically, it is important to consider their absence, for the outcome of the process might be biased due to the ignorance of some vested interests.

Small and medium-sized enterprises (SMEs) clearly belong to this category. The weakness of SMEs in the European policy arena is documented by several case studies. As pointed out by in Chapter 6, small waste management firms did not participate in the discussion of technical standards regulating landfilling and incinerating (directives 89/369 and 89/429). Neither were they involved in the national policy arena, with the partial exception of Italy, where the association of municipality-owned firms has some visibility. Their influence on regulation is basically due to the fact they exist, and that if stringent environmental standards are approved and enforced, they are driven out of business. Three other clues amongst others picked up in case studies signal the imbalance between large and small firms. With regard to the end-of-cycle motor-vehicle regulation, the car manufacturers association is the leading industry interest group although the atomized industry of shredders is more concerned by the project in terms of impact on its business. Packaging producers were less intensively involved in the packaging waste regulation devising process than large food and detergent companies and retailers. Small pesticide producers entered the regulatory game related to the new registration system later than the large agro-chemical companies. One may also notice that Directorate General

XXIII — the Commission department in charge of SMEs — did not exert any influence on the drafting and amending of environmental proposals.

Unlike large firms, SMEs cannot appoint a regulatory affairs manager. Moreover, the cost of forming an interest group and strengthening the coalition is higher for a large number of small firms than for a few firms of an oligopoly (cf. Chapter 3). The distinction between large and small firms is relevant in this book to the extent that it entails the dichotomy between passive and active firms in respect to regulatory matters, that is to say between firms which are able to change their regulatory environment and those which cannot. SMEs are regulation-takers except at the local policy arena. They can influence major or municipality administration, in particular with respect to relaxing enforcement procedures (cf. Chapter 5).

Counter-intuitively, the green interest groups have been noted as not being a major player in the regulatory game. Their direct influence on the devising of regulations is rarely observed. This calls for some explanations. One may distinguish two steps in the genesis of environmental regulation. The first is the emergence of the idea that a public intervention is necessary and a regulation must be set. There is a growing awareness that a case of pollution has become a problem that must be solved. Green groups obviously play a strong role in raising pollution issues and pressurizing policy-makers to legislate. The second step, on which the book is focused, relates to the devising phase of environmental policies. In this phase green groups play a minor role. Environmentalists are a very heterogeneous party in terms of organizing, claims and behaviour. Most green groups are local. Only a small number are internationally organized. In comparison to firms, their lobbying activities in Brussels are considerably less developed. One must note, however, that greens have their representatives in the European Parliament. This would provide them with an indirect canal to influence the regulatory process.

In fact, it does not, for the European Parliament has not yet appeared as a key player. We have shown in the previous section, that the Maastrich Treaty extended the co-decision principle to environmental matters. But this change is too recent to be perceptible in the examined directives. Moreover, they are important exceptions: energy and taxation are exempted to the new principle.

As regards public authorities, the key players of the European regulatory game are the Commission and the Member States through the Council of Ministers. It is important to note that the Commission cannot be viewed as a single regulatory agency. The Commission is divided into Directorates General whose views and objectives may differ. Proposals of environmental directives are generally drafted by Directorate General XI which is in charge of the environment but are amended by other DGs. Proposals are the outcome of a compromise within the Commission. This is soundly documented by the case of the eco-tax project. The consensus on the regulatory project has been particularly difficult to reach and the wrestling matches between DGs have been intense. The carbon tax was initiated by

DG XI (Environment) which supported it as a unilateral measure whereas other DGs such as DG III (Industry) wanted it conditionally on other countries following suit. DG II (Economic and Financial Affairs) favoured a pure CO_2 tax whereas DG XVII (Energy) a pure energy tax. The latter also supported a tax levied at production whereas DG XXI (Customs and indirect Taxation) supported a tax levied on consumption.

The Council takes the final decision whether or not to adopt environmental regulations. As we mentioned before, qualified majority vote has been introduced only recently for environmental matters and most environmental directives have been passed under the principle of unanimity. As a rule, the achievement of a compromise on environmental proposals between Member States has been a conflictual and laborious decision.

A key aspect to underline is the interaction between the European and the national levels of the regulatory process. In the past, European environmental policies were primarily aimed at harmonizing different national legislation. The chain of influence was simple. The position of Member States in the Council was determined by the existing regulations in their countries and their economic interest in removing obstacles to internal market and obtaining a harmonized standard close to their own. Nowadays the chain of influence is more complex, for in most cases the formulation of new environmental regulations takes place simultaneously at the European and national levels; and each influences the other. By preparing in advance their own regulations, Member States may better position themselves at the European level and may pre-empt the future European legislation. Reciprocally, intention and first reflections on regulatory proposals within the Commission may trigger and speed up national regulation devising processes. The best example of this complex interaction between the European and national regulatory arenas is given in Chapter 7 by the regulation of end-of-life vehicles. The initial intention of Germany to set a stringent legislation with respect to car recycling stimulated the French government to reflect on its own scheme. The latter quickly agreed with French car manufacturers on a flexible and voluntary policy. In turn, the French voluntary agreement nurtured the setting of a European-wide legislation. Finally, the European directive, still in discussion, is likely to influence the German policy arena where the initial proposal has been blocked by the car manufacturers' obstruction.

As regards industry, the key players are large firms. The pre-eminence of large firms in the regulation devising process is observed at all levels. They make up most industry interest groups and active industry associations. This pre-eminence is especially impressive in the energy sector case study. Chapter 4 shows how energy producers are creative in setting up new interest organizations related to the environment and developing channels of influence to high executives from public authorities.

As a general pattern, a firm's influence on environmental policy takes the form of inter-firm co-operation. Coalitions of firms prevail. Lobbying from single firms appears as a complement rather than a substitute to interest grouping. The only case where an interest group is made up of only one firm is provided by monopolies. As EDF is the largest producer, not to say the single, of electricity in France, it is the only industry party involved in negotiating the French regulation devoted to emissions from energy facilities.

One also observes very large coalitions based on the networking of several industrial interest groups. This networking has been mainly observed in the regulatory processes dedicated to CO_2/carbon tax and waste recycling. Lobbying between industry associations and other forms of inter-industry co-operation has been a key feature of the business involvement in opposing the eco-tax project. Coal, gas, oil, and electricity industries coalesced to fight the European proposal and to develop very broad-based industry support for their campaign, in particular from energy users, gathered in cross industry groupings named IFIEC (Industrial Federation of Intensive Energy Consumers) and business associations such as UNICE (European Industrial and Employers' Federation), BDI (Federation of German Industry), CBI (Confederation of British Industry) or ICC (International Chamber of Commerce). The same phenomenon of large inter-industry alliances has been observed with regard to recycling regulations. In France and the UK, material suppliers, equipment producers, car manufacturers, the secondary materials and scrap industry quasi acted in a single interest group. Similarly, suppliers and users (material and packaging producers and conditioners in France, conditioners and retailers in Germany) organized a regulatory network to influence the process of devising the means of achieving packaging waste recovery (cf. Chapter 7).

It is important to notice that these inter-industry regulatory networks work under the leadership of a group of firms: oil companies in the case of carbon/energy tax, car manufacturers in the case of end-of-life-cycle motor vehicles, conditioners and retailers respectively in the French and German cases of packaging waste. As a consequence, the regulator is confronted with a dominant source of information instead of obtaining contrasted data from competing industry interest groups.

2.2 Rivalry between Member States

Environmental policy is a factor which may affect the competitiveness of existing industries and the location of decisions of firms. This makes room for strategic behaviour on the part of government to use environmental regulations to strengthen national competitiveness.

The question of whether international trade is influenced by environmental standards was largely studied by economists at the beginning of the nineties. The findings of their empirical as well as theoretical investigations are ambivalent. Whether a laxist environmental policy would result in higher growth in industrial activity, in particular in under-developed countries, or on the contrary whether a first mover advantage would be delivered to those countries which adopt a stringent environmental policy are unsolved questions.

As far as EU countries are concerned, it is clear that environmental policy is not purposely designed for gaining a competitive advantage. It is a simple but wrong view to think that, say, Germany is implementing a very ambitious environmental policy to primarily boost its green technology exportations, or Italy does not enforce environmental legislation with the perspective of enhancing the competitiveness of its industry and attract foreign investments. At the national level, policy processes are largely idiosyncratic. Member states differ in several aspects such as legal system, green groups power, government centralization, industrial organisation, geographic conditions and so forth, which influence their environmental objectives and actions. One encounters for instance the highest environmental targets in Germany and the weakest enforcement in Italy; an emphasis on command and control regulation and technological aspects in Germany whereas the United Kingdom is keen on economic incentives and self-regulation, etc.

However, the positions of Member States at the Council, during the negotiation of future EU environmental policy, conspicuously reflect their national economic interests.

The negotiation of the Large Combustion Plant directive (88/609) is a sound example. Germany pressurised the Commission to regulate SO_2/NO_x emissions. Germany was the first EU country to impose strict controls on these pollutants with the Federal Emission Control Ordinance of 1983. The enlargement of such measures to other countries would alleviate the extra cost of abatement that the German industry alone had to bear. France and Belgium with large nuclear programmes were largely indifferent to the proposal, whereas the UK, the most polluting emitter due to the sources of its power generation, opposed it. Another example is given by the directive proposal on landfilling. The proposal was opposed by UK because it forbids co-disposal. Co-disposal is the joint disposal of municipal and hazardous waste in the same site. This technique is only used in the UK, and British firms, such as Leigh or Biffa, have developed a considerable expertise in managing it. These firms currently confront the British subsidiaries of waste disposal multinationals (e.g., Waste Management Inc., Générale des Eaux) which reject co-disposal as part as their corporate environmental policy. Clearly, a ban on co-disposal would favour the latter firms and damage British firms. The UK Department of the Environment officially took a stand for co-disposal in September 1993 and acts at the Council on this issue as the spokesman of the industry.

The German position *vis à vis* Large Combustion Plant Directive has illustrated the exporting of a regulation to level the playing field for the interest of national industry. Exporting of a regulation through pressure on the Commission to regulate may also serve to boost the market of the national industry. For instance, the United Kingdom was the first EU country to set an environmental management system standard — the BS

7750. As a result, consultancy and auditing firms specialized in environmental management grew in number and rapidly developed an in-house expertise. Subsequently, the UK government strongly encouraged the adoption of a similar regulation which gave birth to the EMAS regulatory act (cf. Chapter 8).

Finally, the most sophisticated strategy is observed when several Member States compete to pre-empt the future environmental regulation. It takes place when the regulated area is completely new, and thus neither the Commission, nor the Member States' have previous experience. The member state which moves first, will learn first, and its proposal is likely to strongly influence the Commission as a source of inspiration. In turn, such pre-emption may secure competitive advantage for the national industry. This kind of rivalry has been illustrated above with the battle between France and Germany in relation with car-recycling regulation. One encounters another pre-empting race between these two countries in the case of packaging waste. The German Ordinance aimed at reducing the landfilling packaging material and increasing its recycling was adopted in June 1991. Just before, the French minister for the environment announced a target recovery, less ambitious than the German one, and asked the chairman of the BSN food group to reflect on the means of reaching the target. As a result, a voluntary agreement was signed in France between industry and government to set a consortium — Eco-Emballage SA Eco-Emballage SA is a variant of the German Scheme — the Dual System Deutschland. But it differs in a few aspects which reflect different national industry interests. For instance, the French system is in the hands of packaging users not of retailers like in Germany. The purpose is to secure the competitiveness of the French food industry. The French decision to implement its own scheme has strongly influenced the drafting of the packaging waste directive (94/62), in particular by lowering the initial objectives of recovery.

In all the above-mentioned examples there is a converging interest between a national industry interest group and the public authority. The latter has appeared as the spokesman of the former on the European stage, and the conflicts between regulators have in fact reflected a conflict between industry interest groups. One will see now that competition on regulation between industry interest groups can follow more direct routes and is not limited to battles between national industries. Competing on regulation through national public authorities involved in international forums is only one form of inter-firm regulatory rivalry.

2.3 Inter-firm competition on regulation

As a general pattern, the introduction of a new regulation is divisive and raises conflicts between firms. It creates losers and winners absolutely and relatively. For instance, the waste management industry as a whole is an absolute benefiter of waste policies. They boost the growth of its market.

However, small enterprises specializing in waste collection and landfilling are relative losers and large firms relative winners for they benefit from a technological advantage on waste sorting, incinerating and material recovering. Firms from the energy sector would be the loser if an eco-tax is adopted. The energy demand is expected to decrease. But power generation with gas would be better positioned than electricity producers using fuel or coal. Regulatory conflicts between different firms are differently localized depending on the case. The conflict may take place between different segments of one industry (e.g., between innovative agrochemical producers and the formulators); between large and small firms (e.g., in the waste management case); between firms in different but related industries (e.g., along the vertical chain or horizontally by material in the packaging industry); between firms in different countries (as exemplified in the previous section).

For environmental regulation confers and redistributes rewards and losses among industries, it offers firms a new arena to compete in besides the traditional arena of the market. The interesting aspect lies in interaction between these two arenas: competition on the market and competition on the regulation. Each influences the other.

Interfirm competition on regulation reflects competition on the market. This works in two ways. Firstly, the participation of firms into the regulatory process depends on the market structure. Interest grouping is easier for large firms in a small number than for small enterprises in a large number. Consequently, the presence of SMEs is rare, whereas the presence of large firms is pervasive. Secondly, a firm's preference for the outcome of the regulatory process, and subsequently its regulatory strategy, are determined by its position in the market. The case of pesticides detailed in Chapter 4 soundly highlights this general pattern. The agro-chemical industry is divided into two strategic groups. The first groups large chemical firms like Bayer or Rhône-Poulenc which specialize in R&D intensive products. The second is dominated by smaller firms specializing in 'me-too' pesticides. The former was the first interest group to be organized. It claimed a stronger protection of innovation. This directly threatened the market share of smaller producers who in turn entered the regulatory arena.

Interfirm competition on regulation influences the competition on the market. The rivalry between the industry interest groups influences the outcome of the regulatory process, which in turn will influence the firms' position in the market. A sound example is given with waste disposal policy. It is a major determinant of the waste management industry structure. It influences the choice of technology, the rate of growth of the industry, the competitive balance between large and small firms, and even the ownership. In Italy and the UK, private waste management firms obtained advantages from regulation to the detriment of municipally-owned firms. In the European Union non-hazardous waste producers whether they are households or firms, have not been involved in the regulation devising process. They were not able to counter balance the interest of waste treatment firms for the proximity principle which is likely to strengthen the local monopoly of waste facilities.

It is interesting to notice that when different firms and industries organize themselves in a single regulatory network, as in the case of packaging waste in France, it may lead to a regulation which freezes the competition on the market for the best environmental quality. The introduction of a regulation to cope with packaging immediately raises a potential change in the market share of different materials. Packaging materials such as metal, plastic and paper have a different environmental performance, in particular with regard to recycling. However, the way firms coalesced in France resulted in a recovery scheme of packaging waste where fees are not differentiated according to materials (see Chapter 7).

A last interesting pattern to note is that potential losers seem to be more represented and active in the regulation devising process than winners. But this is connected with more dynamic aspects we will now examine.

2.4 The entry of firms into the regulation devising process and the evolution of their strategies

To simplify, the first steps of the regulatory game can be viewed as follows: a regulatory project triggers the entry of a first industry interest group because of its potential absolute losses; firms obstruct it to obtain a less costly solution and at the same time attempt to get a relative gain (i.e., a competitive advantage) over some competitors (firms from another segment of the industry, from a related industry, from a foreign industry, etc.); this triggers the entry of a second industry interest group into the process and most of time the entry of a new public authority which shares the same interests than the new interest group; then the process becomes more and more complex with increasing numbers of participants.

The involvement of first industrial entrants is systematically triggered by a clear prospect of losses. This does not mean that there are no potential industrial winners from environmental policies, but that there is an asymmetry between winners and losers. As pointed out in Chapter 3 firms might be more sensitive to a loss than to a gain of the same level. Moreover, at the beginning of the devising process relative gains related to competitive advantage are very uncertain. One might say that environmental policy related to climate change would benefit the gas and nuclear industries, but this advantage was very hard to assess on the basis of the early drafts of the eco-tax directive. It depended on whether the tax would cover the energy content in addition to CO_2 emissions, and the balance between these two components. This was only specified later in the process. On the contrary, the international competitiveness of the European energy sector was very much at stake. Losses were obvious since it was unlikely that all firms in the world would be subjected to a similar policy.

The first entry triggers the involvement of new industry interest groups. The objective of the first entrant does not only consists in obtaining a less stringent policy. It also consists in orienting the process against competitors. Firms disadvantaged by a pure CO_2 emission tax lobbied the Commission to adopt an energy tax which would affect the nuclear industry. The latter reacted to this initiative. Large agro-chemical companies entered the process to oppose a drastic standard for pesticide residues in water and the introduction of cut-off criteria for the registration of new molecules. They lobbied the regulator to withdraw these two points, but they also demanded better protection of registration dossiers to increase their market share to the detriment to small 'me-too' producers. The latter organized a rival industry interest group and fought the initiative of the oligopolistic firms.

Public authorities, especially national ones, are active players in this development of the game which raises new potential gains and losses and thus attracts new participants.

The German electricity supply industry did not succeed in obstructing the tightening of SO_2 and NO_x emission standards in their country, but made their government press the Commission to adopt a similar regulation. A similar example is the entry into the European regulatory process of French conditioners and the administration. This entry was triggered by the potential advantage that the German industry would obtain if German authorities led the European regulatory process in packaging waste.

The strategy of firms changes during the evolution of the regulation devising process. Supporting public authorities may for instance follow a phase of obstruction. A sound example is provided by French car manufacturers which at the beginning of the process strongly opposed the Ministry of the Environment with regard to the regulating of end-of-life-cycle motor vehicles. They argued that car disposal accounts for only 4 per cent of all waste and that the industry had already achieved a high rate of recovery. 72 per cent of a car is recycled and this was achieved without any regulations. At the second stage, viewing future legislation as a credible threat and taking into account their reputation, car manufacturers undertook self-regulation. For instance, Peugeot co-operated with CFF (the largest shredding company in France) and Vicat (a cement works) in a pilot project for treating discarded cars. This phase of voluntary initiatives was followed by a strategy of support for the French authorities after the announcement of a very strict German bill. The precedent of the catalytic converter, interpreted in France as a victory for German car manufacturers, was very much in mind. French companies and policy makers were afraid that the future European Directive would be inspired by German regulations. This co-operation led to a contract between industry and government in March 1993. Industry undertook to reduce waste disposal to a maximum of 15 per cent per car as from 2002 (on a weight basis). Nowadays, there is an alliance between French car manufacturers and the administration to influence the future European directive.

Changes in regulatory strategy are caused by the entry of new interest groups and public authorities and the subsequent modifications of the contents of the proposal.

2.5 Changes between initial and final proposals

A major finding provided by case studies is that significant changes are noticeable between the contents of the initial and final regulatory proposals. The revisions concern both the objective of pollution abatement (via a reduction of the target, the introduction of exemptions or conditional clauses, etc.) and the measures to achieve it (i.e., choice of policy instruments and system of enforcement). In addition, one observes an enlargement of the regulatory goal to include non-environmental objectives. These changes are documented to be caused by the entry and strategy of industry interest groups and public authorities.

The following illustrations can be briefly mentioned. The original European regulations in pesticides proscribed more than 0.1 microgram of any pesticide's residue in drinking water. This is a very stringent standard since it means a decrease by one-half of the use of pesticides registration in agriculture. This reference was dropped from the final version of the Directive. The initial proposal of the Commission on the sulphur content of petroleum products had included the introduction of a 0.1 per cent sulphur limit for industrial/marine gas oils and the tightening of existing standards on heavy products (e.g., diesel oil). These two objectives were not adopted in the Directive 12/93. The initial goal of the French Ministry of the environment was to reduce waste disposal to 10 per cent per car as from 2002 on a weight basis. As the outcome of the process, a 15 per cent objective was finally retained. Some changes in the pollution reduction objective are indirectly obtained through the postponement of the compliance date (e.g., the achievement of recycling targets related to packaging waste), the inclusion of exemptions (e.g., a partial exemption to the eco-tax for energy intensive industries), and the introduction of conditional clauses (e.g., the adoption of the EU eco-tax only if similar measures were adopted by other OECD countries).

Important changes have also been observed with respect to the measures. The first draft of the German decree on packaging waste was based on the obligation for retailers to take back and recycle their packaging. The German regulation that was finally adopted includes the possibility for firms to use an alternative route. They can contract with a specialized network of packaging waste recovery: the so-called Duales System Deutschland. In France, at the beginning of the regulation devising process related to car recycling, a mandatory standard was planned. The final proposal refers to a voluntary agreement. The implementation of an Eco-Management and Audit Scheme, the so-called EMAS regulation, was initially proposed by the Commission as mandatory. The adopted regulation stipulates that the adoption by firms is voluntary. When the regulation devising process related to hazardous waste started, the idea was to stop the illegal traffic by increasing control procedures rather than by restricting its transportation. At the end of the process, the limitation of transporting waste (proximity and self-sufficiency principles) was adopted.

The final proposal also includes non-environmental objectives which were not mentioned in the initial draft. The eco-tax process is a sound example. The creation of employment and the setting of fiscal reform was progressively integrated into the proposal as new objectives.

To sum up, the initial draft contains a simple solution close to that prescribed in environmental economics text-books and propose a high environmental objective whereas the legislation that is finally adopted (or the final proposal if the regulation is not passed) is very complex, less ambitious and looks like a strange animal from a strictly environmental point of view. The best illustration is given by the case of eco-tax. An initiative, thought as *simplissimus*, progressively changed into a monster where the largest polluters are partly exempted whereas energy sources which do not emit CO_2 are also taxed.

This first chapter has provided the main descriptive features of the European fabric. It has focused on the *hows* of the regulatory process. The second chapter will survey the different economic theories aimed at explaining *why* the regulatory process exists and what purposes it serves.

NOTES

1. François Lévêque, Professor of economics, Deputy Director of CERNA, Centre of Industrial Economics, Ecole Nationale Supérieure des Mines de Paris, 60, bld St Michel, 75272 Paris Cedex 06, France, tel: 33140519091/9071; fax: 33144071046.
2. The Single European Act opened a door to qualified majority vote with the new article 100. However, as we mentioned, most European environmental regulations were adopted by the Council in reference to article 130 which requires unanimity of Member States.

REFERENCES

Hannequart, J.P. (1993), *Le Droit Européen des Déchets*, Bruxelles: Institut Bruxellois pour la Gestion de l'Environnement.

Institute for European Environmental Policy (IEEP) (1994), *The State of Action to Protect the Environment in Europe*, Bruxelles: European Environment Agency, mimeo.

Kay, J. and J. Vickers (1990), 'Regulatory Reform: An Appraisal', in Majone G. (ed.), *Deregulation or re-regulation? Regulatory Reform in Europe and the United States*, London: Pinter Publishers, pp. 223—251.

Lévêque, F., M. Angel and M. Glachant (1992), *Interaction between Environment Policy and Industry Policy*, Paris: OECD, Synthesis Report DSTI/IND(92)48.

Skea, J. (1995), 'Environmental technology', in H. Folmer, H. Opschoor and H.L. Gabel (eds.), *The Principles of Environmental Economics: A Guide for Students and Decision Makers*, Aldershot: Edward Elgar, pp. 389—412.

3. The regulatory game

François Lévêque[1]

This chapter provides the reader with the analytical framework which irrigates the economic analysis of the European fabric of environmental policy. The analytical framework has four main strands. As a general orientation, the regulatory process is stylized as a strategic game. Two main players are considered: the industry and the regulator. Industry groups firms organized in interest groups and the regulator is viewed as a set of public authorities belonging to different regulatory levels and pursuing different and conflicting goals. The second strand is the theoretical background which is based on economic theories of regulation rather than traditional environmental economics. The former allows the highlighting of the rationale of the regulatory process and the motives of the players whereas the latter largely ignores problems of information collection and institutional aspects. The two last strands are specific elements of stylization of, respectively, a firm's involvement and modes of regulation. They are advanced to provide the reader with a better understanding of the behaviour and patterns observed in the regulation devising process as surveyed in the second chapter and detailed in the next five chapters.

Reference to strategic game is obvious to analyse the European fabric of environmental policy. The rationale and the general stylization of the process as a game throughout the book is the following.

A small number of participants are involved in the process. In each examined case study, no more than a dozen public authorities and interest groups can be circumscribed as exerting a key influence. These players are mutually interdependent. The payoff of each participant depends upon the action of the others. Each participant is aware and takes into consideration the interests and reactions of the others. He elaborates and makes his decision according to his anticipations and the expectations of the others. Concerned parties spend a lot of time exchanging information, proposals, promises, threats, etc. Bargaining is very pervasive. The regulatory process is dominated by the redistribution of income and the creation (and destruction) of competitive advantages. Here are rooted the stakes and the rewards for the players.

The regulator is viewed as a set of public authorities belonging to different regulatory levels (European, national, local) and areas (environment, industry, finance, etc.) and pursuing different and partly conflicting goals. This means that public authorities themselves interact strategically. They bargain with each other. The vertical relationships between the regulatory levels are marked with an institutional economic competition. The stylized fact is to consider that each vertical public authority is seeking to increase the wealth and the competitiveness of its territory. This suits especially with respect to the conflicts between Member States to influence and pre-empt the European legislation. The horizontal relationships between specialized public authorities are stylized as driven by the ranking of different objectives. Each specialized public authority is in charge of, and supports, a public interest concern (pollution reduction, unemployment decrease, development of exports, decrease in public expenditures and budget deficit, removing barriers to competition, etc.). The institutional rivalry which takes place between the specialized authorities during the genesis of environmental legislation results in a set of ranked objectives which characterizes the proposal of regulation. The public interest for the environment is then balanced and rendered compatible with other legitimate public concerns. This applies in the case of the discussion between the different Directorates General of the Commission.

The co-ordination between public authorities is not isolated from the industry party. The multiplicity of the goals of the regulator opens up the route for firms to enlarge the scope of the regulation, the number of issues to be weighed up, and thus the number of regulatory decision-makers. Some industry interest groups may support some public authorities in the game. This enlargement could go across different regulatory areas (e.g., from environment to employment) or to a higher regulatory level (e.g., it could pit European Union policy making with subsidiarity).

The regulatory process is not a static game, it is a repeated game whose outcome is not known *ex ante*. It depends on the strategic actions and decisions of the participants. There is a set of possible outcomes and the choice of the outcome is at the core of the conflict between the players; each player has different preferences according to the losses and benefits that the outcome entails. The first uncertainty is whether any environmental legislation will pass. The process may be blocked by an inflexible obstruction from a party like in the case of the eco-tax project. Once the perspective of a legislation is likely, the uncertainty moves towards the fixing of the objectives, in particular the environmental collective objective (i.e., the amount of pollution to curb), and the choice of the measures to achieve them, in particular the selection of the policy instrument. The regulatory game is dynamic for decisions are sequential and the game goes through several iterations. But above all, it is stylized as dynamic in a broader sense: knowledge is increasing and behaviour and rules change during the process.

1. THEORETICAL INSIGHTS

The analytical framework is based on the economics of regulation rather than environmental economics.

Environmental economics is indeed poorly equipped to analyse the genesis of environmental regulations. In environmental economics, the analysis of public policy is centred on its effects. Positive and empiric studies focus on studying the economic impacts of different policies and instruments. This *ex post* approach addresses several critical issues such as the consequences of environmental policies on a firm's organization, industry competitiveness, employment, economic growth, and international trade. In case negative effects overweight positive ones the general reflex is to infer that a wrong policy instrument has been used. The policy-makers' inclination to use command-and-control rather than economic incentives is viewed by environmental economists as the major policy failure.

Environmental economics has paid much attention to the question of policy instruments and their efficiency. Policy instruments are the measures that public authorities have to use to remedy the environmental externalities. Two categories are currently distinguished. Economic instruments are measures such as taxes, subsidies, tradeable permits, or deposit-refund systems. They use market-based incentives to channel economic activity in environmentally desirable directions. They leave actors free to respond to certain stimuli in a way actors themselves think most beneficial. The second category is named by environmental economists as command-and-control, or regulation, or regulatory approach. It groups instruments like emission standards which require economic agents 'to set one or more output or input quantities at some specified level or prohibiting them from exceeding (or falling short of) some specified levels' (Baumol and Oates, 1971). Environmental economists support the use of economic incentives for they are more efficient. Unlike command-and-control, these instruments orient actions of pollution reduction according to their relative costs. Via a tax, pollution reduction takes place first for the part of the pollution which is less costly to reduce whereas in the case of a uniform standard each polluter has to limit the same amount of emission whatever his cost. The cost of achieving a pollution abatement of one unit, say a ton of CO_2, is higher with a uniform standard. Moreover, economic instruments present a dynamic advantage: they allow a larger freedom of adjustment and provide stronger incentives for developing new technological ways of reducing pollution. In short, economic instruments have a clear advantage in terms of effects.

In terms of cost of regulation, that is to say the cost for the regulator to obtain the information he needs to set the optimal policy, the relative performance of the different instruments is less clear-cut (Glachant, 1996). Before passing a new regulation, the regulator needs to know the benefits of pollution reduction and the abatement costs. This represents a high quantity of information which is costly to collect. The benefits of pollution reduction depend on the costs of environmental damage and the valuation of environmental amenities. The abatement cost depends on firms according to the technology they use and their location. All this information is very atomized for, as a rule, the number of polluters and pollutees is high. Theoretically (Weitzman, 1974), the setting of an optimal tax or an optimal standard (a standard specific to each firm depending on its abatement cost) requires the same amount of information. However, taking into account that information is not obtained by the regulator in one go but requires an iterative process of adjustment, the tax has an advantage. The fine tuning of the environmental objective according to abatement cost can be monitored through a single parameter, the price. In the case of an optimal standard, the adjustments have to be made by changing the quantities of emissions of each firm.

Informational costs and procedures of data collection are largely ignored by environmental scholarships because of the labour division which prevails in economics. In the simplest and oldest model of environmental economics, the regulator is viewed as omniscient: he possesses, or may collect without cost, the required information. This vision is that of welfare economics as proposed by Pigou (1946) from which environmental economics is derived. The regulator acts perfectly; only market failures are considered. In a subsequent model, the so-called second best approach (Baumol and Oates, 1971), the setting of environmental policy is divided into two steps: the choice of the environmental objective and the choice of the instrument. The former is considered as a policy matter. The objective is the outcome of an administrative process whose study is left to the lenses of policy science. In this second model, the difficult problem of the valuation of externalities is overcome by considering the environmental goal as exogenously given. The single issue is the choice of the instrument which minimizes the cost to achieve the policy set objective. Nowadays, the setting of the environmental objective has been re-integrated into environmental economics with the development of cost-benefit analysis. However, the focus is primarily on the valuation of benefits and the different methodologies to put a price on environmental resources. The collection by the regulator of firms' information related to abatement cost and, more generally, the relationships between the regulator and the regulated industry are not topics that environmental economics addresses. They are left to the economics of regulation.

Before briefly surveying this discipline, it is interesting to note that direct public intervention is viewed by environmental economists as natural, as *aller de soi*. In the presence of an externality, only the government is able to reconcile polluters and pollutees. By definition, the market cannot do it for externality marks one of its shortcomings. Moreover, bargaining between polluters and pollutees is also excluded. Such bargaining has been proposed as an alternative solution to public intervention by Coase (1960). It has been strongly criticized by environmental economists. Firstly, it was interpreted as a typical justification of *laissez-faire*. Secondly, it was pointed out that the conditions for decentralized negotiation to be effective are very limited. One requirement, in particular, is that only a very small number of polluters and pollutees exist and that they mutually know their preferences and costs. If not, the cost of contracting between the parties becomes so high that it outweighs the potential benefits of the negotiation and thus impedes the bargaining. Given this cost, parties have no interest in moving from the initial state. It is noteworthy that the obstacles to achieve an optimal pollution reduction related to information and opportunism of agents are not specific to bargaining. They may also be pointed out in the case of public intervention. There is no reason to assume like most environmental economists that intervention of public authorities has no cost and is the single best way of regulating the environment. As documented by voluntary initiatives and voluntary agreements between industry and government, in some contexts self-regulation and co-regulation may appear as most cost-effective (cf. Section 3 of this Chapter).

The economics of regulation has a normative and a positive side. The normative one is aimed at devising and prescribing optimal regulations. The purpose is to limit both market and regulatory failures which result in inefficient allocations of resource. The positive side is interested in explaining why regulations are what they are. It attempts to understand the mechanisms of the offer of regulation from policy-makers and the demand from industry.

Market does not spontaneously lead to an efficient allocation or Pareto optimal allocation (i.e., an allocation of resource where no economic agent can be made better off without making another agent worse off) in three situations. The first is where the industry has certain characteristics in terms of demand or costs. The best known example is the natural monopoly: left to its own devices, the market may give rise to imperfect competition (failure to meet demand at the lowest cost and destructive competition) and permanent excess profit (monopoly rent). This is the main cause addressed by economics of regulation which has especially emphasized the regulating of public utilities. The second circumstance is where there is asymmetry of information on product (or service) quality and the consumer has no way of assessing the quality of the goods (or services) available. This allows companies to engage in unfair opportunistic conduct. This is typically the motive of public intervention to restrict adulteration and short measures. Asymmetry of information is often regulated through self-arrangements between firms. It is particularly developed in professions such as actuaries, lawyers, medical practitioners, or stock exchange operators. They adopt a common code of practice which economizes the cost of search for consumers and secures the reputation of all the profession. Asymmetry of information between buyers and sellers is especially serious when the quality cannot be assessed by the former after their purchase. The perspective of a repeated purchase by the consumer if he is satisfied cannot act as an incentive to the seller to provide the right quality level. This is the typical case of environmental performance of products. Unlike the speed of a motor vehicle or the longevity of an electric bulb, the consumer has no alternative but to trust producers or third parties like green groups or independent experts. The third market failure occurs in the presence of externalities. It arises when economic agents impose costs on (or deliver benefits to, in the case of positive external effect) third parties which are not involved in the transaction. A famous example, for it was mentioned by the founding father of environmental economics, Alfred Pigou, and later discussed by Ronald Coase, is that of damage due to sparks from railway engines. Steam powered trains occasionally caused fires in surrounding woods and forest owners were not compensated by the railways. Another example is the textbook illustration where a leather factory pollutes a river which causes fish destruction and then affects anglers. Forest owners or anglers stay outside the market transaction between the polluting firms and their clients but their welfare is affected by the transaction. Such negative externalities are the fundamental justification of environmental policy.

The existence of a market failure is a necessary but not a sufficient condition to regulate. Like the market, the regulator may be confronted with informational, institutional and technological constraints which will lead him to fail in allocating resources. The efficiency of public intervention is constrained by regulatory failures. Regulatory failures are rooted in three circumstances: the regulator may lack information, he may not be credible with respect to future commitment and he may be self-interested. These circumstances render perfect regulation impossible to achieve, that is to say to reach a Pareto optimal allocation. It is only possible to attempt to be close to it. Such a vision corresponds with an important change in the basic hypotheses of the governmental intervention as considered in traditional welfare economics (and in current environmental economics) where the regulator is seen as a benevolent maximizer of welfare, and an omniscient (i.e., he knows a firm's cost) and fair (he does not behave opportunistically) economic agent.

The most addressed informational constraint is that of information asymmetry between the regulator and the regulated firm. For instance, the regulator is typically less informed than the firm about abatement costs and technology of pollution reduction. Using the term of principal/agent — a theory which examines strategic interaction between economic agents — there is a problem of hidden information, or adverse selection. To set an optimal environmental policy, the regulator must know the cost of the polluting firm. But, it is not in the interest of the firm to provide this information. On the contrary, since the regulation will negatively affect its revenues, the firm is motivated to overestimate abatement costs and underestimate its emissions. To limit this manipulation, the regulator must set up an incentive system which is aimed at making a firm reveal true information. Then and only then, he would be able to devise the optimal regulation.

For institutional reasons in relation to legislation and administrative rules, it is difficult for the regulator to commit itself to incentive schemes, in particular in long term contracts. For instance, if the choice of policy in the first period reveals information about a firm's technology, the regulator may have an *ex post* incentive to act opportunistically by exploiting it in future periods. Anticipating this, the firm will revise its strategy for the first period which will result in an *ex ante* inefficiency. When the regulator cannot precommit future environmental policy, there is a risk of underinvestment in green technology. Industry will prefer not to make irreversible expenditures to curb pollution.

The third but not least important source of regulatory failure is where the regulator does not act for the public interest but pursues its own specific objective. A public utility regulator or an environmental agency may for instance collude with the regulated industry or green groups, respectively. This means that the regulator reports wrong information to the government in order to support the interest of the group it acts for. To limit such a risk of capture, regulatory economists prescribe setting an incentive scheme between the government and the regulatory agency which will align the personal interest of the regulator to social welfare. Political and regulatory institutions are viewed as organizational arrangements aimed at limiting the potential for regulatory capture.

This is the normative version of regulatory capture.

The positive economic theory of regulatory capture denies that the regulator or the government is pursuing a public interest goal. It is inspired by policy science theories which suggest that regulatory bodies are in fact created to serve industry interests (the conspiracy theory of regulation) or that regulatory bodies start by using their discretionary power independently but will be progressively captured (the life-cycle theory of regulation) by business. Regulation is viewed as a pure mechanism of redistribution. It does not originate from a market failure but is provided in response to the demand of interested parties struggling between themselves to maximize the incomes of their members. The regulation is viewed as a commodity: regulatory payoffs are exchanged between interest groups and policy-makers according to the rules of supply and demand. The reward to suppliers is political support in terms of votes or campaign contributions, jobs in the political afterlife, and so forth. As summarized by Foster (1992) 'different interests compete for favours using whatever favours they have to offer in exchange for cash, expected votes, ideological support, etc.'.

The seminal contribution was that of the Chicago economist George Stigler who pointed out in 1971 that 'the central tasks of the theory of economic regulation are to explain who will receive the benefits or burdens of regulation, what form regulation will take and the effect of regulation upon allocation of resources'. Like policy science theories, his own theory predicts that the regulator will be captured by the industry. The reasons are that industry has most to lose or gain and has a better ability to organize itself into an interest group. It has therefore both the incentive and the capacity to dominate regulation to the detriment to consumers and taxpayers. The individual economic actor has no power to influence the regulator and thus collective action is the only means to obtain access to the market of regulations. The cost of interest grouping depends on the size of the group and on the proximity of the interest to its members. As a consequence, small homogeneous groups will have lower organization costs and greater performance in their collective action. This is inspired by the Olson theory of collective action (Olson, 1965). Stigler's theory also predicts, and this is pure Chicago school, that the outcome of the regulatory process would be economically efficient. Differences between outcomes depending on the administrative rules and regulatory institutions would affect only the distribution of income between the parties.

In this simpler form the positive economic theory of regulatory capture was challenged by the wave of deregulation which took place in the United States during the mid- and late 1970s. It concerned various sectors, such as railroads, airlines, trucking, communication, and so on. It falsified the statement that regulation is necessarily captured by the regulated industry. As a rule, regulated firms as potential losers of liberalization fought strongly against deregulation. The deregulation, it was argued by policy-makers, pursued public interest goals. During the same period, there was also an impressive growth in environmental legislation. Obviously, environmental regulations were pushed by public opinion rather than business. Generally speaking, the strengthening of environmental policy does not result in an additional benefit for firms but conversely in an extra cost — the expenditure to reduce pollution. Regulation economists were obviously prompted to consider these new trends. This gave birth to a second set of theoretical and empirical investigation (Becker, 1983; Keeler, 1984) which includes a mixture of public and private interest considerations. A policy-maker is viewed as serving a broader constituency than the regulated producer. According to these new investigations, achieving public interest goals is not prevented by involvement of interest groups. Decisions of policy-makers are aimed at increasing social welfare and redistributing this increase among interest groups in order to obtain their political support.

There is no place here to go beyond a simplified overview of the economics of regulation. However, main gains in realism of the theories have to be mentioned. They concern the objectives of the regulator and the institutional arrangements in government. The objective of maximizing social welfare or maximizing the private interests of the interest groups which offer the highest rewards is oversimplified. It is currently considered that the regulator pursues multiple goals rather than maximizes a single objective function. A multi-argument objective function is more realistic but the multidimensionality of goals induces a severe difficulty. Some dimensions, in particular social ones, are hard to measure and each goal has to be weighted relatively to others to permit an aggregation. As a result, theory loses in predictive power and falsification. The regulatory outcome can always be rationalized as the achievement of a political equilibrium between the various public interests. Another gain in realism is considering the internal organization of the state (Tirole, 1994). The policy device of new regulation, say an environmental regulation, does not depend on a single player, the environmental agency. The regulator is a set of public authorities rather than a single agent. The institutional arrangement concerns the division of labour between different departments (e.g., ministry of employment and ministry of the environment), between geographic levels (e.g., local/national/EU levels) and between hierarchical levels (agency/government). Policy making is then decided by considering a complex chain of principal-agent relationships. For instance, the government acts as an agent for the citizens and as a principal for the regulatory agency who, in its turn, supervises the regulation process.

To sum up, the rationale of the phase which precedes the enactment of new environmental legislation appears as very different depending on economic theories. According to environmental economics, the regulation devising process can be outlined as follows. There is a market failure, an externality which is identified; public intervention is required to remedy it; this is the role of a specialized agency which proceeds by evaluating the benefit of pollution and selecting the policy instrument. As said before, the regulator is a benevolent maximizer of welfare and neither regulatory failures nor the institutional environment of the agency are considered. The perspective of positive economics of regulation differs radically. Regulation is viewed as a mechanism of wealth redistribution and not as a mechanism aimed at curing resource misallocation. The regulatory process is a marketplace where interest groups compete to obtain rents. Finally, from the normative side of economics of regulation, public interest is the objective of public intervention but there are constraints, mainly informational, to achieve it. They prevent the decision-making process from being efficient. Within this perspective, the clearing of asymmetries between the regulator and the regulated is the *raison d'être* of the regulation devising process. The regulatory process is viewed as a phase of collecting information and the institutional arrangements as made to limit the potential of regulatory capture. It explains why environmental policy encourages the participation of business in devising new policies: firms possess the information they need. Industry is then *de facto* involved in the regulatory process.

2. A FIRM'S INVOLVEMENT IN THE REGULATION DEVISING PROCESS

The strategic use of the regulation devising process may be at least as important to firms as the traditional decisions on price, entry or innovation. It may be used as a powerful weapon of inter-firm competition.

Early work investigating the effect of regulation on industry treated firms in the industry as a single coalition. Firms were equally interested in regulation and equally affected. Their objective when becoming involved in the regulatory arena was rent-seeking and they were considered as the benefiters of regulations. Nowadays, it is commonly recognized that regulations are divisive between firms and the industry as the whole is not systematically the winner, especially in the case of environmental regulations. Environmental regulations are pushed by pollutees and public opinion rather than by industry which is one of the major polluters.

2.1 A firm's objective

A firm's objective in its involvement in the regulatory game is twofold. It seeks to minimize the abatement cost, in particular by bargaining a less stringent environmental objective, and to gain a competitive advantage.

There are two different effects of environmental policy on industry. A proposed regulation aimed at curbing pollution entails an absolute and a relative effect for firms. The former is the effect of the regulation which is the same for all firms. If one supposes that firms within the regulated industry are homogeneous, the introduction of the environmental policy will increase similarly their costs. However, this increase will be transferred to the market price. Assuming that the price elasticity is negative, firms will be confronted by a lower demand. The absolute effect is a change in demand which affects all firms of the industry. It is important to note that, as well as an increase in abatement costs, there is a growth in the market for green technologies and services. In this case the absolute effect of environmental regulation is positive for industry. Affecting demand is the first mechanism which creates winners and losers within the industrial sector.

However, regulations do not typically affect all firms within industry in the same way. The industry contains differentiated sub-groups of firms according to peculiar features such as cost, location, size, the quality of products, reputation, and so forth. This difference raises the possibility that a regulation can create a comparative advantage for some firms in the industry and leads to a shifting of market share within the industry. The essence of rivalry in the regulatory arena is that a firm will try to exploit the differential effect of a regulation on itself against its rivals. This, of course, may attract a riposte from competitors, and therefore in turn also encourage their interest grouping and their entry into the process. In other terms, the abatement cost may differ amongst firms competing on the same market and this may lead to the presence of rival industry groups.

As pointed out by Oster (1982), a firm may even encourage the passage of regulation which increases industry costs and reduces industry demand. The firm may encourage such a regulation because it differentially damages its rival, and thus rearranges market shares at the same time as it reduces the total market. For instance, Bayer will be affected more by the new regulation of pesticides than DuPont because, on average, the environmental performance of DuPont's products is better. There is a potential conflict between the two firms as regards the tightening of the environmental standard. Their common interest is to obstruct the new regulation. It will reduce the size of the European pesticide market. However, a change in the standard is in DuPont's interest for it will gain a market share over Bayer.

Taking into account these two effects, one may stylize the objective of a firm's involvement in the regulatory process as twofold: minimizing the abatement cost and gaining a competitive advantage. Decreasing the absolute cost of pollution reduction can be achieved through two mechanisms. Firstly, firms can influence the regulator to adopt a less stringent environmental objective than the objective included in the initial proposal of regulation. This means a higher threshold of emission standard, a lower level of taxation, an exemption, etc. Secondly, firms may convince the regulator to use more cost-effective measures of achieving the environmental objective. This may mean for instance, a flexible rather than uniform standard, a postponement of the compliance date to benefit from technological investment, a voluntary agreement rather than a mandatory requirement, and so forth.

The balance between the two objectives depends on whether demand is sensitive to price and abatement costs are heterogeneous between firms. We may expect that the higher the elasticity, the more firms are involved in the process (for the higher the stakes), and that the more heterogeneous the abatement costs, the more intense the rivalry between firms in the regulatory arena. These statements must be considered all other things being equal. The *ceteris paribus* condition is noteworthy since other variables interfere in a firm's involvement and regulatory strategies.

2.2 The factors which affect industry involvement

Whether a firm enters the game to influence the regulator primarily depends on the regulatory stakes. Four attributes of stakes must be considered to understand a firm's involvement (cf. Table 3.1). The first is the level of the stakes (gains or losses) and whether they are absolute or relative. The higher the expected gains or losses, the more likely a firm's influence is. Moreover, the game may be limited to a *face à face*, an opposition (or a collusion) between the industry interest group and the regulator, or may be open to several competing industry interest groups. This is a critical aspect for rivalry improves the information of the regulator. The second attribute is the distribution of the stakes. A firm's involvement depends on whether the stakes are atomized amongst a large number or concentrated in a few hands. The larger the number of stakeholders, the less likely their involvement in the process is (Olson, 1965). In large groups there is a strong incentive for individuals to free-ride, that is to say not to bear any costs of organizing and lobbying, and to wait for the success of the other who paid for it. The access to the regulator is thus differentiated. The third attribute is uncertainty. As pointed out by Noll and Owen (1983), if the effects of a regulation cannot be predicted beforehand with reasonable accuracy, the incentive to contribute to a lobbying effort is obviously reduced. Uncertainty may be greater about certain circumstances than about others. At the beginning of the devising process, gains (in particular those related to competitive advantage) are uncertain whereas losses (in particular absolute ones) are more predictable. This induces an asymmetry between the presence of gainers and winners into the process and a bias in favor of the *status quo ante*. The fourth dimension, whether the stake is a gain or a loss reinforces this asymmetry. As pointed out by Kahneman (1991), one may assume that firms are more sensitive to a loss than to a gain of the same value.

Table 3.1 The factors which determine a firm's involvement and their effects

Factors	The more likely a firm's involvement	Consequence for the devising process of regulation
Level of regulatory stakes		
• absolute	The higher the demand elasticity to price	One or several sources of information for the regulator
• relative	The broader the differentiation of abatement cost	
Distribution of stakes (atomized/concentrated)	The smaller the number of stakeholders	Biased access to regulator
Uncertainty of stakes	The lower uncertainty of stakes	Asymmetry between industry winners and losers
Gain or loss	A loss rather than a gain	Asymmetry between industry winners and losers
Credibility of the regulatory threat	The higher the threat is credible	The moment of entry into the process
Market incentives to curb pollution	The higher the incentives	Allows self- and co-regulation

From a policy-making perspective, it is very important to consider the attributes of stakes. The involvement of a firm (or an industry interest group) is only a biased proxy of the vested interests. The presence of an industry interest group and the absence of another is not only due to their different payoffs, it is not a sufficient condition to infer that the second has no stakes or they are lower than the stakes of the former.

Whether the regulatory threat is credible or not is another factor which affects a firm's involvement. It explains the moment industry enters the process. When the regulatory project is considered by business as a no future perspective, there is no reason to intervene in the regulatory arena. A sound example is provided by the eco-tax project of the Commission. The opposition from the energy sector to the eco-tax really began in October 1991 when the details of the proposal was released. Business did not react before, although it had access to the early drafts of the Community's climate strategy document. The initial industry judgment was that since the Community produces only a small proportion of global CO_2, drastic action to reduce emissions was unlikely, especially at a time of economic recession. A carbon tax was considered as too innovative, and the barriers to its adoption too great, for it to be a serious threat. Anticipated barriers included conflicts of interest between the different parts of the Commission, differences in the energy structure of the Member States and the North/South divide within the Community.

It is important to mention a last factor of industry participation: the co-presence of market incentives with regulatory incentives. Regulatory pressure is not the single cause of a firm's action in pollution reduction, albeit the dominant one. Market incentives related to a consumer's willingness to pay for greener products or related to the reputation of a firm and its brands may push a firm to 'green' its strategy. These incentives are independent from public intervention but they may combine with regulatory stakes. The regulatory payoffs relative to the cost of lobbying may be insufficient to incite a firm to enter the regulatory arena, but an additional payoff provided by the market may lead the firm to move towards an intervention. Furthermore, the presence of market incentives allows modes of regulation like co-regulation where industry is more pro-active (cf. next section).

In the regulatory game, firms may follow two strategies depending on whether they expect a gain or a loss. The strategy of obstruction has been observed as very widespread. It results in the lowering of pollution objectives, and even in the killing of the proposal (e.g., the eco-tax project). The strategy of obstruction is triggered by both absolute and relative losses. Typically, obstruction based on expectations of absolute costs is observed as the strategy of the first entrant into the process, whereas the second type of obstruction develops later with the emergence of rivalry between different industry interest groups. The strategy of support is less frequent. It occurs mainly within the perspective of a relative gain rather than an absolute one. As said before, there is no evidence of environmental regulations purposely designed for industry and operated for its benefit. The initial environmental proposals come from elsewhere (green groups, citizens, those affected by pollution, etc.). Potential absolute winners from industry are circumscribed to firms producing green technologies and services (including waste management firms). They only represent a small part of industry. The industry winners are thus mainly relative ones. In some cases, they succeeded in obtaining a more stringent regulation than that initially considered by the regulator. For instance, the catalytic converter standard —

supported by Bosch and German car manufacturers — was adopted in the EU for low-powered engine cars, although only big-engined cars were the target at the beginning of the process (Hourcade *et al.*, 1992). Similarly, the pro-active strategy of DuPont *vis-à-vis* CFC regulation led to a revision of the Montreal protocol towards a shortening of the phase-out period of CFCs (Gabel, 1995).

Because of the level of the stakes (larger perspective of losses than gains for industry) and because of the asymmetry between winners and losers, the general pattern is a lowering of the environmental objective included in the draft proposal due to obstructive industry groups rather than an increase caused by industry supportive groups.

3. THREE MODES OF REGULATION

The book documents a rich variety of environmental policies. However they may be ranged in only three generic modes of regulation: public regulation, self-regulation and co-regulation. The first two are distinguished depending on who sets the rules of the game: the State or the economic agents themselves, respectively. In the first case, the environmental policy is the outcome of an administrative process. In the second case, the regulating of pollution is the result of a collective action and a bargaining process between firms. The third mode, co-regulation, is a hybrid form between public regulation and self-regulation. The aim of this section is to present the three categories, in particular to stylize the circumstances in which they take place and to discuss the conditions necessary for them to be successful (i.e., to pass and enforce regulation).

3.1 Public regulation

This mode of regulation is largely addressed in literature. Only a brief presentation will be provided here. Public regulation is primarily an administrative process where the environmental objective and the train of measures to achieve it are both set by public authorities. Nevertheless, the industry via lobbying is very present to influence the regulator's choice.

Public regulation is typically represented in the book by the cases of pesticide registration and CO_2/carbon tax. The definition of the new environmental objective related to pesticides was set in the Uniform Principle directive 94/43. It introduced in particular the mandatory obligation to re-register old but always in use products. The aim is to reject active ingredients of which environmental performances are below the new standard. The measures (e.g., enlargement of the patent duration, sharing of the re-registration costs between firms) to achieve the objective have raised an intense rivalry between firms (see Chapter 4). The EU-wide target of stabilizing CO_2 emissions at their 1990 level by the year 2000 was decided in October 1991 by the Council. Then the Commission was given the task of devising a strategy for achieving the stabilization objective. The emission taxation was proposed as a major measure. As documented in Chapter 5, this proposal raised strong conflicts within the Commission and an intense obstruction from industry.

To be successful, public regulation requires sufficient power of coercion of the regulator to resist the obstruction power of regulated firms. Public regulation takes place when the market does not provide incentives to firm (or incentives enough) via, for instance, reputation effects, to increase their expenditures in curbing pollution. Energy producers and energy intensive industries have no interest in spontaneously reducing their CO_2 emissions, nor agro-chemical companies to re-register the old active ingredients.

The drawbacks of public regulation are well-known. The potential for capture due to the informational asymmetry between the regulator and the regulated firms is high. A second major potential failure deals with the representation of all the industry interested parties. A pattern of under-representation of certain groups of firms has been noticed and explained in the previous section. It is important to emphasize the role in this mode of rivalry between industry interest groups. It increases the regulator's information and reduces the obstruction power of industry. That is what the case of pesticides regulation and *a contrario* the case of eco-tax proposal document (one reason it fails to be passed has been the absence of pro-tax industry interest groups). Ensuring the access to all industrial interests and enabling competition between industry interest groups are means that the regulator can use to achieve more effective public regulations.

3.2 Self-regulation

Regulatory pressures are not the only incentives which may push firms to adopt a more benign behavior *vis-à-vis* the environment. In some circumstances, firms may undertake a collective action to cope with an environmental concern without direct governmental intervention. They voluntarily choose both the environmental target and the measures to achieve it. What are these circumstances?

The mode of self-regulation is currently extending in the field of the environment. It corresponds with the growth in the number of so-called self-initiatives or voluntary actions (CEC, 1994; Gunningham, 1995). The typical example is provided by the case of the Responsible Care Programme detailed in Chapter 8. Responsible Care Programme is a chemical industry action which calls on companies to demonstrate their commitment to improving all aspects of performance which relate to the protection of health, safety and the environment. It was initiated in Canada. Responsible Care has been aimed at re-gaining confidence from customers and public opinion. It started at the end of the 1980's as a response to large accidents such as in Bhopal (India) and in Basel (Switzerland). An important component of this voluntary action concerns the development of environmental performance indicators and their dissemination outside the industry. These indicators are designed to measure the environmental progress achieved by chemical firms.

Environmental self-regulation is featured with two major obstacles: free-riding, and lack of credibility. A charter of good environmental practices, an eco-label which asserts the environmental performances of a product, or a technical standard which ensures the compatibility between a waste product and a recovery scheme, share a characteristic of a public good (Lévêque, 1995). Some firms may be tempted not to comply with the prescribed rules and avoid the compliance cost whereas simultaneously they will continue to benefit from the collective gain (e.g., reputation effects or network economies). To overcome this problem of free riding, the coalition must implement control and policy measures. Its board has to be attributed with a coercive power and must act as a regulatory agency. A second obstacle is that self-regulation has a bad image. People often consider *a priori* that voluntary actions only result in cosmetic effects. Self-regulatory schemes involve regulation of the industry, by the industry, for the industry (Gunningham, 1995). The absence of a third party reduces the credibility of eco-labels and green codes of practice in the eye of public opinion. Trust and confidence of the public may be long and difficult to gain without an external oversight. An answer to this obstacle consists in demanding an oversight from third parties as environmentalist associations. As watchdogs and verifiers, they may increase the credibility of industry self-commitments. This explains why alliances between industry and green group organizations, like WWF, are more and more observed.

Market incentives (e.g., provided by reputation effects or network economies) are pre-requisites for this mode of regulation to be successful. In essence, the private regulator is self-interested. His duties are to serve the interests of the firms of the coalition, not those of other parties. Environmental protection and private profit do not necessarily coincide. Nevertheless, there may be a substantial overlap between public and private interest. For instance as documented by Responsible Care, making investments in pollution reduction has been perceived by the chemical industry as necessary to address a long term perspective of a decrease in demand due to its tarnished image.

Another condition is a low differentiation of abatement costs between firms. The perspective of relative gains weakens the maintain of the coalition and makes room for free-riding. One difficulty the Responsible Care Programme is confronted with is that small and medium-sized enterprises of the chemical industry are lesser benefiters than large international companies. They are less affected with the bad reputation of the chemical industry as a whole for they are less visible to green groups and consumers. They are less equipped with internal resources dedicated to environmental affairs to implement the programme. Their commitments are more difficult (i.e., costly) to control.

Pure self-regulation, that is to say without any public intervention, can be successful in very limited conditions since the following are required: (i) market incentives, (ii) small number of players and homogeneous costs of pollution reduction, (iii) organized watch dogs (green groups), to overcome free-riding and lack of credibility of self-commitments.

A public intervention may enlarge this narrow scope for self-regulation in several ways. Government can increase the incentives to self-regulation by posing a threat of regulatory intervention. This may work when *ex ante* market incentives are not high enough to encourage industry to undertake a self-initiative. The threat creates an additional expected gain to industry: the avoided net cost of a government regulation.[2] Such a synergy between market and regulatory incentives to trigger self-regulation is documented by the case of industrial waste in France. Concern for contaminated areas emerged in France in the early 1990s. Very toxic industrial waste had been discovered in a privately owned landfill in Monchanin. In response to such a worry, large French companies involved in highly polluting sectors such as the chemical, oil and raw material industries set up a collective organization, l'Association Française des Entreprises pour l'Environnement, to cope with such old contaminated areas. Fearing a national version of the US super-fund, they created a private fund which was monitored by the industry itself rather than by the government (Lévêque and Nadaï, 1995).

Government may also intervene directly to support the self-regulatory arrangement. It may use, for instance, its inspectorate bodies to contribute to the controlling and policing of free-riders. It may increase the credibility of industry self-commitments as a third party (e.g., in participating in standardization committees related to industry eco-labeling). However, industry may fear that 'since government has its foot in the door, there is no way of limiting the degree or type of intrusion' (Gunningham, 1995). Industry may fear, in particular, that government will force it to adopt a higher, less flexible environmental objective.

Such intervention of public authorities in self-regulation makes this mode closer to co-regulation.

The main advantage of the mode of self-regulation lies in information costs and flexibility. Information is less costly for the private regulator (i.e., the board of the coalition) to collect and interpret than for the regulatory agency. Furthermore, the mode of self-regulation offers the possibility to better ensure a fine tuning of the pollution reduction actions according to changes in the market and technological circumstances.

The major potential failure lies in the risk of cartelisation. Self-regulation may be explained by considerations of efficiency but also by the self-interest of the firm to avoid competition. Self-regulation is considered by anti-trust regulators as very suspicious. Competition restriction has been especially suspected in the case of monopolistic recovery and recycling schemes of waste. Is self-regulation just a cartelization? Or does it reflect specific market and technology circumstances where there is no possible equilibrium without alliances between firms (Telster, 1985)? This is not the place to attempt to cut the knot. The important point is to pay attention to dynamic aspect. As stated by the regulatory cycle theory, a self-regulatory arrangement may be perfectly set for, and able to achieve, an efficiency purpose and be progressively perverted by the incumbents as a means to create entry barriers to competitors.

3.3 Co-regulation

Co-regulation is a third category which covers the case where the interactive relationships between public authorities and firms are especially pervasive and close. Such cases are documented in this book with the regulating of specific waste recycling (Chapter 7) and of eco-auditing (Chapter 8). Co-regulation is a hybrid form between self- and public regulation for, like self-regulation, the set of measures to achieve the environmental target is set by industry whereas, like public regulation, the environmental objective continues to be set by public authorities.

A typical example is provided by packaging waste recycling in Germany. By 1990, a project of ordinance was set by the Federal Ministry for the Environment. It included: a set of stringent objectives (80—90 per cent recycling by 1995, excluding incineration); a mandatory returnable system for certain kinds of packaging (e.g., beverage packaging); and an obligation for the retailers to take back the packaging placed on the market via a system of containers in the close vicinity of the points of sale. The ordinance was strongly opposed by most industrialists but resulted also in a pro-active strategy on the part of the retailers and packagers. They created a working group aimed at designing a counter-proposal on the measures of achievement of objectives. In January 1991, the counter-proposal emerged: the so-called Duales System Deustchland which exempted the distributors from their obligation to take back packaging waste, relying on a fee-system paid to a consortium who would take charge of reaching recycling targets. As pointed out in Chapter 7, the DSD was clearly a unilateral initiative by industry. The government was not involved in the reflections of the working group.

Two stylized facts characterize the circumstances of co-regulation: shared uncertainty between players and a gain for firms from collective action.

Several projects of legislation are very new. They are aimed at controlling pollution which has never been controlled before (e.g., car or packaging waste recycling). Firms themselves are unable to assess their abatement costs. Their regulatory payoffs are unknown. The single element of certainty that they are confronted with is that a policy will pass, given the strong commitment of policy-makers or the strong green group pressures. In such cases, the key point is not an asymmetry of information (Agerri et al., 1994), but shared uncertainties between players. The information must be discovered during the process which then ensures a role of a collective learning, as documented by the case of car recycling.

In this case, the initial uncertainty was three-fold. Firstly, the future state of legislation was not known in advance, particularly with respect to the rate of recycling to achieve, the liability principle and cost-sharing (that is, who will be responsible for paying — the owner of the vehicle, the last holder, or the manufacturer). Secondly, technology was embryonic. Several technological options were open, ranging from the very labour-intensive dismantling to the use of melt-reactors which separate the steel contents by means of energy emitted from organic components of cars. Thirdly, the future recovery and recycling system might be based on the current waste network (which includes breakers) or on a new system in which dismantling is controlled by car manufacturers and scrapping companies. Thanks to pilot projects and practical experiments connected with the regulation devising process, information has been gradually collected and exchanged, and firms as well as regulators have been able to specify their preferences.

The second stylized fact is that, like self-regulation, co-regulation takes place when a collective gain is attached to inter-firm co-operation in setting the measures. Collective learning described above is one. Gains in reputation and network economies are also observed. Co-regulation is especially pervasive in eco-labeling or specific waste regulations. In other words, co-regulation takes place when incentives to curb pollution provided by market are additional to regulatory incentives.

Co-regulation possesses two specific advantages compared with the other modes. *Vis-à-vis* self-regulation, the advantage for industry is that public intervention secures firms collective action. The presence of government limits the problem of free-riding and mutual coercion. Regarding public regulation, the advantage for industry is that co-regulation ensures more cost-effective measures. Firms are more likely to identify the cost-economizing route to achieve the environmental target than public authorities.

But this raises a question: why is the setting of the measures not *always* left to the hands of industry? The answer lies in the connection between the setting of the objective and of the measures. The setting of the environmental objective appears as a conflictual issue between the regulator and the polluting industry (Glachant, 1996). As losers, firms attempt to block the process, or to obtain a less stringent objective than the initial one. The setting of the measures is less conflictual since the interest of both the industry as a whole and the regulator is to minimize the costs to achieve the environmental objective. However, an agreement on the measures on the part of industry implicitly contains an acceptance of the objective, and impedes firms from continuing to obstruct. It does not seem possible to both obstruct the objective and co-operate with the regulator to select the cost-economizing measures. This is documented for instance in the packaging waste recycling in Germany. Paper producers developed a strategy of obstruction along the entire regulatory process. They did not participate in the devising of the counter-proposal related to the implementation of DSD. Moreover, the setting of the objective and the measures are not always clear-cut during the regulatory process and for some instruments, like tax, the objective and the means cannot be disconnected.

The potential regulatory failures of co-regulation appear as intermediary between those of self-regulation and those of public regulation. It is noteworthy that the potential of capture of the regulator by industry cannot be neglected within this mode. It has been observed that the public regulator is here confronted with a large regulatory network which groups several industries. Encouraging rivalry between industry interest groups may pose a threat to the obtaining of the collective advantage that learning and co-operating in setting the measures entail.

NOTES

1. François Lévêque, Professor of economics, Deputy Director of CERNA, Centre of Industrial Economics, Ecole Nationale Supérieure des Mines de Paris, 60, bld St Michel, 75272 Paris Cedex 06, France, tel: 33140519091/9071; fax: 33144071046.
2. That is to say the cost the industry bears in the case of governmental regulation, minus the cost that the industry bears in the alternative case of self-regulation. As a rule, the avoided cost is positive because self-regulation is supposed to be less costly for firms than a government regulation because of the greater flexibility it gives them.

REFERENCES

Aggeri, F., A. Hatchuel and P. Lefebvre (1994), 'Waste Car Policy: Shared Uncertainty In The Regulatory Process' in Sorensen, K.H. (ed.), *The car and its environments: the past, the present and future of the motorcar in Europe*, Brussels: European Commission, Social Sciences, pp. 256—272.

Baumol, W.J. and W.E. Oates (1971), 'The Use of Standards and Prices for Protection of the Environment', *Swedish Journal of Economics*, **73**(1).

Becker, G.S. (1983), 'A Theory of Competition among Pressure Groups for Political Influence', *Quarterly Journal of Economics*, **XCVIII**(3), pp. 371—400.

Chrysalis Environmental Consulting (1994*), Voluntary Approaches and Sustainable Development*, CEC Discussion Paper (5).

Coase, R. (1960), 'The Problem of Social Cost', *Journal of Law and Economics*, **III**, October, pp. 1—44.

Gabel, H. (1995), 'Environmental management as a competitive strategy: the case of CFCs' in Folmer, H., H. Opschoor and H.L Gabel. (eds.), *The Principles of Environmental Economics: A Guide for Students and Decision Makers*, Aldershot: Edward Elgar.

Foster, C.D. (1992), *Privatization, Public Ownership and the Regulation of Natural Monopoly*, Oxford: Basil Blackwell.

Glachant, M. (1996), *Efficacité des politiques environnementales et coûts d'information*, Ecole Nationale Supérieure des Mines de Paris: CERNA, PhD Thesis.

Gunningham, N. (1995), *Environment, Self-regulation and the Chemical Industry: Assessing Responsible Care*, Australian Center for Environmental Law: Environmental Law and Policy Papers.

Hourcade, J.C., J.M. Salles and D. Thery (1992), 'Ecological Economics and Scientific Controversies: Lessons from Recent Policy Making in the EEC', *Ecological Economics*, 6, pp. 211—223.

Kahneman, O. (1991), 'Anomalies: The Endowment Effect, loss Aversion, and Status Quo Bias', *Journal of Economic Perspectives*, 5.

Keeler, T.E. (1984), 'Theories of Regulation and the Deregulation Movement', *Public Choice*, 44, pp. 103—145.

Lévêque, F. (1995), 'Standards and Standard Setting Processes in the Field of the Environment: An Overview' in R. Hawkins, R. Mansell and J. Skea (Eds.), *Standards, Innovation and Competitiveness*, Aldershot: Edward Elgar.

Lévêque, F. and A. Nadaï (1995), 'A Firm's Involvement in the Policy-Making Process', in H. Folmer, H. Opschoor and H.L. Gabel (Eds.), *The Principles of Environmental Economics: A Guide for Students and Decision Makers*, Aldershot: Edward Elgar.

Noll, R.G. and B.M. Owen (1983), *The Political Economy of Deregulation: Interest Groups in the Regulatory Process*, Washington D.C.: American Enterprise Institute.

Olson, M. (1965), 'The Logic of Collective Action: Public Goods and the Theory of Groups', *Havard Economic Studies*, **CXXIV**.

Oster, S. (1982), 'The Strategic Use of Regulatory Investments by Industry Subgroups', *Economic Enquiry*, 20, pp. 604—618.

Pigou, A.C. (1946), *The Economics of Welfare, fourth edition*, London: Mac Millan.

Stigler, G.J. (1971), 'The Theory of Economic Regulation', *Bell Journal of Economic and Management Science*, 2(1), Spring, pp. 3—21.

Telster, L.G. (1985), 'Co-operation, Competition, and Efficiency', *Journal of Law and Economics*, **XXVIII**, pp. 271—295.

Tirole, J. (1994), 'The Internal Organization of Government', *Oxford Economic Papers*, 46, pp. 1—29.

Weitzman, M.L. (1974), 'Prices Versus Quantities', *Review of Economic Studies*, **XLI**(4), pp. 477—491.

4. From environment to competition — the EU regulatory process in pesticide registration

Alain Nadaï[1]

1. INTRODUCTION

Pesticides are made of chemical molecules combined in a formulation. They are used by farmers to kill pests, weeds and fungi. Their very large use generates environmental damage through the remaining residues in soil and water and their adverse effects on wildlife when they are sprayed on fields. Pesticides pollution has become a major concern in the European Union (EU) for the green lobbies, the regulators and the agrochemical industry. Until 1991, this pollution had been regulated in most individual EU countries through a mandatory system of product registration. Before a pesticide could be sold in any member state, it had to comply with that country's environmental and toxicological standards. In 1991, an EU pesticide regulation was adopted. It harmonized the national pesticide policies and was therefore part of the building of the single market. This gave the EU regulatory authorities the opportunity to adopt higher environmental requirements, as well as the chance to decide on a review process for all of the 700 active ingredients currently used in pesticides sold on the internal market.

We analyse the process that led to the adoption of this regulation, examining the influence different players had on its final content. These players include the Member States' representatives, the European Commission, the green lobbies and the agrochemical firms. Because the agrochemical firms had diverging interests and organized themselves into two opposing and formal trade associations, this case study affords a clear and accessible view of a firm's involvement and strategies in the devising of regulatory policy.

The second section analyses the competition in the agrochemical industry and the impact environmental policy might have on this competition. Two groups of firms (i.e., innovators and imitators) having different issues at stake in such a regulation are characterized. It is argued that the market is not able to directly pay back innovators for their investments in green products. Therefore, the regulator may have to modify the protection of innovation in the sector in order to allow innovators to comply with new environmental requirements. By doing this the regulator faces the diverging interests of firms.

The third section examines the development of the new EU pesticide regulation. It divides the regulatory process into three distinct phases, focusing on the interest groups involved, the issues at stake and the output of each phase. It shows how the process shifted from political and environmental issues during the first phase to issues of competition within the agrochemical industry during the third phase. It analyses the extent to which firms influenced the final contents of the regulation and points to regulatory strategies of firms.

The fourth section draws final conclusions on the links between competition on the market arena and competition on the regulatory arena.

2. COMPETITION IN THE AGROCHEMICAL INDUSTRY

Listed here are some key features of the competition existing in the agrochemical industry, that must be taken into account before the EU pesticide regulatory process can be considered.

2.1 General features

The European and world pesticide markets are controlled by only a few global firms organized in an oligopoly. Table 4.1 shows that the first twelve agrochemical firms totalled around 75 per cent of the world market in 1993.

The agrochemical industry is a science-based industry. The R&D activity has traditionally sustained a product differentiation, thus reducing the competition on price.

Innovation is protected through regulation. The life-cycle of a pesticide[2] (cf. Figure 4.1) illustrates this fact. It begins with an R&D phase. Once a firm has found an active ingredient which is expected to have good pesticide properties, it applies for a patent. This gives the firm a temporary monopoly on the discovered molecule. The current duration of the patent within the EU is twenty years. Toxicological, environmental and biological tests are then undertaken to formalise the properties of the active ingredient. The data are gathered in a *dossier* and the firm applies for the registration of a formulation of this active ingredient. Until the adoption of the new EU regulation in 1991, this registration lasted between 8 and 15 years, depending on the EU country. Once the registration has been granted, the product is launched on the market. The firm then expects to recover the R&D investment and to start making a profit from the product. Yet, when the patent is over, firms which succeed in imitating the molecule get free access to the dossier. They can therefore apply at low cost for a registration and enter the market.

Table 4.1   Sales of the 12 leading agrochemical companies

Company	1993 ($ mill)
Ciba-Geigy	2,790
DuPont	2,014
Zeneca	1,950
Monsanto	1,936
Bayer	1,790
Rhone-Poulenc	1,756
DowElanco	1,604
Hoechst	1,355
BASF	1,149
American Cyanamid	1,100
Sandoz	890
Schering	703
Total	19,037
World market estimates	25,700
Share of world market	74,1%

Source: Agrow Review, n°214

As a result of patent protection, competition on a product may be divided into two phases and the industry into two groups of firms.

During the period of the patent, the firm is assumed to fix its price as a monopolist would. For the sake of simplicity, let us call these products under patent 'specialities'; let us call this segment of the pesticide market the 'speciality market' and the firms selling in this market segment 'speciality manufacturers'. Speciality manufacturers are made up of the main global firms: Ciba-Geigy, Du Pont de Nemours, Zeneca, Rhone-Poulenc, etc. The possibility for these firms to behave as monopolists in the speciality market is dependent on the extent to which their products are successfully differentiated from other specialities. When it is, the speciality manufacturer may not only attract a demand for the new product but also reduce the price competition with the other pesticides.

After the end of the patent, the pesticide's dossier is available free of charge to a firm which achieves the synthesis of a similar pesticide formulation. At this point, speciality manufacturers come into competition with smaller firms. Let us call this products out of patent 'commodities', this segment of the pesticide market 'commodity market' and these small and medium firms '**commodity producers**'. They are numerous. The European Commission lists around 100 agrochemical firms in the EU (European Commission, 1994a). They generally have a small or non-existent R&D capacity. However, once the patent has ended, they are able to copy an active ingredient, to formulate it into a pesticide, and to market it. As a consequence, the competition then shifts to price.

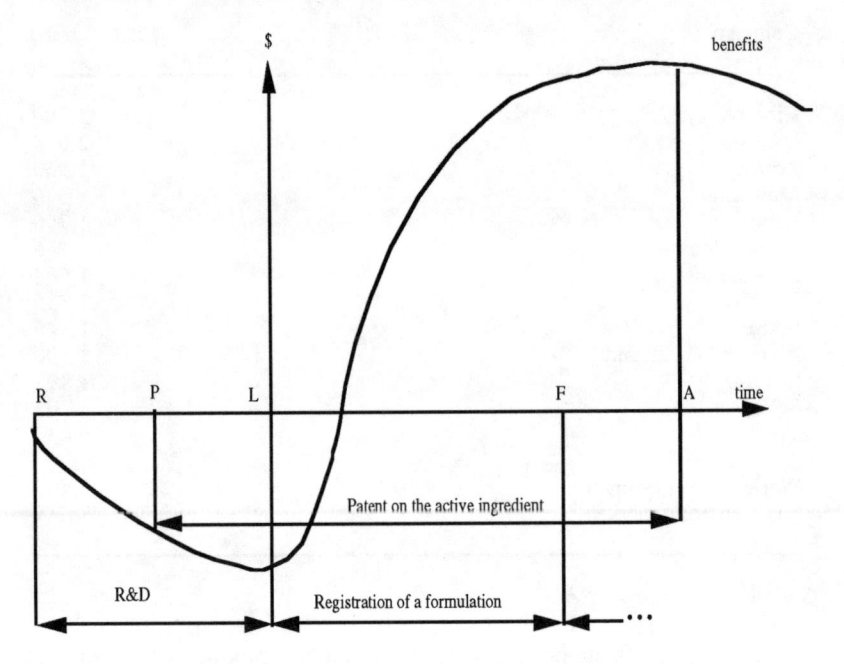

Notes: R=begining of research; P=application for a patent on the active ingredient; L=registration of the formulation and lauching on the market; F=end of the registration and possibility of a new registration; A=end of the patent on the active ingredient.

Source: Bonazzi (1993)

Figure 4.1   The life-cycle of a pesticide

Commodities account for almost half of speciality manufacturers' gross turnover (Nadaï, 1995). Therefore, speciality manufacturers try to protect their active ingredients and dossiers in different ways.

For some active ingredients, technical difficulties in production raise entry barriers and impede other firms from undertaking the production of a copy. One example is the active ingredient Chlorothalonil contained in fungicides for cereals and vegetables. Although the molecule is produced by several firms in addition to the original manufacturer, the Japanese firm ISK, many commodity producers have encountered difficulties when trying to produce it. Some have still not succeeded in their attempt.

For other active ingredients, firms can keep on changing the technical specifications of the product (i.e., nature and degree of the impurities in the formulation, concentration, formulation, etc.). Since imitators are rarely able to keep up with these changes, they cannot pretend to own a perfectly similar product and therefore cannot get free access to its dossier and market. Again ISK's strategy on Chlorothalonil illustrates this. As soon as the patent on the molecule ended, ISK brought to the regulator's attention the fact that an impurity in the formulation (i.e., the hexachlorobenzene) might be potentially dangerous and should therefore be controlled in Chlorothalonil formulations. After a year, the problem was solved by the imitators who demonstrated that this impurity had no adverse effects below a given level of concentration (i.e., 140ppm). ISK then brought another impurity to the regulator's attention taking another year to be resolved, so that during two years pesticides containing non-ISK's Chlorothalonil did not get access to the French market.

A third way to anticipate the end of the patent consists in pricing the product low enough that entry into the market becomes worthless for competitors. The original producer can undertake this strategy because it already benefits from large economies of scale in the production of the molecule. One successful example is the case of Round-up, a corn herbicide, whose price was halved by Monsanto just before the end of its patent.

A fourth strategy is to formulate a pesticide which mixes a molecule which is out of patent with a new and patented one. To the extent that farmers ask for polyvalent products and have a need for the functions of the new molecule, the protection of the new molecule benefits the old one.

A fifth strategy is to patent a technique of production, or a specific use of a molecule. Monsanto patented the most productive technique for the synthesis of Glyphosate. This gave the firm a twenty-year protection period on the technique whereas the molecule was already out of patent. DuPont de Nemours patented Chlorotoluron in 1952, and a technique for its synthesis in 1972.

An alternative strategy is to put pressure on the regulator in order to obtain an extension on the protection of the molecules.

2.2 The environment and competition

The environmental and toxicological requirements on pesticides have been strengthened during the last two decades. This has impacted on the industry by increasing the duration and the cost of the R&D phase. This increase has been reflected in changes in the value of gross turnover and the cost of development per molecule.

The impact on turnover resulted from a shortage of the duration of the temporary monopoly after a molecule has been introduced onto the market. Speciality manufacturers' representatives assert that 'the average effective patent term (i.e., the duration of the patent that protects the product after its introduction onto the market) in Europe was sixteen years in 1968, but is now only nine years and is still on a downward trend' (ECPA, 1994a). Still according to them 'increasing delays in marketing new products as a result of the need to comply with increasingly stringent regulatory requirements imposed by Member States and the EU' are at the origin of the reduction in the effective patent term (ECPA, 1994b). Firms assert that it should even be reduced further with the implementation of the new EU pesticide regulation.

In terms of costs, speciality manufacturers have integrated new toxicological and environmental requirements into their R&D. Early in the R&D phase, firms subject the active ingredients to a series of environmental tests. Some of these are carried out in laboratories, but others have to be carried out in life-size natural environments (e.g. the assessment of the residues in ground water when results in laboratory tests exceed certain thresholds). The latter are very expensive and time consuming. Figures provided by the agrochemical industry show a sharp increase in the R&D cost during the last decade and confirm the large share taken by environmental tests in this cost (Nadaï, 1994). According to the European agrochemical industry, environmental and toxicological tests account for 25 to 40 per cent of the total R&D cost per molecule — this total cost being estimated at around $150 million per molecule.

It is important to notice that in the agrochemical industry, the market does not pay back the investment in environmental innovation. Indeed, the main functions by which pesticide products are currently differentiated on the market are very different from the regulatory requirements (see Table 4.2).

Table 4.2   Profile of a modern plant protection product

What do regulators expect	What do farmers expect
Rapidly and completely biodegradable	Stable formulation, low use rate
Low toxicity to man and wildlife	High efficacy, quick action
No residues in crops	Flexibility in application timing
Feasible synthesis without undue production risk	Reasonable price
Single formulation	Compatibility with other active ingredients, ability to tank mix

Source: Nadaï (1995)

Three reasons may explain this gap between regulator's requirements and market expectations:

- farmers' supposedly low willingness to pay for a cleaner environment,
- the irrationality of public opinion which discourages firms from advertising on very sensitive issues — e.g. carcinogenicity, toxic effects on wildlife, etc. even to point out the relative harmlessness of a particular product — for fear of bringing these issues to the public's attention,
- asymmetries of information between firms and consumers which characterize the environmental quality of goods. Because the consumer cannot verify this quality, he has no reason to trust firms when they announce a high environmental quality. Reducing such asymmetries would require the firms to participate in a system of product labelling (Lévêque and Nadaï, 1995). Such a device implies an exchange of information among firms on the quality of their products. In the case of the agrochemical industry this is not desirable because it would facilitate imitation.

This brief examination of competition and environmental innovation in the agrochemical industry leads to the conclusion that the question of profitability must be tackled by the regulator within the system of protection of the innovation. Indeed, inasmuch as the market does not compensate the increase in environmental quality, the regulator faces the decision of whether or not the profits of the speciality manufacturers are sufficient to finance the investments in environmental innovation. Information on these profits is obviously asymmetric. The European Crop Protection Association (ECPA) asserts that EU-based agrochemical companies' profit margins decreased during the last decade — from 10.5 per cent of sales in 1981 to 6.8 per cent in 1990. Whether or not this reflects reality, whether this is due to increasing regulatory requirements, to increasing imitation and competition or to a decrease in the final demand (EU agriculture crisis), these are open questions. If the regulator over-estimates the profits, it may reduce innovative activity in the industry. If he underestimates them, it may over-protect the innovations and limit farmers' access to them by delaying competition on price. The regulator is therefore faced with a trade-off between the profitability of innovation for firms and their potential diffusion. He has to adjust this trade-off in a context of asymmetric information. He can use two variables: the content of the new regulatory requirements (which influence a firm's cost of compliance with regulation) and the duration of patent. Obviously, speciality manufacturers and commodity producers have diverging interests concerning the setting up of these variables. These conflicting interests are at the core of the pesticide regulatory process, which we will now analyse.

3. THE PESTICIDE REGULATORY PROCESS IN THE EU

3.1 General features

Over the past 20 years the European pesticide policy has been based on four main regulations.

The Directive 91/414 concerns the harmonization of national registration systems. It is the core regulation of the process. A first draft, issued by the Commission in the mid—1970s, was a dead end. Two successive drafts were proposed by the Commission in the late 1980s and early 1990s before the final text was adopted in 1991.[3]

The Directive 94/43 details the requirements for an active ingredient or a pesticide to be accepted for sale on the European market. A first draft was issued by the Commission in 1991 and the final text was adopted in 1994.

The third regulation is a project related to the enlargement of patent duration. In the late eighties, negotiation between industry and Commission on a supplementary patent certificate (SPC) regulation emerged as a separate topic at the EU level. Indeed, in 1989, the European Commission was working on a regulatory text on SPC for the pharmaceutical industry. The agrochemical industry, represented by its international trade association — the 'Groupement International des Associations Nationales de Fabricants de Produits Agrochimiques' (GIFAP) — argued that, given its similarity with the pharmaceutical industry, it should also be included in this regulation. In 1990, the European Parliament refused this inclusion but the idea of a separate SPC regulation concerning the agrochemical industry began to be negotiated between the industry and the Commission. From that point, the stringency of the requirements for registration included in the successive drafts of Directives 91/414 and 94/43, and the additional cost it would generate for agrochemical firms, were used by the agrochemical industry as an argument justifying their need for a SPC.

The EU Drinking Water Directive (COM 80/778) is the last regulation which has to be considered in the analysis of the development of the European pesticide policy. It was adopted in 1980 and regulates the quality of drinking water. It includes very stringent maximum residue limits for pesticides which were taken into account by the Commission when drafting Directive 94/43. Therefore, industry tried to obtain a modification of this Directive, which ended up being re-negotiated.

Our analysis weaves the issues that have emerged on these regulations together in a common picture of the EU pesticide regulatory process. Though losing some degree of precision on the respective development of each regulatory text, this allows us to afford a better understanding of the link between environmental regulation and the regulation of competition in the agrochemical industry.

The regulatory process may be divided into three periods.

3.2 The regulatory compromise between Member States (1976—1991)

This period began in the mid—1970s with the first discussions at the European Commission about a harmonisation of national regulations. It ended with the adoption of Directive 91/414.

The European scene involved various kinds of agent: growers representatives, agrochemical companies, public interest groups and particularly green lobbies, European institutions including the Commission and the Council. This first phase of the regulatory process was mostly driven by green lobbies, the Commission and the Member States. Growers representatives and the agrochemical industry were not very active. The former were strongly involved in the Common Agricultural Policy reform process. The latter, already present at the European level through its international trade organization — the GIFAP — was not deeply involved because its interest was close to that of the Commission. Both wanted to obtain a system of single registration of pesticide formulations at the EU level: the Commission because this was part of the achievement of the single market, and the large agrochemical firms because they hoped that such a system would generate economies of scale in the registration activity, which could compensate for the extra cost associated with more stringent regulatory requirements.

Green lobbies were active in the process from its outset. They lobbied vigorously through the Directorate General of the Environment (DG XI) at the Commission and through Member States like Denmark and Germany. Green lobbies' positions varied. For the 'greenest', (e.g., Greenpeace) the main target was a global ban on all pesticides. Others (e.g., Friends of the Earth) emphasized the unreliability of the scientific research and the consequent risk of basing a regulatory decision on it. They were in favour of a major reduction in pesticide consumption and of a public debate on pesticides uses and features.

The Commission's priority in this phase of the process was to reach a political compromise between the twelve Member States in order to render possible the adoption of an EU pesticide regulation. Its goal was to ensure a genuine harmonization of markets and regulatory practices, which required the maximum reduction of the degree of liberty of the Member States in the new European regulatory framework. Yet, the regulatory text adopted in 1991 remained a very broad and flexible compromise. In other words, the Commission did not really succeed in fulfilling its goal. This was due to diverging interests among the twelve Member States.

Member states were influential as part of an ad hoc Committee (i.e., the Standing Committee) in the Commission and because they make up the Council. They have practised registration at the national level for years. This gives them power as technical experts but also brings into play huge differences in practice from one state to another. Regarding pesticide regulation, each state had set up a national compromise under pressure from public opinion, the national parliament, national growers associations, etc. This national compromise was defended by each member state in the negotiations. Member states can be split into two groups according to their behaviour in the discussions over Directive 91/414.

Group 1 brought together France, United Kingdom and Ireland. They were used to working flexibly at the national level in terms of requirements and registration decisions. In this group only a minimum of data was generally required for pesticide registration and regulators were used to asking for additional studies if the case justified them. Spain and Belgium often joined this group in the regulatory game.

Group 2 brought together Denmark, Germany and the Netherlands. Generally involved in intense political debates about environmental concerns, these countries shared the characteristic of being less flexible and implementing many more requirements. Basically, they were the countries in favour of the implementation of fixed thresholds regarding the way of interpreting the results of tests on active ingredients (the so-called 'cut-off' criteria, see below the example of the ground water parameter). Luxembourg and Italy often joined group 2 in the discussions.

Both groups accepted the new EU Directive because they expected that its contents were compatible with their national particularities in making decisions:

- group 1's need for flexibility in decision making meant that only part of group 2's requirements could be included in this Directive,
- group 2 hoped for its part that a higher level of environmental and health protection would progressively be implemented through future additional requirements to the Directive.

Denmark was the only European state opposed to the compromise because it could not expect to preserve its own stringent way of regulating the pesticide market within the new regulatory framework.

Such a logic has led to three main effects on the final compromise: a global increase in the minimal and systematic requirements adopted; the possibility of implementing further requirements in the future (urged by group 2); a decision which has postponed many questions and problems to further steps in the process.

Directive 91/414 sets up a two-tier system of registration which was implemented in July 1993. It deals with five main aspects.

1) Active ingredients are registered at the EU level. Their dossiers are submitted for examination by a committee of member state experts which decides whether the active ingredient may be authorized on the EU market. The authorized active ingredients are registered on a so-called positive list.

2) National registrations of pesticide formulations are harmonised. Pesticide formulations containing only active ingredients registered on the positive list are registered at the national level. However, these national decisions have to respect a principle of mutual recognition: Member States have to either adopt the same decisions on a given pesticide or to argue their divergence according to differences in their natural environments. This last point gives room for differences between the national decisions.
3) Registration of active ingredients and pesticide formulations are made according to new criteria and requirements. However, these criteria and requirements were not included in the 1991 Directive. They had to be included in six annexes which were planned to be adopted as separate regulatory texts after 1991. In particular, the annex VI, called 'Uniform Principles', was a key issue for the agrochemical industry. It was aimed at including the new toxicological and environmental criteria (neurotoxicity, ecotoxicity, etc.) and at detailing the procedures and the level of stringency to be implemented on the different criteria for (re) registration.
4) All active ingredients currently sold on the EU market must be reviewed within ten years. This review will be carried out at the EU level according to the new criteria and requirements. For each of the active ingredients the result of the review will be: a) full authorization and registration on the positive list or, b) registration with restriction of uses (to certain crops or conditions of use) or, c) a ban.
5) Industrial property rules and data protection are harmonised. In as far as the re-registration of the active ingredient will lead to the production of supplementary data by the firms, these data will be protected for five years.

The 1991 Directive was the main outcome of this phase. Yet, it raised several pending issues. Because the contents of the Uniform Principles had not been adopted, uncertainty remained on their main consequences for firms. Two kinds of costs, whose values were dependent on the criteria that would be included in the Uniform Principles, were indeed at stake for firms:

- an additional cost for registering the specialties, to be borne by the speciality manufacturers who have to undertake new tests,
- a cost of re-registration of commodities to be borne by all firms.

Speciality manufacturers argued their demand for a supplementary patent certificate regulation on the basis of these potential extra-costs. By doing this, they connected two different regulation devising processes: the already ongoing one concerning supplementary patent certificates, and the one concerning the environment and the registration of products.

3.3 The involvement of speciality manufacturers in order to limit the stringency on environmental requirements (1991—1994)

The second period was characterized by the effective involvement of speciality manufacturers in the process. They attempted to control the trend towards increasing stringency of environmental requirements pushed by group 2 Member States. Their involvement became significant with the establishment of a European pressure group, the European Crop Protection Association (ECPA). It was founded in 1992 by national agrochemical associations and thirteen leading agrochemical firms operating in Europe. This association works with few permanent staff but establishes an extensive scientific network between its members. ECPA members employed a total of 5,000 environmental and toxicological experts. This gives it a huge capacity for processing and generating information.

This period ended with the implementation of the Directive 94/43 and with some pending issues: the opposition of the ECPA and the Commission concerning the revison of the Drinking Water Directive (COM 80/778), the ECPA's demand for an extension in the protection of data and patents.

The issues at stake for speciality manufacturer

Speciality manufacturers wanted to limit as much as possible the increase in their net cost of compliance with the new regulation.

Their first strategy consisted in limiting the stringency of the new environmental requirements. These requirements had been fixed in the first draft of the 'Uniform Principles' issued by the European Commission in April 20th 1993. This draft included ecotoxicological decision-making criteria in several area (i.e., birds, terrestrial vertebrates, fish, daphnia and beneficial arthropods) that were far too stringent, according to the ECPA (*Agrow*, N°184, May 21st 1993). Some of them were cut-off criteria. A cut-off criterion consists of a threshold value for test results beyond which a molecule is banned. These criteria were devised according to a protection principle concept that was supported by some of the European Commission's experts, the group 2 Member States and the green lobbies. The rationale of the concept is that due to scientific uncertainties (e.g., the absence of assessment of the cross effects of different pesticide residues on human health and environment) stringent requirements have to be implemented so as to prevent unknown adverse effects. This logic is opposed to the risk-benefit balance previously implemented in EU countries for pesticide registration. Through ECPA, speciality manufacturers put pressure on regulators to cancel cut-off criteria. The most illustrative example was the dispute on a reference to the drinking water parameter (i.e., the so-called parameter '55', Directive 80/778) that had been included in the Uniform Principles. This parameter specified very low maximum limits of pesticide residues in drinking water: $0,1\mu g/l$ for any pesticide residues and a $0,5\mu g/l$ total limit for all pesticide residues whatever their toxicity.

Above such a limit the concerned pesticides should be restricted in their use or banned. The position of industry was that such a limit was not scientifically-based and could not be attained by between 30 to 50 per cent of the pesticides currently sold on the EU market (*Agrow*, 1993). Its anticipated cost would therefore be significant. In March 1993, agrochemical industry obtained the Commission's commitment to revise this criterion and adopt variable levels of permitted residues according to the toxicty of each active ingredient.

A second strategy was to attempt to increase their pay-off from protection of innovation through an extension in its duration. ECPA pointed out that the duration of data protection was insufficient compared to the extra cost of R&D generated by the new regulation and to the related decrease in the profits of agrochemical firms. ECPA asked for a supplementary protection certificate on new active ingredients. It also pointed out the uncertainties which remained on the rules of implementation of the review process, and particularly those related to the protection of additional data produced in order to update the commodities dossiers.

The outcomes of the second period

The major outcome is the reduction in the stringency of the requirements included in the Uniform Principles. Cut-off criteria have been withdrawn from the 'Uniform Principles', which were finally adopted in June 1994 (European Commission, 1994b).

Despite this, the dispute concerning parameter 55 remains unsolved since the final text of the 'Uniform Principles' indicates that: 'pesticides will gain permanent registration if their residue limits in drinking water are expected to be below $0,1\mu g/l$. If the drinking water limit is not achieved, but there are actions ongoing that will bring residues of the product below $0,1\mu g/l$, a provisional authorization of five years may be granted. This is subject to the limit not exceeding a toxicologically-based safety limit' (*Agrow*, n°211, 1994).

The ECPA still did not agree with the adopted text. It required the 'Uniform Principles' to be revised in line with new science-based residue limits, when the Drinking Water Directive (80/778) is amended.

The Commission's last proposal of modification of the drinking water directive was issued in December 1994. It moved towards cancelling the $0,5\mu g/l$ threshold for all pesticide residues while keeping the $0,1\mu g/l$ threshold for individual pesticides (*Agrow*, n°224, 1995). It was strongly opposed by ECPA.

ECPA's demand for an extension of the patent on specialities also remained an unsolved issue at the end of this phase. In December 1994, the European Commission transmitted a proposal of Supplementary Protection Certificate (SPC) regulation to the European Council. It would extend the patent life of pesticides up to fifteen years from the date of their first market launch (*Agrow*, n°223, 1995). This represents a seven year extension of the protection (see above, the European industry asserts that the average effective patent term is currently nine years). A transitional scheme is envisaged for products already on the market at the time the regulation would come into force: the proposed system would apply to all products authorized in the EU after January 1st 1985 for which a patent would still be valid when the regulation would take effect.

ECPA's demand for clarification concerning the rules to follow during the review process also remained unsolved.

Both ECPA's claims concerned commodity producers because of the protection of innovation shapes competition in the industry. In 1994, as annex II of the Directive 91/414 was being drafted by the Commission a third event occurred and brought to their attention the risk of not being involved in the process.

3.4 The confrontation between speciality manufacturers and commodity producers (1994—?)

The issues at stake for commodity producers

Commodity producers structured themselves into a formal pressure group — the European Crop Care Association[4] (ECCA) — in 1993. This group began to be really active in the process in 1994, when they thought that their access to new active ingredients was being threatened. According to the 91/414 regulation, the free access to a molecule's dossier after the end of its patent is permitted to producers reaching the synthesis of a 'similar molecule'. Similarity had to be decided on according to specifications listed in annex II of this Directive. In 1994, the Commission was working on a draft of annex II which mentioned the producer's name as one of these specifications. Commodity producers thought that it could mean that similarity was defined on the basis of the producer's name. In this case, even the synthesis of a molecule would no longer have allowed a producer access to the molecule's original dossier. 'Similar molecule' would have meant 'same producer' and a commodity producer's activity would simply have been hindered. This alarmed commodity producers and brought to their attention broader issues at stake in the process.

Among these issues was the Commission's SPC proposal but also the question of the procedures to be followed for the review. Commodity producers dread speciality manufacturers using the review process in order to re-establish temporary monopolies on commodities.

The review process system is complex. The Commission is responsible for the regular publication of a list of active ingredients to be reviewed. Firms which want to keep on selling any of these molecules have, from the date of the publication of each list: i) six months to state their intention to support the re-registration of the molecule; and ii) one year to show that the molecule's dossier meets the new requirements, or to produce additional data in order to update it. Then, the authority has another year to recommend that the active ingredient be registered or to request additional data. Given that the new data will be protected for five years after the re-

registration, firms which provide this data will benefit from a protected market for five years. The straightforward implications are the following. If only one firm applies, it will get a five year monopoly on the active ingredient. If there are several applicants, they have to decide how to share the cost of updating the dossier and the then protected market of the molecule.

In order to tackle these points, the European Commission has proposed to use decentralized negotiations among firms. This means that firms applying for the same active ingredient have been encouraged to negotiate, within task forces, in order to fix the contents of the additional data package, its total cost and the sharing out of this cost among the participants. The way these task forces will be organized is thus crucial. If the rules implemented allow one of the participants to deter other firms from participating, then task forces may allow the re-establishment of temporary monopolies on commodities.

Given that more than half of the gross turnover of speciality manufacturers comes from the sales of active ingredients out of patent (Nadaï, 1995), it can be assumed that in most cases the original manufacturer of a molecule will apply for it. Moreover, a profit maximizing objective may imply the attempt to expel other firms from its market in order to re-establish a temporary monopoly. Speciality manufacturers will therefore oppose task forces, whereas commodity producers will support them. The positions of the ECPA and the ECCA reflect these interests. ECPA argues that 'the reasonable steps to set up a task force can only be judged as "reasonable" by the parties involved', and that 'a firm deciding not to organise a task force should not necessarily be considered as having failed to take "reasonable steps"'. In other words, it defends the possibility for firms not to organise task-forces (ECPA, 1994a). ECCA argues that task forces should be mandatory when there are several notifiers for an active ingredient.

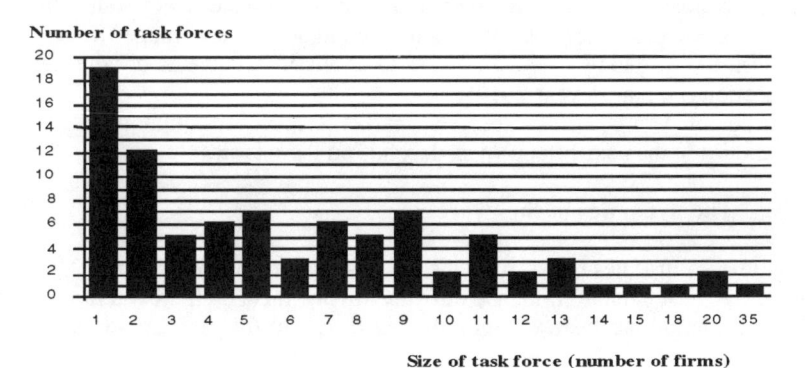

Figure 4.2   *The distribution of task-forces for the review process in 1994*

Source: European Commission, 1994(a)

The first list of ninety active ingredients was published by the Commission in 1994 and firms applied. Figure 4.2 shows that most of these molecules are currently defended by more than one firm, which makes the above considerations relevant.

The future outcomes of the third period
At the moment (November 1995), one outcome has been achieved. It is the decision to specify active ingredients on the positive list only by their physical and chemical characteristics. This change was due to pressure from the ECCA. In fact, ECCA obtained the guarantee that the name of the producer of the active ingredient, which is still included in the dossier as information, will not be considered as a specification of the molecule.

Three major issues are still pending. They concern the drinking water parameter, the SPC regulatory text and the outcome of the review.

In June 1995, the European Parliament approved the first reading of the Commission's Supplementary Protection proposal. The Council and the European Parliament (second reading) still have to give their advice on this proposal. Concerning the drinking water issue, no further steps had been made. The review process still has not been undertaken on the first commodities. Therefore, the foregoing considerations on the possible re-establishment of temporary monopolies on commodities do not have any actual answers. However, a theoretical analysis of this point (Nadaï, 1995) confirmed this possibility under restrictive conditions concerning competition and information on the molecule (i.e., number of firms, market shares, intensity of price competition, information on the molecule's profitability for the competitors).

It is worth mentioning that an important number of patents on active ingredients are due to end before 1998. This highlights the importance of the issue at stake on the speciality market. Indeed, depending whether the SPC is adopted before or after 1998 and depending on the review outcomes, the effective protection of these active ingredients may range from no extension (i.e., end of patent in 1998) to almost twelve years of additional protection (i.e., up to year 2010).[5]

In other words, the respective market shares of commodities and specialties in the next fifteen years depends on these issues.

3.5 The dynamics of the process

Figure 4.3 illustrates the story of the EU pesticide regulatory process. Up to now, the most evident influence of firms' involvement on the content of the new regulation has been to limit the stringency of the new environmental requirements.

Three strategic variables have been negotiated during the process between the regulator and the firms.

The first one is the cost of compliance of agrochemical firms with the new regulation. The regulatory game consisted in adjusting the

From environment to competition 69

environmental requirements. These requirements became very stringent during the first phase of the process when green groups and group 2 Member States were actively involved in the negotiations whereas agrochemical firms were absent. During the second phase, this cost was reduced as a result of ECPA's pressure on the regulator. The reduction was embodied in the changes in the drinking water parameter and the cancelling of cut-off criteria. Speciality manufacturers and commodity producers have the same interest concerning this variable. They want to diminish the abatement cost. As a result of group 2's pressure the Commission is interested in reducing pollution which in turn leads to an increase in firms' cost of compliance.

	Phase 1 1991	Phase 2 1994	Phase 3
Input	EU political agenda.	EU pesticide regulatory text	Review process supplementary. Protection certificate.
Logic	Building the single market.	Limiting the stringency on environmental requirements.	Sharing the pesticide market.
Interest groups	Green Lobbies involvement (1989).	Specialty manufacturers involvement (ECPA)	Commodity manufacturers (ECCA) Specialty manufacturers (ECPA)
Outcomes	EU registration and re-registration framework.	Uniform principles (Annex IV), reduction in cut-off criteria.	Specification of active ingredients only by their physical and chemical features.
Pending issues	New environemental requirements to be devised.	Proposal of supplementary protection certificate regulation (extension of the average effective patent term from nine to fifteen years). Proposal of change in the drinking water directive. Proposal of specification of new active ingredients by their producer's name.	Proposal of supplementary protection certificate regulation (extension of the average effective patent term from nine to fifteen years). Proposal of change in the drinking water directive. Review process on old active ingredients: - re-registrations, restrictions in the use, bans, - new temporary monopolies.

Figure 4.3   The three periods of the EU pesticide regulatory process

The second variable is *the duration of the patent on new active ingredients*. This duration determines, for a given molecule, the value of the temporary monopoly a speciality manufacturer may expect. The longer the protection, the higher the value of the temporary monopoly for this manufacturer. However, such an extension penalizes commodity producers because the longer this patent lasts, the later they are allowed to sell the new molecules. Therefore it is in their interest to limit the extension of patents on new active ingredients. The regulator wants to allow the speciality manufacturers to innovate while not leaving them a rent by over-extending the patent duration. The configuration of interests is thus different concerning this variable: speciality manufacturers and commodity producers have diverging interests. During the second phase of the process, speciality manufacturers demanded an increase in the patent duration and the producer's name was included in the specification of the molecules.

The third variable is the protection of the new data generated by firms for the review process. This variable is strategic to the extent that it also protects the market of the concerned commodity. As most of the commodities are sold by several firms, data protection raises the question of how to share each commodity market among the firms financing the review. As mentioned above, this problem is faced within the implementation of the review process.

Given these conflicting interests, two patterns have been noticeable during the regulatory process and characterise its dynamic.

First, the private cost of compliance value has been successively increased and decreased through bargaining, as a result of the pressure of interest groups on the regulator.

Second, the dynamic suggested is one of a cumulative involvement of interest groups triggered by negative regulatory payoffs emerging in the process. Figure 4.4 illustrates this. The involvement of interest groups was triggered by the emergence, within the process, of highly negative payoffs: firms were reactive to the course of the process. Speciality manufacturers reacted to the increasing number and the stringency of the cut-off criteria included in the first proposal of Directive 94/43. Commodity producers reacted to the threat of extension of the patent.

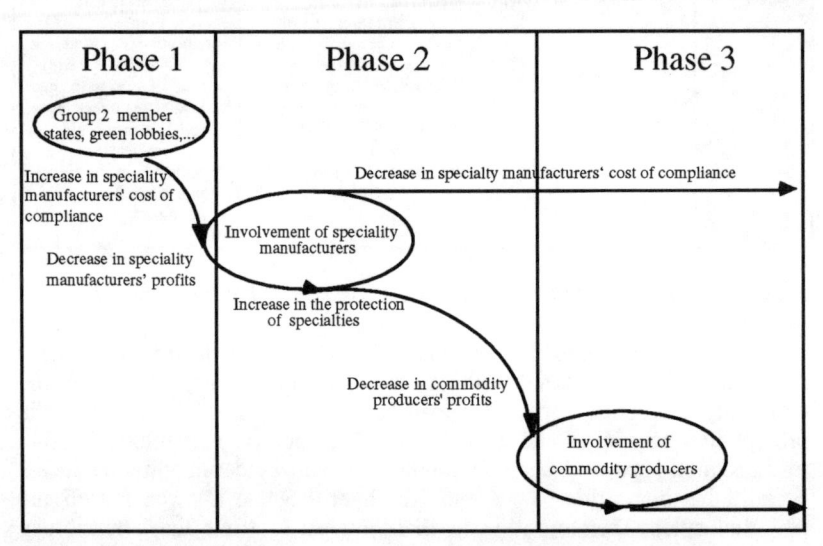

Figure 4.4   The dynamic of the EU pesticide regulatory process

4. CONCLUSION

The story of the pesticide regulatory process in the EU illustrates a shift from political and environmental issues towards issues of competition within an industry. It is also a case where interest groups have clearly influenced the final content of a regulation.

Concerning a firm's behaviour in the regulatory process it shows that, when *deciding to involve* themselves in the regulatory arena, firms seemed to be short-sighted. Their *involvement* in the process is interpreted here as a *reaction* to the course of the process. The competition between firms of the different interest groups seems to have structured the process in that it made the increase in one group's payoff correspond to a decrease in that of the other. The process presents a dynamic which gives a central role to *negative regulatory payoffs* in triggering the involvement of firms.

Once they *have become involved* in the process firms' behaviour seems to have become more strategic and less reactive. They have played on information asymmetries concerning their cost of compliance in order to increase their own gains. This strategy confronts the regulator with two risks. The first is to change the structure of the industry, from a differentiated and innovative one to a commodity one, if it does not provide sufficient payoffs for environmental R&D costs. The second is to allow speciality manufacturers to increase monopoly rents. Both risks would affect the environmental efficiency of the regulation. The first one would reduce the innovative activity towards 'greener' pesticides. The second one may delay farmers' access to 'greener' pesticides by delaying the competition on their price. These risks reflect the trade-off between environmental policy and competition policy in this industry. Since the SPC regulation and the Drinking Water Directive modification have not yet been adopted and since the review process rules are still unclear, the influence of this trade-off on the agrochemical industry remains uncertain. It depends to a great extent on the regulator's decisions. The regulatory process in still under way.

NOTES

1. Alain Nadaï, Researcher, Centre of Industrial Economics (CERNA), Ecole Nationale Supérieure des Mines de Paris, 60, bld St Michel, 75272 Paris Cedex 06, France, tel: 33140519091/9071; fax: 33144071046.
2. A pesticide contains an active ingredient in a formulation. For the sake of clarity, 'formulation' or 'pesticide' refers hereafter to the final pesticide product, whereas 'molecule' or 'active ingredient' refers to the chemical molecule contained in the pesticide.
3. Looking back in time, the successive regulatory texts concerning the EU pesticide registration have been the following:
   —**1976,** *'Proposition de Directive du Conseil concernant le mise en marché des produits phytopharmaceutiques homologués CEE'*, presented

by the Commission to the Council August 4th 1976, edited in the Official Journal **9/9/76**, n° **C 212/3**,

—**1989**, *'Proposition de Directive du Conseil concernant le mise en marché des produits phytopharmaceutiques homologués CEE'*, presented by the Commission to the Council February 16th 1989, **COM (89) 34 final**. This text proposes the adoption of the two-tier EU registration whereas the former (n° C 212/3) proposed a single system of EU registration.

—**1991**, *'Directive du Conseil du 15 Juillet 1991 concernant la mise en marché des produits phytosanitaires'*, edited in the Official Journal August 19th 1991, n° **91/414/CEE**.

—**1994**, *'Directive du Conseil, du 27 juillet 1994, établissant l'annexe VI de la Directive 91/414/CEE concernant la mise sur le marché des produits phytopharmaceutiques'*, edited in the Official Journal JO L227/37, 1/9/94, n°**94/43/CE**.

4. ECCA is composed of 12 firms from seven EU countries (Spain, Italy, France, Netherlands, Ireland, Germany, United Kingdom).
5. If the current SPC regulation proposal (see above) is adopted after 1998, these molecules will not benefit from a supplementary patent certificate. Their review should thus take place in 1998. If, at that time, the molecule's market is shared through the building of a task force during this review, then their protection will end (i.e., 1998). If the current SPC regulation proposal is adopted before 1998, these molecules will benefit from a seven year effective patent term extension. Their review may thus take place in 2005. At that time, if the review process allows an additional temporary monopoly of five years to the original producer, the total extension of protection will be of twelve years (i.e., up to 2010).

REFERENCES

Agrow review (1993*)*, n°184.
Agrow review (1994*)*, n°211.
Agrow review (1994*)*, n°214.
Agrow review (1995*)*, n°223.
Agrow review (1995*)*, n°224.
Bonazzi, C. (1993), *R&D Industrielle et Concurrence: Cas de l'Agrochimie et de la Pharmacie*, Ecole Nationale Supérieure des Mines de Paris: CERNA, PhD Thesis.
European Commission (1976), 'Proposition de Directive du Conseil Concernant la Mise en Marché des Produits Phytopharmaceutiques Homologués CEE', *Journal Officiel*, September 9, n°C/212/3.
European Commission (1989), 'Proposition Modifiée de Directive du Conseil Concernant la Mise en Marché des Produits Phytopharmaceutiques Homologués CEE', Brussels: COM (89) 34 final.
European Commission (1991), 'Directive du Conseil du 15 Juillet 1991 Concernant la Mise en Marché des Produits Phytosanitaires', *Journal Officiel*, n° 91/414/CE.
European Commission (1994a), 'Réglement CE N°933/94 de la Commission du 27 Avril 1994, établissant la liste de substances actives des produits

pharmaceutiques et désignant les Etats membres rapporteurs pour l'application du réglement (CEE) n°3600/92', *Journal Officiel*, L107/8.

European Commission (1994b), 'Directive 94/43/CE du Conseil, du 27 juillet 1994, établissant l'annexe VI de la Directive 91/414/CEE concernant la mise sur le marché des produits phytopharmaceutiques', *Journal Officiel*, L227/37.

ECPA (1994a), *ECPA Views on 'Reasonable Efforts' to Submit a Single Dossier in Compliance with the 'Registration Directive' (91/414/EEC) and the 'Review Regulation' (3600/92)*, Brussels: ECPA.

ECPA (1994b), *ECPA Brief on the Creation of a Supplementary Protection Certificate for Plant Protection Products*, Brussels: ECPA, C/93/PT/1078.

Lévêque, F. and A. Nadaï (1995), 'A Firm's Involvement in the Policy-Making Process', in H. Folmer, H. Opschoor and H.L. Gabel (eds.), *The Principles of Environmental Economics: A Guide for Students and Decision Makers*, Aldershot: Edward Elgar, pp. 299—327.

Nadaï, A. (1994) 'The Greening of the EU Agrochemical Market: Regulation and Competition', *Business Strategy and the Environment*, 3(2), pp. 34—42.

Nadaï, A. (1995), *The EU Regulatory Process in Pesticide Registration*, ERIC Report for the European Commission (DG XII/D-5), CERNA: Paris.

5. The energy sector response to European combustion emission regulations

Antony Ikwue[1] and Jim Skea[2]

1. INTRODUCTION

Energy sector activity has major environmental impacts which have been recognized in laws and regulations for several decades. Economic development in the energy sector is intertwined with regulatory activity to a degree which is unparalleled except perhaps in chemicals and vehicle manufacturing. As a result, the competencies which energy companies have developed in negotiating with policy-makers and regulatory authorities make an important contribution to their overall competitiveness.

The energy sector itself comprises a diverse set of sub-markets. These divide into two broad classes. The first type of market, for primary commodities such as oil, gas and coal, are competitive at a global level. In general, countries act as hosts for multinational companies operating in oligopolistic markets in which competition takes place on an international scale. The second type of market, for some forms of delivered energy such as electricity and natural gas, is characterized by strong elements of natural monopoly. In the 'network industries', the state is heavily involved either through regulation of the prices and profits of privately owned 'utility' companies or through ownership of the companies themselves. So far, electricity and gas distribution has primarily been a national concern. Different systems of organization, ownership and regulation have evolved in different countries and a great diversity of patterns is apparent even within the European Union (EU). Whatever the system, the state has a significant economic stake in electricity and gas supply and this can influence the relationship between the regulator and the regulated with respect to environmental issues. This chapter covers the energy sector in general, but highlights the electricity generation and oil refining sectors which are taken to reflect the crude distinction between the globally competitive and nationally monopolistic components of the energy sector. The role of energy users is also discussed, especially in the context of the carbon/energy tax.

The energy sector gives rise to a variety of environmental impacts including atmospheric pollution, water pollution, landscape effects, public amenity and the disposal of solid and radioactive wastes. However, the dominant environmental issues from the 1970s through to the 1990s relate to emissions of atmospheric pollutants such as sulphur dioxide (SO_2), nitrogen oxides (NO_x) and carbon dioxide (CO_2). These pollutants have been associated with two contentious environmental issues — acid rain/forest dieback in the 1970s and 1980s and climate change during the late 1980s and 1990s. Both the EU and its Member States have been active in developing policies in relation to these problems. Acid rain and climate change are therefore taken as case studies which illustrate the role of energy sector companies in relation to European regulatory processes dealing with environmental questions.

In order to place the relationship between regulatory authorities and energy companies under the microscope, two specific EU regulatory proposals are explored: a) the 1988 Large Combustion Plants (LCP) Directive (proposed in 1983) which limits emission of SO_2 and NO_x in order to mitigate the problem of acid rain; and b) the so-far unsuccessful 1992 proposal for a carbon/energy tax which was to have formed part of the EU's climate change strategy. This latter proposal was modified significantly in March 1995.

The choice of these two specific regulatory proposals, which are separated by approximately a decade, allows a number of useful comparisons and developments within EU environmental policy to be highlighted:

- although Member States have a considerable degree of discretion with respect to implementation, the LCP Directive essentially establishes a traditional framework of administrative controls. The carbon/energy tax, by way of contrast, represents an innovative market-based instrument of the type which the EU, under its Fifth Environmental Action Programme, wishes to exploit to a greater degree (European Commission, 1992a).
- When the LCP Directive was proposed, EU environmental policy was a great deal less developed than it is now. There has been a great deal of mutual learning on the part of industry, the Commission and other EU institutions concerning how regulatory processes can be operated, manipulated or blocked. In particular, various industrial sectors have created European trade associations, such as EurElec (electricity) and EuroPIA (petroleum industry) whose primary task is to press their members' interests when regulatory initiatives at the European level are being developed.
- The balance of power between EU institutions, especially the Commission, and those of the Member States has ebbed and flowed during the 1980s and 1990s. In the 1980s, the EU drew sovereignty from the Member States in the environmental field. In the 1990s, the development and implementation of the subsidiarity principle has, in the

environment policy domain as in other areas, allowed power to flow back to the Member States.
- The introduction of competition (liberalization) into the network energy industries has proceeded to a very high degree in some Member States, notably the UK. At the same time, the EU's energy policy has begun to focus on the problem of creating trans-European networks in electricity and gas. The energy sector has formed an important arena for the interplay between the European Commission's liberalization agenda and its environmental objectives.

The chapter is structured as follows. The following section provides important contextual information on the structure of the electricity generation and oil refining sectors in the EU, focusing on the four largest Member States — Germany, France, Italy and the UK. The organization, ownership and patterns of regulation are described and the key actors are identified. This section also covers energy policy in the four Member States.

The next section presents, in narrative form, the development and negotiation of the LCP Directive, focusing on the role of energy companies and trade associations. The point is made that the regulatory process within Europe does not necessarily come to an end when the Council of Ministers and Parliament agree a Directive. Directives tend to allow for discretion at the national level in developing laws and regulations which give effect to the basic objectives of the Directive.[3] The degree of national discretion and the consequent impacts on competitiveness within the EU may grow as the subsidiarity principle is given greater emphasis. The chapter also covers, therefore, the regulatory process which continued at the national level following the agreement of the LCP Directive. However, this discussion covers only the development of national laws and regulations, not site-specific negotiations between regulatory agencies and companies. These negotiations are considered to be part of the implementation process rather than the regulatory process.

The next section describes the development of the carbon/energy tax proposal and the factors which contributed to its not being agreed. The salient feature here is that a proposal for a market-based instrument proved no more easy — and perhaps more difficult — to negotiate than a traditional administrative measure. The degree to which the intelligence of energy companies and their trade associations failed, in spite of their growing sophistication, to anticipate accurately the intentions of the Commission is also striking.

The penultimate section of the chapter considers the immediate prospects for environmental policy in the energy sector, including the possible extension of oil product standards and the nature of the informal regulatory process which is already under way.

The final section draws together conclusions from the case studies, noting differences as well as similarities. The conclusions relate to:

differences between the approach and effectiveness of the oil and electricity sectors; the significance of liberalization of electricity markets; the special characteristics of environmental issues with a high public profile in relation to regulatory processes; incentives for collaboration between companies and sectors; the use of regulatory processes to mitigate competitive disadvantage; and differences (and similarities) between regulatory processes associated with market-based instruments and more traditional forms of control.

2. ELECTRICITY GENERATION AND OIL REFINING IN THE EU

2.1 Electricity generation

The role of the electricity supply industry
Electricity is vital to the functioning of modern industrialized economies. As a result, the electricity supply industry occupies a privileged position in most countries. State ownership is common and the industry benefits from a considerable degree of government protection. The three components of the industry — generation, high voltage transmission and local distribution — have often been vertically integrated. Competition has taken place only to a limited degree and the industry has generally been subject to some form of 'rate-of-return' regulation by which prices are controlled in order to prevent companies earning 'excess' profits. The state has often intervened in the industry in order to influence the fortunes of related sectors of the economy, especially coal mining and the manufacture of electricity generation equipment.

In recent years however there has been a sustained challenge to the traditional paradigm of centralization, vertical integration, protected national markets and, in some countries, state ownership. Several countries have liberalized fuel and equipment procurement and have encouraged greater competition, especially in generation. The EU has backed up these trends with a Directive relating to the procurement of equipment.

Changes introduced so far fall short of the creation of a single energy market within the EU. Taking the newly privatized UK electricity industry as a marker, the Commission has charted a path towards vertical de-integration and greater competition. Deprived of the certainty provided by guaranteed profits under rate-of-return regulation, electricity suppliers are likely to depreciate investments over much shorter timescales with significant implications for technology choice. To the extent that privatization takes place, public interest commitments to social policy, environmental performance and long-term R&D are also likely to decline.

Electricity companies are highly active participants in the policy process which is redefining the nature of their businesses. For the most part, companies are fiercely resisting change. Within the EU, some national governments, notably France, have also shown little enthusiasm for de-integrating or privatizing their national utilities. Slow progress is expected in Italy, where opposition from management and wider political uncertainties have delayed the privatization of ENEL, the state-owned electricity company. Germany has also announced plans for a liberalization of the industry.

At the same time as the industry is challenged by growing competition, public concerns about environmental issues such as climate change and nuclear power are creating pressure for a fundamental shift in technological trajectory. The Commission has been pressing for the introduction of 'least-cost planning' in the electricity supply industry. Following practice in some US states, this would require companies to balance the benefits of investments in new generating capacity against the active promotion of demand-side measures. This could include investment in more efficient electricity-using equipment on behalf of customers. Least cost planning concepts would be boosted by a pro-active climate strategy. The interventionist concept of least cost planning sits rather uneasily alongside parallel pressures to deregulate the industry. Nevertheless, the promotion of energy efficiency, carbon-free renewable energy and cleaner combustion of fossil fuels is becoming a major issue.

National differences
Although there are broad similarities, the ownership, structure and regulation of the electricity industry in the case study countries vary considerably, reflecting national political preferences and differing resource endowments. In France, the industry takes the traditional form of a public monopoly, with a single, vertically integrated company. Electricité de France (EdF) is responsible for electricity generation, transmission and distribution. ENEL plays a similar role in Italy.

In the UK, the industry was de-integrated and most of the components privatized in the early 1990s[4]. Transmission and distribution remain regulated monopolies but generation has been opened up to competition from new entrants. Competition is progressively being introduced into the supply business, which involves the arrangement of contracts between generators, distributors and customers. At the time of privatization, three companies — state-owned Nuclear Electric and two privately owned companies, National Power and PowerGen — accounted for almost all electricity generation. National Power and PowerGen inherited the stock of traditional 'dirty' coal-fired power stations. Plans to privatize Nuclear Electric's more profitable nuclear reactors were announced in 1995. Independent electricity producers are making a rapidly growing contribution to electricity generation. Independents have been vigorously promoted by the regional electricity companies responsible for distribution and supply. This strategy is intended to weaken the National Power/PowerGen generation duopoly. Nevertheless, the two privatized fossil-fuel generators and the nuclear companies are expected to dominate the generation market for the foreseeable future.

The German electricity industry is fragmented and has an extremely complex structure. A centralized model involving state ownership was rejected in the late 1940s. The nine companies which own and operate the national high voltage grid and the majority of generation capacity enjoy regional monopolies. The industry is exempt from competition and anti-cartel laws. There is a very large number of local distribution companies, many of them municipally owned, and considerable public sector involvement in the sector at the Land and municipal levels. Utilities with public sector shareholders, including RWE, the largest company, controlled about 85 per cent of generation capacity in 1992.

Technology
In most countries, the dominant electricity generation technology involves the pulverization of coal followed by combustion in a boiler which then drives a steam turbine. Oil-fired power stations use similar technology. Technological development over the last decades has involved the pursuit of returns to scale and incremental efficiency gains. The potential of this technology appears to be virtually exhausted. Its advantages have been eroded by the reduction or removal of subsidies for indigenous coal and by emission controls which require investment in end-of-pipe clean-up technology such as flue gas desulphurization (FGD).

In France, the dominant technology is the nuclear pressurized water reactor (PWR). There is also a considerable degree of nuclear investment in Germany, but less so in the UK and Italy. French success with PWRs can be attributed to a high-level policy commitment and design standardization which has allowed economies of scale to be realised.

In recent years, the power equipment industry has 'borrowed' innovations in gas turbine technology from the aviation industry, leading to the development of combined cycle gas turbine plants (CCGTs) which have several advantages over dominant steam plant. They are modular, cheaper to build, have rapid construction times, lead to low levels of emissions and, by combining steam and gas cycles, are considerably more efficient. Current systems use natural gas but, in principle, a coal gasification unit could be fitted to the front end of a CCGT. CCGTs have been the primary vehicle for new entrants to the UK electricity market. There has been a considerable investment by both governments and energy companies in 'clean coal technology' but the most promising designs, pressurized fluidized bed combustion (PFBC) and integrated gasification combined cycle (IGCC) are still at the demonstration stage.

State intervention has had an important influence on fuel/technology choice in each of the countries examined. Cheap oil was the fuel of choice in the 1960s. In the aftermath of the 1970s oil shocks, cost considerations combined with active energy policies led to an increased market share for coal and nuclear power. State sponsored programmes led to the rapid

Energy sector response to combustion emission regulations 81

expansion of nuclear generation in the 1970s and early 1980s, especially in France which had been heavily dependent on imported oil. Public opposition has stalled nuclear programmes in Germany and the UK and has led to the abandonment of the option in Italy. In 1992, nuclear power accounted for some 73 per cent of electricity generated in France, 30 per cent in Germany and 24 per cent in the UK.

The UK and Germany have large coal reserves and their governments have traditionally intervened heavily to ensure that electricity generators utilise domestic coal for the bulk of their electricity generation. This is still the case in Germany, where solid fuels, including brown coal, account for over 80 per cent of the inputs to thermal power stations. German hard coal is very much more expensive than coal available on the world market. Its production has been supported by long-term contracts between electricity producers and the coal industry and by a levy on electricity generation (the 'Kohlepfennig'). Social policy in the hard-coal producing regions, especially North Rhine-Westphalia, has been a key political factor in maintaining support for coal. The long-term contracts are now under review.

Following the recent energy sector privatizations in the UK, the government has removed its support for coal and the market is in steep decline. Gas is now the fuel of choice for new plants and a rapid burst of investment is taking place. Italy is relatively poor in energy resources and public opposition to coal plants has resulted in heavy dependence on oil. Natural gas and geothermal energy also make important contributions.

2.2 Oil refining

The oil industry in Europe

The EU petroleum refining sector exhibits all the characteristics of a mature industry: commodity products, keen price competition and standardization of technology. Unlike in the electricity industry, the market for oil products is relatively open to international trade and substantial product volumes are supplied by external refining centres in the Middle East and the CIS (Barnett, 1994). Globally, the industry is dominated by a small number of vertically integrated firms which undertake the whole sequence of operations from exploration to crude oil production, refining and marketing. Four of these companies — Shell, Exxon, BP and Mobil — have sizeable operations in Europe. Three other categories of refiners are important at the European level: large, often state-owned European firms (e.g., ENI in Italy); companies from oil producing nations (e.g., Tamoil of Libya); and smaller independents.

The European oil industry has undergone a prolonged period of structural adjustment, driven initially by the downturn in demand following the oil shocks of the 1970s and subsequently by stricter environmental regulations and a shift in product demand towards lighter products. After initially adopting a wait-and-see attitude, the industry began to cut back excess capacity in the 1980s. By 1989, EU distillation capacity had declined by 34 per cent. Restructuring is still a major theme as governments reduce their involvement in the industry and companies invest to meet continuing changes in product demand and increasingly stringent environmental standards. Ongoing changes include: privatization of the remaining large state-owned companies (e.g., ENI in Italy); further withdrawals from the sector as product specification and environmental regulations bring financial pressures to bear; greater industry co-operation in the form of strategic alliances and joint venture processing arrangements; continuing moves by non-EU oil producers to integrate downstream by buying refining facilities/marketing chains in their traditional markets; and attempts by EU companies to expand the scope and scale of their activities.

National differences
The top five companies account for some 96 per cent of capacity in France, 78 per cent in Italy, 64 per cent in the UK and 55 per cent in Germany. France and Italy have traditionally had the most tightly regulated oil refining sectors, with the government intervening to shape the market in favour of domestic firms. Both countries have gradually relaxed their hold on the sector. In recent years, the French government has largely sold off its share of domestic companies and Italy has announced its intention to privatize ENI, the state-owned oil giant. National companies remain pre-eminent in both countries, especially in Italy, where the international oil majors have a relatively small involvement and independents play an important role. Germany has the most fragmented industry with eighteen active companies. Unlike in the other countries, German firms are relatively minor players in the international oil industry. UK refining is dominated by the international oil majors, two of which (Shell and BP) are headquartered in the UK. As is often the case, the largest domestic company (the oil giant BP) is a legacy of previous government involvement in the sector. The trade balance in oil products varies across the four countries, but only Germany has a large deficit in all the major products. The UK is unique in being self-sufficient in crude oil as a result of access to substantial reserves in the North Sea.

Technology
Petroleum refineries are technologically complex. The configuration of plant at a specific site is often the result of incremental investments made over a period of time in response to changing market conditions. The key refining process is distillation in which crude oil is separated into various fractions — naphtha used to manufacture petrochemicals, motor gasoline, 'middle distillates' (diesel fuel and gas oil), residual fuel oil and marine bunker fuels. In response to a decline in the demand for heavier oil fractions following the 1973 oil crisis, refiners have invested heavily in 'cracking' capacity which chemically converts heavier oil fractions into lighter products. Sulphur can be captured during the cracking process. The average sulphur content of fuel oil in Europe (and hence emissions from the

combustion of oil products) has declined over the over the last twenty years as a result of the use of 'sweet' (low-sulphur) North Sea crude oil and investment in cracking capacity.

Emissions from the combustion of oil products greatly exceed those directly associated with refinery processes. Product-related emissions are the focus of an increasing amount of regulatory attention. The recently revised EU directive on the sulphur content of gas oil has forced many refiners to make process modifications or add desulphurization capacity. The technology required is well established. However, if changes to other product quality parameters are made, e.g. the aromatics content of motor gasoline, much more expensive processing might be required.

About 80 per cent of the sulphur in refinery products destined for combustion ends up in the heaviest fractions. Reducing the sulphur content of these fractions would be costly and would reduce the competitiveness of residual fuel oils *vis-à-vis* alternative fuels. Refiners are showing growing interest in 'residue gasification' in which solid/liquid residues are converted to gaseous products which are readily desulphurized and can be used as chemical feedstocks or as a fuel (Arthur D. Little, 1992). In Italy, several refiners have announced their interest in integrating residue gasification with CCGT technology to generate electricity.

Energy policy

The energy sector has been a prime target for extensive public sector 'management' as a result of the energy dependence of modern society, the substantial contribution which the sector makes to employment and wealth creation and the tendency towards natural monopoly. In the UK, the only EU Member States to be self-sufficient in energy, the sector contributes about 5 per cent to gross domestic product (UK Central Statistical Office, 1995). Until relatively recently, energy policy was an important policy domain in most countries, with the need to gain access to cheap and secure energy supplies a prime consideration. The wider social and economic implications of energy sector activity were also important considerations. Import restrictions, subsidies and other forms of intervention have been widely used to protect domestic companies and exploit their powerful influence on other sectors of the economy. Behind the shelter of these national barriers, energy companies have grown to be amongst the largest and most powerful in their domestic economies.

The interventionist energy policies which followed the 1973 and 1979 oil crises have, since the mid-1980s, been replaced with a more relaxed view of energy markets. Reductions in energy prices and new sources of supply have eased anxieties and the sector has started to lose some of its strategic significance. Energy is increasingly becoming a commodity like any other and national governments have started to weaken their traditionally close ties with the sector. The availability of natural gas and the abandonment of EU restrictions on its use in power stations has been an important factor allowing improved environmental performance in the electricity sector.

Only the European Commission itself has a separate 'department', Directorate-General XVII, devoted specifically to energy policy. The UK dismantled its Department of Energy in 1992, moving most of its functions to the Department of Trade and Industry and some, relating to energy efficiency, to the Department of the Environment. Neither France, Germany nor Italy has a distinct energy ministry. Throughout Europe, liberalization and environmental concerns have replaced the traditional energy policy agenda. Energy companies are struggling to come to terms with the erosion of their privileged position.

The government of the energy-rich UK has gone farthest in withdrawing from the energy sector, exposing it to market forces. Countries which are less self-sufficient in energy, such as France and Italy, have proceeded more cautiously. Policy-makers have been reluctant to lose control of the wider social and economic impacts of energy sector activity. Even in a free market economy like Germany, politicians are reluctant to reduce state intervention, fearful of the high social cost and loss of supply security that may result. The importance of energy costs as a factor in competition between Member States is however helping to drive the process of change. With the European Commission actively promoting liberalization, the policy actions of individual nations are constrained to a greater degree. European institutions have combined with broader consumer, environmental and competitive pressures to nudge countries on to a policy trajectory that mirrors the far-reaching changes occurring in the UK.

3. COMBUSTION EMISSIONS: THE LARGE COMBUSTION PLANTS DIRECTIVE

3.1 Overview of the process

The Large Combustion Plants (LCP) Directive (European Commission, 1988) was proposed in late 1983 in order to reduce emissions of SO_2 and NO_x, believed to be associated with acid rain and the forest dieback experienced in Germany and Central Europe in the early 1980s. The Directive affects fossil fuel-fired power stations (but not gas turbines or CCGTs) and boiler plant at petroleum refineries and larger industrial installations.

The regulatory process associated with the Directive was particularly long-drawn out. Although the Commission proposed the measure in 1983, a considerably modified version was approved only in November 1988. The Directive itself contains emission limits for new plants and national emission targets through to the year 2003. Individual Member States were required to forward their implementation plans to the Commission by June

1990. In fact, the regulatory process, involving negotiations between regulatory authorities and industry, continues inside several Member States as dynamic adjustments are made to national emission policies.

The development of the LCP Directive began at a time when the EU was a very different forum for decision-making: there were only ten Member States; Directorate-General XI of the Commission (DG-XI), the Environment Directorate, was beginning to flex its muscles at a time when public concern about environmental issues was growing; all environmental decisions made in the Council of Ministers were unanimous; and the European Parliament had virtually no meaningful role to play. The scene was set for Member State governments to defend the interests of indigenous industries while the Commission, or at least DG-XI, viewed itself as being in the bureaucratic vanguard of the environmental movement.

The LCP case study provides a concrete illustration of a number of contemporary features of the EU regulatory process with respect to environmental issues:

- the opportunity which EU environmental policy-making offered for competitive concerns arising from a purely national regulatory process to be considered in a wider European context;
- the role of EU institutions in transmitting environmental concerns from one country to another; and
- the alignment of Member State government policies with the interests of their own industries.

The story of the LCP Directive began in one Member State, Germany. Domestic legislation to deal with an environmental problem of a specifically German nature, forest dieback, was believed to have competitive implications for German industry through impacts on electricity prices. The German Federal Government pressed the European Commission to propose a similar measure which, apart from reducing environmental burdens across Europe, would also serve to even out competitive conditions — or 'spread the misery' in the words of German industrialists at the time. After several years of negotiations in the Council of Ministers, in which each Member States defended its own economic rather than environmental interests, a significantly modified Directive was agreed. This was followed by a set of regulatory processes at the national level which were concerned primarily with competitive issues between companies, or groups of companies representing different subsectors of the energy market. The remainder of this section tells this story in more detail, concluding with an assessment of the wider lessons.

3.2 The German prologue

The proposal of the LCP Directive was preceded by a five year domestic regulatory process in Germany. The particular form which this process took was strongly influenced by the relationships of the German electricity industry with the Federal Government and the governments of individual Länder. During the 1970s, the Land governments which are responsible for licensing new power stations had begun to impose strict SO_2 emission standards, based on interpretations of guidance developed by the German Society of Engineers (VDI). The actual standards set varied from one Land to another. The electricity industry, represented by its powerful trade association, VDEW, pressed for uniform, legally defined emission standards set at the Federal level which would pre-empt the actions of individual Länder. Standards proposed by the environmentally-ambitious Federal Environment Office (UBA) in 1978 were not however acceptable to the electricity industry because they were to be applied to existing as well as new plants, implying huge costs for retrofitting FGD plants at existing power stations. The Federal Economics Ministry (BMWi), effectively representing the electricity industry at Cabinet level, temporarily killed this proposal for uniform emission standards.

The situation was changed completely by broader political events in the period 1981—83. The full story of how the narrower economic interests of both the electricity industry and energy-intensive electricity users were overruled in an emotive national debate is told by Boehmer-Christiansen and Skea (1991). Only the basic outline is set out here.

In 1981, it became apparent that the health of German forests, which cover a significant proportion of the land area and are an important cultural symbol, had entered rapid decline. One hypothesis given great prominence in the national press was that SO_2 emitted from power stations was a major factor causing this decline. In fact, the health of German forests stabilized in the mid—1980s and it is now believed that a more complex combination of factors, including air pollution, caused forest dieback.

At the same time, the Green Party had begun to enjoy considerable electoral success, threatening the viability of the coalition (SPD/FDP) government. The government was attacked on the forest dieback issue by the main opposition parties, especially the Bavarian-based CSU. Farmers and foresters represented an important constituency for the CSU. In addition, there was resentment in Southern Germany about the flow of funds from South to North as a result of the Kohlepfennig, the levy on electricity production used to subsidize the Northern hard coal industry. Tight emission controls were seen by the CSU as another way of attacking SPD support for hard coal. The conditions were created for a political competition between the main political parties to establish their 'green' credentials.

Following the coming to power of the new CSU/CDU/FDP coalition government in October 1982, the 1978 proposals for uniform Federal emission standards were resurrected in the form of a strict new Federal law, the GFAVo or Large Combustion Plant Ordinance. This required the retrofitting of FGD plant to all existing power stations fired either on hard coal or lignite by 1988. Together with subsequent controls on NO_x, the total cost to the German electricity industry was to be DM 21 bn.

The specific interests of the electricity industry and energy-intensive users were over-ruled in this high-level and very public debate about emission standards. Through a working group established by BMWi, industry argued strongly that the costs of compliance with the GFAVo would significantly affect its competitiveness. There were also concerns on the part of the electricity supply industry that large users (e.g., BASF) close to the French border would have incentives to take supplies from EdF, thus eroding the privileged monopoly position of the German industry. The industry's arguments were countered by macro-economic as well as political considerations. Large-scale investment in FGD on the part of cash-rich utilities was seen by some as a useful counter-cyclical push which would help to stimulate the economy at a time of a recession.

Having lost out in the German regulatory process, industry saw EU environmental policy as a possible means of relieving the competitive disadvantages created by domestic legislation. Industry therefore pressed the Federal Government to promote similar rules at the EU level. Germany was able, at the time, to exert influence over relevant parts of the European Commission. Within six months of the enactment of the GFAVo in June 1983, the Commission had produced a first draft of the LCP Directive. This was greeted with astonishment by some Member States, especially the UK, for whom the German debate about forest dieback had no political resonance.

3.3 The EU regulatory process

Overview
The primary forum in which the EU regulatory process took place was the Council of Ministers. The process was essentially one of intergovernmental bargaining. Governments represented the interests of their own industries which were consulted extensively in developing negotiating positions. Regular Council meetings held once, or perhaps twice, during each six-month Council Presidency marked the milestones of the regulatory process. As negotiations dragged on, the Commission lost authority and the initiative passed to those Member States holding the Council Presidency. Both the UK and Germany held the Presidency during the latter phase of the negotiations (1986—88). The German Presidency used its considerable authority to draw negotiations to a close in June 1988.

The four countries covered in this book each had a distinctive approach to the LCP proposal. For Germany, with strong domestic legislation in place, environmental and competitive interests went hand-in-hand. It was a strong advocate of the proposed measure. France did not play a major role because SO_2 emissions had declined significantly as a result of investment in nuclear power. Italy's pattern of emissions was unusual in that a significant proportion of emissions was accounted for by petroleum refineries as a result of a low level of coal use in power stations. Italy was also not an active player in the negotiations. This can be attributed to a more relaxed approach to the implementation and enforcement of EU rules. The initial UK position was adamant opposition to the proposal. Later, critical linkages between domestic energy policy and the EU regulatory process forced a compromise. The UK became the key player opposing the draft Directive and several countries with reservations 'sheltered' behind the UK's dominant position. A closer examination of linkages between UK industry, energy policy and negotiating strategy on the one hand and the EU regulatory process on the other provides the framework for the remainder of this section.

The early stages 1984—85
In late 1983, the Commission proposed that each Member State should reduce its SO_2 emissions from pre—1987 combustion plant by 60 per cent by 1995 starting from a 1980 baseline. The negotiations which got under way coincided with a turbulent period in the development of the UK electricity industry. The industry was then under national ownership, though firm proposals for privatization appeared just before the agreement of the LCP Directive. In England and Wales, the industry was dominated by the Central Electricity Generating Board (CEGB) which was responsible for all generation and high voltage transmission. During 1984—85, the CEGB was embroiled in the year-long coal miners' strike, playing a key role in minimising the economic impacts and 'keeping the lights on'. At the time, there was an unusually close relationship at the highest levels between the CEGB and the Government. In May 1984, at a high-level meeting called by the Prime Minister, Mrs (now Baroness) Thatcher, and attended by the Chairman of the CEGB, Sir Walter (now Lord) Marshall, the decision was taken to resist pressures to reduce the UK's SO_2 emissions pending further scientific research into the phenomenon of acid rain. Representatives of the Department of the Environment argued for limited emission controls at that meeting but were overruled by a powerful axis formed by the CEGB, the Department of Energy and the Prime Minister's office.

The rationale for resisting the LCP proposals and the parallel UN Economic Commission for Europe '30 per cent Club' were attributed publicly to the lack of direct scientific evidence for a link between the UK's SO_2 emissions and acid rain damage. There were however other factors underlying the UK Government's position:

- a run-down in the CEGB's debts was contributing to a low public sector borrowing requirement, a key element of the Government's macro-economic strategy. The reduction in debts was also an important element of the preparations for privatization, to take place later in the decade. Major investment in retrofitting power plants would have slowed, or reversed, the debt run-down, and would have frustrated both policies.

- the introduction of acid rain controls could have been perceived as an anti-coal measure by elements of the labour force in the coal industry who continued to work during the strike;
- a general distaste for regulatory controls and placing burdens on business, especially if these were 'imposed' from outside the UK.

There was a great deal of overlap between the CEGB's and the Government's thinking. However, there were additional factors at play within the electricity supply industry and the Department of Energy, its sponsor within the government system:

- it was believed that SO_2 emissions would fall rapidly in the 1990s with the planned construction of large numbers of nuclear reactors;
- the development and design of FGD units which, under the nationalized regime, would have fallen almost automatically to the CEGB's engineering division would have taken the organization's resources away from what were seen to be the primary tasks — building nuclear plant and moving incrementally on to the next generation of larger scale coal-fired generation plant;
- Sir Walter Marshall, the Chairman of the CEGB, genuinely believed in the 'better science' argument;
- CEGB experience with crude FGD systems operated since the 1930s had prejudiced the organization against the technology; and
- under a 1979 reorganization, CEGB environmental planners who had internally advocated the construction of at least a pilot FGD plant had been subsumed within the division responsible for the large 'defensive' scientific research programmes on acid rain.

This background was reflected in the EU regulatory process. It was very important for the Commission to obtain significant commitments from the UK within the framework of the LCP Directive. The UK was a major industrial economy, the largest SO_2 emitter in the EU and a major contributor to acid rain damage. The Commission's early strategy was to isolate the UK from its less vocal supporters — essentially the 'cohesion' countries, Greece and Ireland — by offering them significant concessions. In view of the UK's firmness, this strategy failed and became untenable when Spain and Portugal joined the EU in 1986. Thereafter, the Council Presidencies led the negotiations and significant changes were made to the Commission's original proposal. Instead of a single, uniform SO_2 emission reduction for each Member State by 1995, the Presidencies moved towards non-uniform emission reductions, based essentially on political acceptability, to be implemented in multiple stages by the early years of next century. This would cut compliance costs by ensuring that a larger proportion of emission reductions could be met by 'business-as-usual' investment in cleaner electricity generation technologies. It also meant that the German objective of levelling the playing field by raising abatement costs in other countries had already been frustrated.

Regulatory progress 1986—87

A more normal distance between the CEGB and the UK Government was re-established following the end of the miners' strike. In July 1986, the CEGB volunteered to accelerate its emission reductions during the 1990s by retrofitting FGD to three major power stations. This programme was only one-sixth the size of the German programme but represented a significant investment nevertheless. This remarkable voluntary gesture could have been taken only by a nationalized body which could refer back to environmental obligations in the legislation which established its terms of reference. A privately owned company could not have justified an unforced, value-destroying investment of £600m to its shareholders.

The declared reason for the revision of the CEGB's position was a re-assessment of the scientific evidence linking SO_2 emission to acid rain damage in Scandinavia. There has also been speculation that the CEGB had its arm twisted informally by the Government. Whatever the truth, the voluntary decision yielded several benefits for the UK Government:

- the Prime Minister was able to visit Norway in late 1986 with a gesture to placate Scandinavian opposition to UK acid rain policy; and
- the UK, which had the Presidency of the EU Council of Ministers in late 1986, could table a more dignified proposal for the resolution of the debate about the LCP Directive than it would otherwise have done.

In fact, the UK used its Presidency to embarrass other major countries which had played a low-key role in the negotiations. The UK for example proposed a 91 per cent SO_2 emission reduction for France by 1995. There was no expectation on anyone's part that the UK would have been able to conclude negotiations.

Agreement on the LCP Directive

UK domestic developments proved critical to the concluding stages of the regulatory process at the EU level. By early 1988, relationships between the Government and the CEGB had deteriorated to a very low point. In 1987, the Government had announced its intention of privatizing the electricity industry. This was supported by the CEGB, but it soon became apparent that the Government intended to de-integrate the industry, split the CEGB into several component parts and introduce competition into generation. The CEGB had argued forcefully that its organizational identity and monopoly powers should remain intact. From late 1987 onwards, the CEGB management's influence over the UK's position on the LCP Directive became minimal.

Privatizing the CEGB successor companies required the development of prospectuses which, to satisfy potential investors and comply with financial

Energy sector response to combustion emission regulations 91

law, had to characterize the companies' financial prospects in clear and certain terms. Uncertainties over the LCP Directive and the implications for the investment plans of two successor companies with fossil power station assets were a significant deterrent to investors. For this reason, there were huge pressures on the UK government to conclude negotiations on the LCP Directive during the German Presidency of the EU in the first half of 1988. In June, the UK conceded the staged SO_2 emission reductions shown in Table 5.1. The CEGB was not consulted about the UK's final negotiating position. At the time, it was believed that the UK's programme of investment in FGD at coal-fired power stations would need to be doubled to 12,000 MW (still only one third of the German programme) to comply with the Directive. The significant disparity between the size of the German FGD programme and that in the UK indicates clearly that any intention that the LCP Directive should level the competitive playing field in Europe had been frustrated.

Table 5.1 SO_2 emission reduction requirements for existing plant under the LCP Directive

Country	SO_2 Emissions (ktonnes) 1980	Initial SO_2 Reduction Proposal 1995	Final Agreed SO_2 Reductions 1993	1998	2003
Germany	2225	60%	40%	60%	70%
France	1910	60%	40%	60%	70%
Italy	2450	60%	27%	39%	63%
UK	3883	60%	20%	40%	60%
F, I, G, UK	10468	60%	30%	48%	65%
EU 12	14430	60%	23%	42%	57%

Source: European Commission, 1988

3.4   The subsequent regulatory process in the Member States

In all of the countries examined apart from Germany, the regulatory process continued at the national level following the negotiation of the LCP Directive. In Germany, the regulatory process associated with SO_2/NO_x control is effectively over following the major investments of the 1980s and early 1990s.

As a result of investment in nuclear power, France had expected to comply with the LCP Directive requirements without adopting any specific measures. However, shortfalls in nuclear production have raised the use of coal above expected levels and a small amount of investment in FGD has been required. This has caused few problems for EdF which, as a nationalized utility, enjoys close links to the French government.

In Italy, more tensions have arisen within and between the nationalized energy companies. In 1993, the newly-created Italian Environment Ministry created controls which would force emission reductions by the end of the century. ENEL is employing a diversified strategy to fulfil its obligations. It will make some investment in pollution control equipment but will also impose tight product specifications on suppliers of residual fuel oil. Some suppliers (e.g. Tamoil of Libya) have ready access to low sulphur crudes while others, notably ENI, the state oil and gas company, do not. ENI has inevitably tried to influence ENEL's purchasing strategy at the political level but has not succeeded, partly because of the dominant position of ENEL as a major purchaser in the Mediterranean fuel oil markets. Italian refiners have advanced plans for investing in integrated gasification combined cycle (IGCC) plant which will burn high sulphur residual oil while producing electricity. This electricity can be readily sold as a result of liberalization measures in the electricity sector.

The most complex regulatory process at the national level has taken place in the UK where electricity privatization and its aftermath have had a considerable influence. When the LCP Directive was agreed, the soon to be privatised electricity sector was still operating within a technological paradigm developed under the nationalized regime. Essentially, the industry had intended to build as many nuclear power stations as possible and fill in any capacity gaps with traditional, albeit larger scale, coal-fired plant. Within this framework, investment in 12,000 MW of expensive FGD plant appeared to be the only option for complying with the LCP Directive.

By the end of 1989, this technology strategy fell apart. Nuclear power stations were withdrawn from the privatization because the associated liabilities were not acceptable to potential investors. At the same time, plans to build new coal-fired stations were withdrawn because of high capital costs and the prospect of long-drawn out public inquiries. Potential new entrants were considering building clean CCGTs to challenge incumbent generators. National Power and PowerGen were forced to follow suit in order to protect their positions within the generation market.

By 1989—90, it became clear that plans for investment in CCGTs would result in the UK complying comfortably with the requirements of the LCP Directive without the need for significant investment in FGD. Yet, only 18 months before, British negotiators had convinced EU colleagues that the UK could not accept more stringent SO_2 emission reduction targets because of the excessive costs of FGD investment. The Department of the Environment clung to the 12,000 MW retrofit figure it had used in negotiations for several months. Investment in FGD technology became, for environmental pressure groups, a totem of the British Government's commitment to its environmental policy. The coal industry also lobbied for a large FGD programme because it believed that it would establish a continuing market for high sulphur British coal.

The electricity companies argued forcefully however that commitment to building FGDs should not become part of the UK's formal programme for compliance with the LCP Directive. From their point of view, FGD investment would be non-productive and would impede their ability to compete in a liberalised electricity generation market. The formal programme needed to be determined in advance of the publication of the prospectus for the sale of National Power and Power Gen.

In the event, a compromise was agreed between the Department of the Environment and the generators. A commitment to build 8,000 MW of FGD was incorporated in the compliance programme. 6,000 MW was already under construction as a result of the CEGB's voluntary measure in 1986. An adjustment was made to PowerGen's initial debt structure to provide it with the resources to construct the additional 2,000 MW. In the event, PowerGen has not undertaken the investment and the electricity sector is emitting about 30 per cent less SO_2 than permitted under the UK's national programme for compliance with the LCP Directive. The stations which have been fitted with FGD units are shut down from time to time because emission controls have pushed up operating costs and rendered them uneconomic. The regulatory process within the UK has further widened the gap between the competitive intentions underlying the LCP Directive and the actual consequences of implementation practice.

3.5 Lessons from the Large Combustion Plants Directive

The LCP case study provides mainly negative lessons about environmental policy within the EU. Dating from a time which precedes qualified majority voting, subsidiarity and the new emphasis on partnership between the Commission and industrial interests expressed in the Fifth Environmental Action Programme, the case study in fact demonstrates a great deal what can go wrong with environmental policy:

- the Commission was too ambitious in pressing forward a measure, drawing heavily on the practice of one Member State, on which it had not consulted sufficiently widely. But for electricity privatization in Britain, the measure would, perhaps, never have been agreed.
- competitive considerations and the alignment of Member States behind their industry's interests was probably a more potent factor determining the policy outcome than was environmental ambition;
- in spite of, or perhaps because of, five years of protracted negotiations, the original ambition of equalizing competitive conditions across the EU was far from realized. The subsequent regulatory process within Member States served to widen the gap between ambition and achievement;

- informational asymmetries, between Member States in Council negotiations and between Member States and their industries, served to create a large gap between expectations and outcomes, especially in the UK, where the rate of institutional and organizational change in the energy sector was rapid;
- a regulatory process which ostensibly covered all countries has resulted in entirely different compliance strategies in the different Member States. This is a symptom of the very great diversity in the organization and management of the energy sector in different countries. Sovereignty is cherished in a sector of strategic importance over which Member States are reluctant to release control;
- in the 1980s, the lobbying activities of the sectors concerned was weaker at the European level. The electricity supply industries in the different Member States had little incentive to combine forces because their interests with respect to the LCP Directive diverged after German legislation had been enacted.

4. CLIMATE CHANGE: THE CARBON/ENERGY TAX PROPOSAL

4.1 Overview

Like the LCP Directive, the European Commission's 1992 proposal for a carbon/energy tax (European Commission, 1992b) has proved highly controversial. As with acid rain/forest dieback in the early 1980s, climate change a decade later was a novel, high profile issue which gave the Commission sufficient confidence to propose a radical new measure. Once again a controversial measure faced the difficult hurdle of a unanimous decision in the Council of Ministers.

There were differences though. No one country actively sponsored the tax measure and scepticism about the proposal was more widely spread — although the UK can again be identified as the leading opponent. Those countries which had already introduced some form of carbon tax, e.g., Denmark and Sweden, had applied the tax only to domestic and service sector consumers, leaving price-sensitive industrial consumers immune from the impacts. Thus, there was no compelling reason for any one country, on competition grounds, to press for the measure to be adopted at the wider European level. Competitiveness considerations were in fact critical in focusing opposition to the tax proposal. Also, most energy sector companies across the EU (apart from those with gas and nuclear interests) were against the tax proposal as were energy-intensive industrial users. There was little difference in the nature of the business inputs to the regulatory process in different Member States. By the 1990s, the scope and sophistication of industrial lobbying in Brussels had grown considerably and pan-European trade associations fed their views directly to the Commission and other EU institutions — though country-level lobbying was far from absent.

4.2 Climate policy and the origins of the carbon tax

EU action on the issue of climate change began in 1988—89 just as Europe began to experience a series of hot summers and as the Green Parties performed remarkably well in the European elections. In 1988, the Commission reviewed for the Council of Ministers the scientific state-of-the-art relating to climate change and the status of international diplomatic activity. At this stage, the Commission was well behind some Member States who had already published quite detailed policy papers on the climate issue.

By 1990, prompted by its more environmentally ambitious Member States such as Germany and the Netherlands, the EU took the decision to take a pro-active role in negotiating the Framework Convention on Climate Change (FCCC) due to be signed at the UN Conference on Environment and Development (UNCED) in 1992. This conference represented a landmark in international environmental diplomacy and attracted many world leaders. Several Conventions were opened for signature at the Conference. The close linkages between climate change and energy policy led to an unprecedented joint Council of Environment and Energy Ministers in October of that year. At the meeting, Ministers agreed a (non-binding) EU commitment to stabilize CO_2 emissions at their 1990 levels by the year 2000. The Council statement promised specific policy proposals and, for the first time, raised the possibility of fiscal instruments.

At this early stage, there was no agreement regarding the means for achieving the target. The Commission was asked to devise a strategy for doing so. DG-XI (Environment) took the lead role but the issue also concerned DG-XVII (Energy), DG-XXI (Customs Union and Indirect Taxation), DG-II (Economic and Financial Affairs) and DG-III (Industrial Affairs). Within a month of the October Council meeting, the Commission had produced a draft document sketching the outlines of a strategy which included regulatory measures and standards; collaboration and agreements with industry and fiscal/financial measures.

By July 1991, most elements of the strategy had been developed in greater detail and the strategy document was presented to the Council late in 1991. DG-XXI had been strongly opposed to new tax measures and, as a result, the proposals were put forward very tentatively. The Economic and Financial Affairs Council (ECOFIN) and the Environment Council simply called on the Commission to further develop the strategy proposals. In the event, the final EU strategy 'framework' document was produced only just in time for UNCED in June 1992. The controversial draft Directive proposing a carbon/energy tax was published too late to allow any discussion by the Council of Ministers prior to UNCED. This prevented any public disagreements over the controversial tax proposal undermining the EU's negotiating position. Apart from the proposed carbon/energy tax, the other elements of the EU's climate strategy (European Commission, 1992c) were: a) a monitoring mechanism for CO_2 and other greenhouse gas emissions; b) a set of conventional measures relating to the promotion of energy efficiency and renewable energy sources; and c) the use of EU funds to offset the impacts of the tax in economically less-favoured regions of the EU.

During 1992—94, the protectiveness of Member States towards their energy sectors resulted in a weakening of the EU's climate strategy. The policy packages on energy efficiency and renewables were agreed in 1993 — but they were modified significantly and now take the form of a common framework for action by individual Member States. The monitoring mechanism was also agreed in 1993 but there have been considerable difficulties involved in agreeing protocols for communicating information and securing the provision of data by Member States. The carbon/energy tax became the only component of the climate strategy with a truly EU dimension. The remainder of this section focuses on that measure and the role of business in its development.

4.3   The development of the Carbon/Energy Tax Proposal

The role of the European Commission

Under the Fifth Environmental Action Programme which was proposed in 1992, the Commission had begun to promote economic instruments which would allow polluters discretion to choose their own methods of regulatory compliance and would, in theory, result in lower compliance costs. The concept of a fiscal measure fitted well with this new thinking. The new Programme also promoted the idea of partnership and consultation with the 'key actors' (i.e., industry). The Commission's approach to the carbon/energy tax in practice relied less on this philosophy. Industrial interests played almost no direct role in shaping the formal tax proposal. Business input came at a later stage.

The carbon tax proposal originated within DG-XI rather than being borrowed from the policy of any Member State. A major driver was the desire to be 'new and ambitious'. The initial ideas were very sketchy and DG-XI approached DG-II for its views. DG-II was not initially keen. It would have preferred a package of 'no regrets' measures of a more conventional nature. DG-XI argued that the publicity which would inevitably be associated with such an innovative measure would raise public awareness and would, in the end, make it easier to promote than a traditional regulatory package. Despite DG-II's initial misgivings, an alliance between the economists of DG-II and the environmentalists in DG-XI emerged. The initial outline tax proposal expressed a preference for a pure carbon tax, arguing that the only rationale for a general energy tax would be 'political'.

Energy sector concerns brought DG-XVII into the discussion. Strategic energy objectives had slipped down the EU's policy agenda and DG-XVII had failed to get a specific energy chapter included in the Maastricht Treaty. There had even been discussion about whether the continued existence of an Energy Directorate was necessary. The climate issue, although it held risks, offered a chance for DG-XVII to revitalize progress towards the EU's energy efficiency objectives and perhaps place security of energy supply, DG-XVII's distinctive policy theme, back on the political agenda. DG-XVII consequently played an active role in the development of the carbon/energy tax proposal. This can be seen by the subsequent treatment of its 'client' sectors (e.g., electricity) in the tax proposal.

Initially, DG-XXI was strongly opposed to the inclusion of a fiscal measure in the Commission's climate policy strategy. Its attention had been focused on the difficult task of harmonizing value added tax and excise duties under the Single Market initiative. The proposed carbon/energy tax was an unwelcome addition to an already full and complex agenda. The taxation Commissioner was scrupulously lukewarm when discussing the proposal, emphasizing the importance of first 'exhausting' other non-fiscal measures. However, despite her misgivings, political pressure forced DG-XXI not only to accept the idea but to take the lead in promoting its development from early 1992 onwards. The challenge of reconciling existing tax practice with the environmental and economic efficiency concerns of other DGs had important implications for the shape of the tax proposal.

There was little input from DG-III and the business sector during the early stages of the regulatory process (October 1990—October 1991). DG-III later played a more important role, pressing for a greater emphasis on traditional measures, exemptions for energy intensive industry and the tax being conditional on other OECD countries taking similar measures. The main economic interests taken into account were those of the steel and chemical industries ('clients' of DG-III) and the energy industry, especially coal and nuclear (clients of DG-XVII).

The result of these different interests was a considerable debate on the details of the tax proposal. The key issues were:

- the split between the carbon and energy components of the tax (DGs II and XI favoured a pure carbon tax, DG-XVII a pure energy tax);
- the point of taxation (DG-XI favoured a tax on production, DG-XXI a tax on consumption);
- exemptions for energy intensive industry (supported by DG-III); and
- implications for competitiveness (DG-III wanted the measure to be conditional on other countries following suit, others, including DG-XI, wanted a unilateral measure).

In the end, a simple measure in principle turned into a remarkably complicated proposal in practice as the interests of the relevant DGs and their 'clients' were accommodated in order to construct a consensus for the measure within the Commission as a whole.

Put simply, the basic elements of the 1992 proposal were:

- a tax equivalent to $10/barrel of oil, split 50:50 between the carbon and energy components;
- a seven-year phase-in period with the tax starting at $3/barrel;
- conditionality on comparable action on other OECD countries;
- revenue neutrality, i.e., an undertaking that other taxes would be cut back to compensate for the new fiscal measure;
- the exemptions of most forms of renewable energy, but not nuclear power, from the energy component of the tax;
- exemptions for sectors of industry whose competitiveness would be adversely affected by the measure; and
- the possibility of setting investments in energy-saving measures against the tax.

The role of the Council of Ministers

It is impossible to understand the development and fate of the carbon/energy tax proposal without reference to the role of the Council of Ministers. Although the Maastricht Treaty introduced qualified majority voting on environmental issues, there were specific exceptions made for measures 'primarily of a fiscal nature' and measures 'significantly affecting a Member State's choice between different energy sources and the structure of its energy supply'. For several reasons then, the carbon/energy tax proposal is of particular sensitivity to Member States and is subject to a unanimous decision-making procedure in Council. Any decision over the tax would be taken by ECOFIN. There is a large overlap of interest between various economic interests (some energy companies, energy-intensive industry) and Member States, such as the UK, which are opposed to the tax.

In the early days of the EU climate change strategy, the Council of Ministers encouraged the inclusion of a fiscal element. Apart from this encouragement, Member States contributed very little (directly) to the development of the actual proposal. Prior to the 1995 enlargement of the EU, six Member States (Belgium, Denmark, Germany, Luxembourg, Netherlands and Italy) supported the tax proposal. Broadly speaking, support for the tax mirrors the ambitiousness of a country's CO_2 emission reduction target. For these countries, the tax forms an integral component of their CO_2 reduction strategy and without it, they would struggle to attain their national targets. Italy had the Presidency of the Council in October 1990 when the EU's CO_2 stabilization target was established and has since been a consistent supporter of the tax.

The four 'cohesion' countries — Greece, Spain, Ireland and Portugal — which are eligible to receive support from the Cohesion Funds established under the Maastricht Treaty have been cautious towards the proposal. They believe that the tax would have negative economic impacts, but also believe that they could derive advantage from a compensating use of the Cohesion Funds. Spain and Ireland are especially cautious because of their degree of dependence on carbon-intensive solid fuels.

France and the UK have idiosyncratic policy positions. French policy is that all industrialized countries should introduce a graduated tax which reflects the costs of climate impacts and which avoids distortion of competition and the relocation of industry. France favour an EU-level carbon tax but is opposed to any energy component. This reflects the country's major investment in nuclear power. The UK is opposed to an EU-level tax, reflecting a wider political concern about a perceived loss of sovereignty to Brussels. Moreover, the UK has raised domestic taxes on household heating and transport fuels and the Government's current position is that further tax increases on energy products are not necessary.

4.4 The anticipated impacts on business

The carbon/energy tax is designed to encourage structural change away from carbon intensive fuels and energy intensive products and processes. Economic analyses show that the aggregate effects would be small as long as the tax is phased in gradually and the principle of revenue neutrality is observed. A small number of sectors, however, would be particularly affected by the tax. These include: the energy industries; 'highly sensitive' industries such as iron and steel, cement, glass and clay products for which energy makes up 10—20 per cent of costs; and 'moderately sensitive' industries such as chemicals, paper and ceramics where energy accounts for 5—10 per cent of costs. There are potentially some winners from the introduction of the tax, though the positive effects are small and diffuse. The service sector may benefit because the prices of services will fall relative to those of goods and because it is mostly sheltered from international competition. Energy costs are relatively more important in the southern Member States (Spain, Portugal) than they are in the north (Britain, Germany).

For manufacturing industry in the UK for example, the full $10/barrel tax would raise the price of bulk fuels (coal, residual fuel oil, interruptible gas) by 50—80 per cent if no exemptions were available. The price of premium fuels (distillate oil, gas sold on firm contracts) would rise by around 30 per cent and electricity by around 20 per cent. These price changes would significantly affect the competitiveness of energy-intensive sectors and individual fuels. Coal markets, already threatened by competition from gas and the likely withdrawal of subsidies, would be particularly affected. The introduction of a tax could also force oil refiners to reconsider their strategies for marketing residual fuel oil, particularly as tighter sulphur controls are being developed in parallel. A further withdrawal of oil from the bulk fuels market would be likely.

4.5 Business and the regulatory process

Industry wakes up

Prior to the development of the carbon/energy tax proposal, only a few sections of industry had begun to contemplate seriously the prospect of fiscal measures in environmental policy. UNICE (Union of Industrial and Employers' Confederations of Europe) had taken a broadly supportive stance, provided that prior consultation with industry took place. Only those firms particularly affected by the CO_2 abatement issue responded to the 1990—91 versions of the Commission's climate change strategy document. At this stage, details of the tax were still very sketchy and firms (mainly from the energy sector) focused on the wider issues surrounding the CO_2 debate. Most companies did not attach any credibility to the discussion of a tax. They believed that conflicts of interest between the different parts of the Commission and differences in the energy structures of the Member States presented too great a barrier to the adoption of the measure.

When more details of the tax were released in October 1991, there was genuine surprise in the business community. By December 1991, the oil industry and other energy sector companies had circulated letters and briefs to prominent political figures, policy makers at the national and EU levels and the media. Lobbying at this stage was emotionally highly charged. The oil, coal, electricity and energy intensive sectors predicted direct impacts on competitiveness and employment. A great deal of political capital had however been invested in the proposal and Commission officials were reluctant to make changes so close to the UNCED Conference.

The formal tax proposal in May 1992 created a sense of almost disbelief in the business community. Activities undertaken independently by companies, national trade associations, European trade associations and industry confederations such as UNICE added up to a major anti-tax campaign.

Business responses

In any given sector, business responses across the EU were remarkably uniform. Business was much more sophisticated in its response to the tax proposal than it had been to regulatory proposals relating to acid rain. Very few companies or sectors took the line that conclusive evidence for climate change did not exist and that action was unwarranted on grounds of scientific uncertainty. Only the coal industry, which could have been hit very severely by the tax, took that line. Broadly speaking, most companies publicly acknowledged the possibility of a climate threat and supported the EU's CO_2 stabilization target while opposing the mix of measures chosen, in particular the proposed carbon tax. Privately, many individuals within companies were more critical of the state of scientific knowledge about climate change. Predictably, the gas industry and, even more so, the nuclear industry chose to emphasize the risks of climate change and at least tactically supported fiscal measures.

Much of industry's criticism of the tax came from the heart rather from than the head. Little credence was given either to the economic analyses which were used to justify the tax or those carried out by independent analysts. As well as the uncertainties inherent in economic modelling, there was uncertainty over detailed aspects of the tax, such as the point of application (upstream or downstream in the energy sector), the treatment of electricity, the split between CO_2 and energy and the operation of industry or country-specific exemptions. Companies chose to criticize the Commission's analyses rather than publishing their own work. Material which did reach the public was predominantly of a defensive nature.

Industry's criticisms of the tax proposal generally took the following lines:

- the appropriateness of a tax. Governments would be prudent to adopt a precautionary approach to climate change but measures should be taken on a no regrets basis, i.e., measures should make economic sense even if the fear of climate change should prove unfounded.
- energy efficiency. Many energy-intensive processes are close to the theoretical limits for energy efficiency. A tax would force cuts in domestic output rather than improving energy efficiency. A tax could reduce profitability and hence the ability of companies to invest in energy efficiency measures.
- inadequate use of conventional measures. Not enough is being done to promote the adoption of beneficial energy efficiency measures by companies. There is still a large untapped potential for energy conservation projects with short to medium paybacks at current energy prices. Governments do not do enough to reduce non-market barriers to energy efficiency.
- voluntary measures. In some sectors, voluntary measures could lead to reduced CO_2 emissions without the negative economic impacts of a carbon/energy tax.
- pursuing economic efficiency. The benefits of a carbon/energy tax would be outweighed by existing anomalies caused by taxes and subsidies in energy markets. Financial assistance to the coal industry for example comes to $6.8bn in Germany, $1.72bn in the UK, $200m in France and $90m in Italy.
- fiscal neutrality. The EU has no competence to raise taxes and Member States will decide if and how reductions in the overall tax burden will be made. Governments are unlikely to forego the opportunity to utilize this additional revenue for budgetary purposes. The tax will not be revenue neutral in all countries, thus leading to distortions in competitiveness.

In practice, the detailed text of the carbon/energy tax proposal addressed almost all of these points. Exemptions for energy-intensive industry and rebates tied to investments in energy-saving projects would minimise the economic impacts in almost all sectors. The key issue remains one of trust.

Industry does not trust governments to introduce such a measure without turning it into a revenue-raising device at some point in the future. The tax is seen as 'the thin end of a wedge'.

Industry tactics

The sectors particularly affected by the proposed carbon/energy tax (energy, chemicals, steel) tend to be dominated by a relatively small number of large, long established, well organized and resource-rich companies. These companies play an important role in national economies and over the years, have developed an extensive network of political, industrial and government contacts. For the most part, because of the potential impact of national and EU climate change strategies on their activities, they have monitored the debate closely. From its early days, they have been involved in shaping the overall 'industry' position on the issue.

One of the earliest tactics was to develop broad-based industry support for the anti-tax campaign. Major energy companies are well represented on committees in industrial confederations and they have used their position to argue the case against the tax. As a result, broad-based industry associations such as BDI (Federation of German Industry), CBI (Confederation of British Industry), ICC (International Chamber of Commerce) have joined the criticism of the tax. International industry coalitions have also been used to maintain resistance to the idea of a tax in countries outside the EU. Support for the anti-tax lobby in the United States for instance is an important component of some EU firms' anti-tax strategy. National lobbying has been carried out by companies and their trade associations, but at the EU level the lead has been taken by Brussels-based industry associations. Some of the most active on the issue include: EurElec (electricity), EuroPIA (oil), CEFIC (chemicals), EuroMetaux (non-ferrous metals), EuroFer (ferrous metals), IFIEC (industrial energy consumers). Companies with Brussels-based representatives have also taken an active role in Europe.

Considerable effort was put in to lobbying participants in the regulatory process at all levels, from members of the public to civil servants and politicians. As well as contacting decision makers and the major proponents of the tax (usually environment ministries), strong representations were made to those DGs (III, XVII) within the Commission which were felt likely to represent industry's interests. Representations have also been made to finance ministries which, across the Member States, tend to be sceptical of the proposal. Within the EU contact was made with Council working groups, Member States' Permanent Representatives and appropriate Committees of the European Parliament. In addition to formal lobbying, large companies, business confederations and established industry groups enjoy privileged access to policy makers through personal friendship and unattributable briefings.

Some organizations have offered voluntary energy efficiency/CO_2 reduction programmes in exchange for the dropping of the tax proposal. For example, CEFIC proposed a voluntary energy efficiency programme aiming at a 15 per cent improvement in energy efficiency in the chemicals industry between 1990 and 2000.

Industry's anti-tax position was strengthened by the fact that there is no strong pro-tax lobby. Manufacturers of insulation products, for example, believe that more targeted regulatory measures or financial assistance schemes for energy efficiency would better promote their activities (Grubb, 1992). In addition, such companies are often members of larger industrial groupings which, in aggregate, would be adversely affected by the tax.

4.6 Lessons from the carbon/energy tax case study

The carbon/energy tax represents the EU's first attempt to adopt a major economic instrument in support of environmental policy. Under almost any criterion, the regulatory process has failed. A variety of lessons can be drawn from this experience. Some relate to business and its regulatory relationships:

- although the rhetoric of market instruments is superficially attractive to business, the case study shows that the devil is in the detail. Economic instruments like the carbon/energy tax which have as their intention a fundamental change in the 'normal' economic environment are unattractive. This has led to the ironical position of companies asking for traditional command-and-control regulation.
- Most multinational companies now find it in their interest to take a more pro-active position on environmental issues. Although there are incentives on both sides for a more co-operative relationship between business and public authorities, the carbon/energy tax case study shows that there are still conditions under which industry will adopt a negative approach to proposed environmental measures. Lobbying activity of the simplest and most traditional kind offered potential payoffs (in terms of killing the tax) which were well in excess of either the direct costs or any loss of public image.
- Supranational industry federations are becoming increasingly important in the regulatory process as companies turn to collaborative action as a means of maximizing the impact of interest representation.
- A relatively small number of large organizations had the influence, resources and ability to gain access to personnel at all levels of the regulatory process.

Others relate more to the public policy-making process:

- The policy instrument chosen led to the perception that there were a large numbers of losers — in this case business and consumers — while there were few identifiable winners.
- Existing policy-making structures are not adequate for dealing with environmental problems which have significant impacts across several

jurisdictions. Inter-service feuding, inadequate consultation with interested parties and political interference have resulted in a complex and ambitious regulatory proposal. Although there has been lip service to the 'integration' of environmental concerns into other policy areas, the truth is that there are few mechanisms in place to facilitate such an integration.
- Policies developed under conditions of political urgency lead to a lack of consultation with interest groups. This is particularly likely to happen with headline grabbing issues like climate change which have tight, high profile deadlines such as the UNCED conference.

5. FUTURE DIRECTIONS

5.1 General trends

Although there are no new high-profile environmental issues facing the EU energy sector, the legacy of the last fifteen years is a considerable amount of unfinished business. DG-XI and other parts of the Commission, national administrations, energy companies and their trade associations form a loosely-linked and extensive regulatory policy network. A number of specific inter-related regulatory initiatives remain on the agenda. EU environmental policy-making as it impinges on the energy sector can be seen as a continuous game in which the players grow ever more sophisticated and able to judge the others' moves and intentions. Concern on the part of the Commission about the energy industry's ability to block, weaken or delay measures has led to a recognition of the need to consult heavily before making formal proposals. This is especially necessary as the EU's formal decision-making procedures, e.g., the co-decision process undertaken by Council and Parliament, become more complex. The remainder of this section describes briefly the main features of the regulatory processes which are likely to be under way over the next decade.

5.2 Climate change

Independent analysis suggests that the EU may well just achieve its CO_2 stabilisation objective for the year 2000, perhaps more through luck than policy design (STOA, 1995). DG-XI continues however to project a substantial overshoot in an attempt to inject more urgency into the development of the EU climate strategy. The first Conference of the Parties to the Climate Convention, comprising national delegations which oversee its implementation, considered the prospect of emission reduction targets for industrialized countries for around 2010 in March 1995. If such a protocol to the Convention were to be agreed, the EU would need additional policy measures in order to sign up. The EU might even need additional policy measures to keep CO_2 emissions below their 1990 levels after the year 2000.

In spite of failure in the Council and major opposition from industry, the carbon/energy tax has remained the centre-piece of the Commission's policy approach. Continued interest in ecological tax reform in some new and existing Member States has encouraged the Commission to retain an interest in the carbon/energy tax concept. Towards the end of 1994, the Commission did acknowledge that the original proposal had failed. However, it re-proposed the tax in March 1995, specifying it as an optional measure which could be adopted at the discretion of individual Member States. The basic principles are:

- the tax must be adopted using the same structure as in the original 1992 proposal (50:50 energy/carbon mix for example), but Member States may adopt it to any degree they wish, i.e., from 0 to 100 per cent of the original $10/barrel rate. This ensures that any parallel national taxes would be compatible and could be harmonized at a later date;
- the condition that the tax is dependent on similar action being taken in other OECD countries is dropped because individual Member States are able to judge whether or not to adopt the measure; and
- Member States adopting the tax may provide exemptions for energy-intensive industry to protect the competitiveness of relevant sectors *vis-à-vis* EU non-adopters and non-EU countries.

If this proposal were adopted, some Member States would probably proceed with the measure. These include the Scandinavian Member States, Belgium, Luxembourg, the Netherlands and Germany. The impacts on industry would however be minimal because generous exemptions at the national level would be likely unless all Member States were to adopt the tax. Although the Commission's tactic means that any adoption of the tax will be slow, it makes it much more difficult for industry to block because the locus of decision-making becomes distributed round the Member States. This will weaken the role of the effective Brussels-based trade associations.

5.3 Integrated Pollution Prevention and Control (IPPC)

Several energy facilities, including power stations, petroleum refineries and larger combustion processes, are covered by the draft Directive on Integrated Pollution Prevention and Control (IPPC) which is expected to be adopted during 1996. This provides for the application of best available technology (BAT) to relevant plants with eight-year timetables for the upgrading of existing plant to new plant standards. BAT notes, prepared by the Commission, will consider discharges to air, water and land within a unified framework. Application of the BAT principle to individual facilities will be the responsibility of individual Member States.

The degree of discretion which Member States will in fact enjoy is not yet clear. The approach of the energy industry in each Member State appears to depend on the indigenous regulatory culture. UK companies, for example, argue for greater discretion for regulators at the implementation level. This accords with UK practice from which companies have derived considerable benefit. German companies, facing different regulators in different Länder, may prefer a more top-down, uniform approach. Under these circumstances, companies and trade associations will prefer to operate at the national level to gain the support of their own governments.

5.4 Revisions to the Large Combustion Plants Directive

The original LCP Directive made provisions for revisions to the national targets for existing plant in 1994 and revisions to emission limits by July 1995. Both of these deadlines have passed without action, although the Commission has been consulting intensively over the new plant limits. The treatment of existing plants would have the greatest economic impact. The Commission's course of action has not yet been decided. One option is to do nothing and retain the existing national targets. This would have the support of many energy companies. Other options are to tighten up the national targets or to replace the targets with a formal requirement that existing plant should meet new plant standards by a specified date. The Commission is showing some inclination to follow the latter route, implementing it by establishing the LCP Directive revision as a 'daughter' Directive to IPPC. Many energy companies would be strongly opposed to the latter option because it would set a precedent which would weaken Member State discretion in implementing the IPPC Directive.

5.5 The sulphur content of liquid fuels

The LCP Directive has had the effect of significantly reducing emissions from: a) coal-firing; and b) larger installations. As a result, an increasing proportion of SO_2 emissions derives from oil-firing and smaller plants which are difficult to regulate through a conventional system of emission limits backed up by monitoring and inspection. For this reason, the Commission is keen to push forward measures which will cover smaller plant and maintain progress in reducing emissions. The draft Liquid Fuels Directive is DG-XI's response. However, it faces a major fight with the well-organized European oil industry which has close links to several parts of the Commission and has, in the past, been very effective in defeating or weakening measures which it opposes. A Fuel Oil Directive proposed in 1975 was withdrawn as a result of industry lobbying.

The Liquid Fuels Directive is technical in nature and the regulatory process is far from complete. As of July 1995, no formal proposal had been agreed by the Commission. As it stands, the current draft provides for: a limit on the sulphur content of residual fuel oil; a higher limit if ambient air quality meets defined limits at the location where the fuel is to be burned; and two separate limits for marine bunker fuel depending on whether the oil is to be burned in coastal or international waters.

The oil industry is opposed to this measure at the EU level and EuroPIA has played a significant role in discussions with the Commission. Desulphurization measures could cost refiners several $100m per plant and drive some plants out of business in an industry suffering from over-capacity. Part of the oil industry strategy has been to extend the limits to cover solid fuels. If this were to happen, the price relativities between coal and oil in price-sensitive markets would be maintained. However, this proposal, if it were to succeed, would drag the European coal industry into the debate, slowing down negotiations considerably.

There were signs of Member State rivalry early in the regulatory process. In 1990, France made a proposal for a comprehensive approach to SO_2 emissions from the petroleum chain from which the current draft proposal derives. This proposal, which even enjoyed the support of French subsidiaries of the multinationals, would have significantly disadvantaged the Dutch refining industry which is a major supplier of marine bunker fuel. A vigorous Dutch response set the scene for the more measured regulatory process which is now under way.

CONCLUSIONS

Regulation of the energy sector represents one of the most important and difficult strands of environmental policy-making at both the national and the EU levels. The two regulatory processes described in this chapter have been particularly contentious. There have been some significant developments in the style of EU environmental policy-making during the 1980s and 1990s — notably the new approach to partnership with the business community and the stated preferences for market-based instruments signalled in the Fifth Environmental Action Programme. Nevertheless, this chapter identifies some persistent features of the EU regulatory process which are evident in both case studies.

The regulatory power of the energy industries. The energy sector is economically important and interacts with public authorities in a range of contexts apart from environmental policy. These include: price and profits regulation; public procurement; competition law; and the licensing of oil and gas exploration and production. This puts the industry in a powerful position in which it can 'trade-off' different issues within its multiple regulatory interactions. The plural nature of decision-making structures within the EU provides the industry with a range of levers which it can manipulate. The Council of Ministers, representing the 'federal' dimension of EU decision making, must interact with Parliament and the Commission. The Commission itself is divided into DGs with different, often diverging, interests which companies with sophisticated corporate affairs competencies can readily exploit. The tensions between different levels of decision-making within the EU — in particular the tensions between Member States and the Brussels institutions highlighted by debate over the subsidiarity principle — provide the energy sector with further opportunities to 'manage' the regulatory process.

Differences between electricity generation and oil refining. The most striking difference between the electricity industry and the oil industry is that the latter has been markedly more successful in terms of the measured outcomes of regulatory processes. The oil industry for example succeeded in killing a proposed fuel oil directive in the 1970s and has been minimally affected by other rules relating to combustion emissions. The electricity industry, on the other hand, has taken no regulatory scalps. In practice, the regulatory affairs techniques used by companies in the two sectors differ little. Explanations must therefore be sought in the nature of the relationship between the industries and public authorities.

The strong monopoly element in electricity supply means that the ability of the industry to recover the costs of environmental controls depends on economic regulation rather than trading conditions in a competitive market. In general, authorities have allowed costs to be passed so that companies have maintained profitability. The resistance of electricity companies to environmental controls has more often been motivated by a reluctance to change technological direction than by a fear of reduced profits. Also, differences between companies operating in the electricity sector, in terms of fuel mix for example, has created the opportunity for public authorities to practice 'divide and rule' policies.

The oil industry on the other hand is competitive at the global level and faces problems of structural over-capacity. It fears the bunching of capital expenditure from multiple environmental initiatives and knows that it cannot recover costs in the market-place given the over-capacity. The different oil companies largely share the same problems and have incentives to pool regulatory resources via trade associations such as EuroPIA. In the UK, oil companies wield considerable economic power through their role in exploiting North Sea oil resources. The oil industry thus has both the incentive and the capacity to manage regulatory processes effectively.

Liberalization and environmental regulation. The relationship between de-integration and liberalization of the electricity industry on the one hand and environmental regulation on the other is complex. Both monopolistic generating companies and those operating in a competitive market have an incentive to resist controls. But costs may be easier to recover when the result can be achieved through bargaining with regulatory authorities over price controls. The marketplace may be less indulgent. The privatised generators in the UK for example are not able to recover the costs of operating their FGD units in the context of a competitive market. It is possible that the electricity industry may take on more of the commodity characteristics of the oil industry as liberalization proceeds. There is however still more technological diversity in electricity generation than there is in oil refining and the incentives for regulatory co-operation between companies may be weaker.

High profile environmental issues. It is striking that both of the environmental problems discussed in this chapter have been very high-profile, engaging the attention of the public and the media. In both cases, this led the European Commission to propose measures with major economic implications for the energy sector without carrying out any wide-ranging consultations. In the event, the price was paid in terms of a five-year negotiation on the LCP Directive and a failure to agree the carbon/energy tax. Lack of consultation over the carbon/energy tax was remarkable in the light of the aspirations towards partnership with the business community expressed in the Fifth Environmental Action Programme. In a heady political atmosphere, the temptation to bypass laborious consultation procedures is great. But in both cases the consequences were highly negative.

Incentives for regulatory collaboration. The varying incentives for firms in the electricity and oil sectors to collaborate through trade associations has already been noted. A strong feature which stands out from the comparison of the two case studies a decade apart is the development of trade associations at the European level. This signals strongly the importance which companies attach to the regulatory process at the EU level. European trade associations have emerged in all parts of the energy sector. Previous collaboration on technical issues, for example through the oil industry organisation CONCAWE, has been reinforced by collaborative organisations which are extensions of individual firms' corporate affairs capabilities. The complementary roles of CONCAWE and EuroPIA within the oil industry illustrate this trend.

Member State interests. The tendency of Member States to press the interests of domestic industrial interests through negotiations in the Council of Ministers as well as through the working parties which precede the development of a draft directive by the Commission is a strong feature in the energy sector. This strong axis of interests between the energy industry and national governments is illustrated both by particular cases, for example the divergence of German—British interests over the LCP Directive, and by the procedural provisions in the Maastricht Treaty which require unanimous decisions for proposals affecting strategic energy interests.

'Beggar my neighbour' regulatory strategies. The tendency of both industries and national governments to attempt to develop regulations which will inhibit potential competitors is noted. For example, the oil industry wanted to expand the scope of the liquid fuels sulphur directive to cover solid fuels. In the 1980s, the German Federal Government wanted emission controls extended to all members of the EU. In the case studies covered in this chapter, the motivation was to mitigate, in a reactive way, an actual or perceived competitive disadvantage rather than pro-actively to create a new competitive advantage.

Market instruments and traditional regulation. Comparison of the LCP and carbon tax case studies shows that the regulatory process associated with a market-based instrument is likely to be no easier than that associated with a traditional 'command-and-control' instrument. In fact, the regulatory process associated with the market-based instrument was perhaps more difficult because it created a more fundamental challenge to existing practices and assumptions. Certainly, market-based instruments offer the prospect of greater economic efficiency but the degree of advantage of real measures is less clear. The pure carbon tax proposed by DG-XI would have been an economically efficient instrument. But the associated regulatory process addressed questions of efficiency and equity — efficiency was negotiated out while equity, in the forms of the energy component of the tax and exemptions, was negotiated in. On the other hand, the regulatory process associated with the LCP Directive arguably raised economic efficiency. The compliance regime used in the UK, which post-dates the EU debate, is certainly more cost-effective than the German regime which preceded it.

No-one commands and no-one is in control. The case studies make it clear the term 'command-and-control' bares only the most tenuous relationship to reality as a characterization of actual regulatory processes. The term implies a hierarchical relationship between regulatory authorities and regulated firms for which no evidence can be found in the context of EU regulatory procedures. The Commission, national governments and energy companies have acted together in an relationship characterized by an uneasy mix of partnership and rivalry. The term has entered the vocabulary of environmental regulation and will not go away — but perhaps it should not be used without raised commas.

NOTES

1. Anthony Ikwue, Researcher, SPRU, University of Sussex, Falmer, Brighton, East Sussex BN1 9RF, UK, tel: 441273686758; fax: 441273685865.
2. Jim Skea, Professor Fellow, SPRU at the University of Sussex. SPRU, University of Sussex, Falmer, Brighton, East Sussex BN1 9RF, UK, tel: 441273686758; fax: 441273685865.
3. Indeed, from the legal perspective this is the key feature which distinguishes an EU Directive from a Regulation.
4. The patterns of privatisation were different in England and Wales, Scotland and Northern Ireland. Only the situation in England and Wales is discussed here.

REFERENCES

Arthur D. Little (1992), *Integrated Approach for Sulphur and Sulphur Dioxide Limit in the European Refining Industry*, London: Arthur D. Little Ltd.

Barnett, A. (1994), *European Oil Refining*, London: Financial Times Management Report.

Boehmer-Christiansen, S.A. and J. Skea (1991), *Acid Politics*, London: Belhaven Press.

European Commission (1988), 'Council Directive on the Limitation of Emission into the Air from Large Combustion Plants', *Official Journal of the European Communities*, **L366**.

European Commission (1992a), 'Towards Sustainability: A European Community Programme of Policy and Action in relation to the Environment and Sustainable Development', COM (92) 23 final.

European Commission (1992b), 'Proposal for a Council Directive Introducing a Tax on Carbon Dioxide Emissions and Energy', COM (92) 226.

European Commission (1992c), 'A Community Strategy to Limit Carbon Dioxide Emissions and Improve Energy Efficiency', COM (92) 246 final.

Grubb, M. (ed.) (1992), *Climate Change in the European Community*, London: Royal Institute of International Affairs.

STOA (1995), *Climate Change and Energy Use: Status and Options for European Policy*, Strasbourg: European Parliament.

UK Central Statistical Office (1995), *Annual Abstract of Statistics 131*, London: HMSO.

6. Playing on two chessboards — the European waste management industry: strategic behaviour in the market and in the policy debate

Sebastiano Brusco,[1] **Paolo Bertossi**[2] **and Alberto Cottica**[3]

1. INTRODUCTION

Up to the end of the 1970s, municipal waste management was carried out almost exclusively by the public sector, directly or through publicly owned firms. This situation has now radically changed. Large private firms, often operating outside as well as within their home country's borders, have appeared and grown; the industry's concentration has increased very significantly; and the prevailing technologies have changed.

Section 2 of this paper looks at these developments. Section 3 examines the new regulation that European regulatory agencies have implemented for this industry. We look at regulation issued from the beginning of the 1970s to the present day, in which we distinguish two main phases. The first one resulted in the emergence of a new institutional configuration; the second one in the elaboration of new principles, the 'polluter pays' and 'proximity' principles. Section 4 looks at regulation from a different point of view: that of technical standards setting, that has kept the European Union as well as is Member States continuously busy from the 1970s to the present day. Of all relevant norms, the paper examines not only the content but the process leading to their launch, with particular reference to the role that firms played in it.

Section 5, the final one, attempts to highlight the strategic interaction between the different agents: firms, regulators, environmental organizations and the public opinion. The results of this analysis are that firms fight each other on a competitive arena that grows more integrated and Europe-wide, but that they influence and interact with regulators on two policy arenas. On the European and national arenas, the point of view of large firms, asking for strict environmental standards that local businesses cannot comply with, is the prevailing one. On local policy arenas, on the contrary, small private firms and publicly owned ones score vital points, obtaining from local authorities a less stringent enforcement of environmental regulation than is normally demanded from large firms.

This analysis leads to forecasting a clash between national and international operators on one side and local operators on the other side, with the former demanding that enforcement of environmental standards be carried out by national authorities; this would make the degree of enforcement much more 'level playing' and eliminate, *de facto*, the local policy arenas.

2. THE MUNICIPAL WASTE INDUSTRY IN FRANCE, GERMANY, ITALY AND THE UK FROM THE 1970S TO THE PRESENT DAY

2.1 The situation at the beginning of the 1970s

At the beginning of the 1970s, in the four countries investigated, the municipal waste collection and disposal industry was almost entirely controlled and run by municipalities, which managed the service directly or through companies of which they maintained the ownership. Private operators, who were tendered out the service, were few, and in general small.

Despite the general similarities, there were also differences among the four countries, and it is useful to survey them.

Germany

In Germany the tradition of public intervention in public utilities dates back to the beginning of the century. At the beginning of the 1970s, more or less all medium-sized and large cities had a *Stadtwerke,* i.e., a firm, owned by the municipality, that run waste management as well as electricity, water and gas distribution, and in many cases district heating. Stadtwerke are not on the city's budget; they use commercial accounting systems, and have a good deal of autonomy from the city administration. Their size is rather small, as they serve only one municipality and sometimes its suburban areas. In smaller towns, services were run by the municipality on its own budget, or tendered out to small operators. By far the most widespread disposal technique was landfilling.

France

In the 30,000 French communes (10,000 of which had less than 1,000 inhabitants) the municipal waste collection and disposal service was almost always carried out by firms owned by the municipality (mostly in large cities) or by municipalities themselves (*régie directe*). Private operators were few, and mainly consisted of local firms working for smaller communes. In France, as well as in Germany, co-operation between neighbouring towns to run the service was rare; in France a tradition of integration of the various utilities into one single firm was also lacking. Landfilling was by far the prevailing disposal option for municipal waste.

Italy

In Italy, like in Germany, many publicly owned firms were created before 1930. Some, however, were created after the second World War. At the beginning of the 1970s these firms were about 100, catering for about 25—30 per cent of the population. Their geographic distribution was very uneven. They were more common in large and medium-sized cities than in small towns, and much more in northern than in southern Italy. Also their efficiency and technical skill were unevenly distributed, with northern firms tending to perform better than southern ones. Like their French and German counterparts, Italian publicly owned firms operated only in one city, and sometimes its suburban area. This is a relevant difference with regard to other Italian public companies: many water and gas supply companies are larger than that.

The remaining 70 per cent of Italy disposed of its waste through direct intervention of communes (this option was also used in some large cities, like Naples) or tendered the service to private operators. Again, landfills were the final destination of almost all waste.

United Kingdom

In the UK, as well, at the beginning of the 1970s communes had a very important role. Here, however, municipal waste management in the UK was carried out by a peculiar mixed public-private system. Household waste was collected and disposed of by local authorities; 'commercial' waste (physically indistinguishable from municipal waste, but produced by service or commercial firms rather than households) was dealt with by contractors chosen by the waste producers themselves, who could be either local authorities or private firms. So, under the regulatory framework provided by the Control of Pollution Act (COPA) in 1974, an embryonic private sector, based on free market, could develop from an early stage, supplying its services to commercial waste producers.

Starting from 1974, and following norms contained in the COPA itself, a Waste Collection Authority (WCA) and a Waste Disposal Authority (WDA) were created in each county. The staff of WCAs and WDAs was on the payroll of the municipality. So, in general, waste was managed in a form which was very similar to the French *régie directe,* though in some counties, private companies had access to contracts to collect and dispose of waste on behalf of the local Waste Disposal Authorities.

In the UK, the integration of waste management services with other public utilities was practically nonexistent. The prevailing disposal technique was, as elsewhere in Europe, landfilling.

2.2 The situation in the mid—1990s

In the mid—1990s, the situation had changed significantly.

Germany

From 1970 to the mid—1990s the German private waste management industry grew fast. Private firms now control 50 per cent of a fast-growing municipal waste collection and disposal market. Here, however, it is more difficult than elsewhere (in France, for example) to separate out clearly private sector from public sector waste management: it is not uncommon for the private sector to run publicly owned facilities, or build and run disposal plants on behalf of the public sector.[4] The 'pure private' waste disposal sector, with firms building disposal plants with their own capital and selling their capacity on the market, is dominated by four large firms. The industry is more diversified than elsewhere in Europe; firms specializing in activities such as recycling of particular fractions of waste, sorting, composting and so on are relatively common. Large, well structured firms specialize in the production of machines and other capital goods for waste collection and disposal.

By the 'big four' criterion, and in comparison with other European countries, the concentration level of the industry is, in Germany, quite high. The registered firms are about one thousand, but the four largest ones (Edelhoff, RWE Entsorgung, Otto and Rethmann) control about 40 per cent of the market.

The launch, in the early 90s, of DSD, which is discussed in Chapter 7, was a major drive in the concentration and diversification process. DSD, in fact, has strongly concentrated segments of disposal demand, and has brought a very diverse demand for recycling to the market place. Concentration of demand, then, has given impulse to the concentration of supply.

France

In France, the share of municipal waste disposed of by private operators, close to nil in 1970, had grown to about 80 per cent by the mid—1990s. There are about 200 private firms, but the concentration level is very high. The two largest groups, Compagnie Générale des Eaux (which uses the trademark Onyx for waste management) and Lyonnaise des Eaux, control about 20 per cent each of the market. Two medium-sized operators, Electricité de France and Bouygues-Saur control, between the two of them, about 10 per cent. Only 25 firms run five or more disposal plants; eight of these are owned by the two conglomerates.

The techniques employed by private firms are different from those employed by public firms. The share of landfilled waste is about the same in both cases, but privately owned plants tend to be much larger than publicly owned ones. Publicly owned incinerators have an average capacity of 15 tonnes per day, whereas for privately owned ones the figure is 82. For waste-to-energy incinerators, the figures are, respectively, 183 and 270.

Italy

In Italy, publicly owned firms cover a share of about 30 per cent of the collection (but not disposal) market. With respect to 1970, there has probably been a small increase in the market share of publicly owned firms combined, attributable to an expansion in the suburban or metropolitan areas of the larger firms.

Large private operators have increased very significantly their waste collection market share, from almost nil to nearly 25 per cent. The main feature of the private waste collection industry in Italy is that the majority of this 25 per cent is accounted for by non-Italian firms; Waste Management alone controls 15 per cent of the market; Browning Ferries International another 3.5 per cent. The larger nationally owned firms are Sorain Cecchini, Aimeri, Manutencoop (owned by Lega delle Cooperative) and Fisia (Fiat group) and account, all together, for less than 8 per cent. The concentration process, that in Germany and France was managed by indigenous firms, in Italy benefited mainly foreign groups.

The growth of large firms has eroded mainly the competitive position of small private operators, though in some cases the named firms were tendered services that used to be run by municipalities themselves. A reasonable estimate is that direct intervention of municipalities accounts today for 20 per cent of the Italian market (in 1970 it was about 35 per cent), and local businesses for the remaining 25 per cent.

These estimates, it should be noted, refer to the waste collection market. In waste disposal, the market share of private operators is larger. This does not depend, like in Germany, from an excess disposal capacity of private firms with respect to what they collect. The disposal market in Italy is dominated by firms that can be small or large, but that almost always display a very low environmental profile, that have somehow managed to get a permit to run a landfill.

In many cases, in central and southern Italy in particular, publicly owned firms limit their activity to waste collection, and waste is disposed of in privately owned facilities. The *azienda municipalizzata* of Rome brings the waste collected to the privately owned landfill of Malagrotta (the disposal capacity of which has been declared exhausted five years ago). In the southern region of Puglia two thirds of the cities are served by publicly owned firms, but they have no disposal capacity at all. Only in the best-run regions these firms dispose of almost all the waste they collect.

United Kingdom

In the UK the industry structure was heavily influenced by two laws that have no counterpart in the other countries.

The first one is a disposition of the 1990 Environmental Protection Act (EPA), that ordered municipalities to manage through publicly owned firms the waste collection and disposal activities previously run directly. So, WCAs and WDAs were outlawed, and they had to be transformed into Local Authorities Waste Disposal Companies (LAWDCs). These are owned by counties, but they operate as private sector companies (they are probably closer to the German *Stadtwerken* than to the Italian *aziende municipalizzate).* Two years earlier, the 1988 Local Government Act had obliged local authorities to have competitive tendering for waste collection and disposal services. So, the newly created LAWDCs had no certainty to win the tender against private competitors, even though they ended up winning 70 per cent of tenders within their base counties.

The second norm, also contained in the EPA, sets stringent environmental standards for landfills to be built after 1993, but allowed existing facilities to go on running with old standards. This originated elements of rent, that helped small businesses with local landfills to defend their market niches. Many of these are expected to go out of business when their existing capacity is exhausted.

Although these two norms, in general, are favourable to the growth of the private sector in waste management, in the UK this sector is much less developed than in France and Germany. Consisting in 40 LAWDCs, the public sector controlled, in 1993, 75 per cent of the market. The remaining 25 per cent is divided among about 2,000 small local businesses (with a turnover of £25 million or less), many of them enjoying the rents mentioned above, about twenty large indigenous firms and some multinationals. Among British firms, the most important are Biffa (Severn Trent group), Shanks & McEwan and Leigh. Among multinationals, the most important are Waste Management and Browning Ferries International (USA-based) and Générale des Eaux and Lyonnaise des Eaux (France-based). Unfortunately, reliable market share data are not available; however, the 'big four' concentration index is sure to be significantly smaller to the German and French ones.

2.3 Some general notes

The large firms mentioned above have different backgrounds. In Italy and in the UK American firms play a relevant role; indigenous firms enter the industry almost always through a diversification route. In Germany they enter from businesses that are close to waste management, like Otto (equipment and machines for waste collection) or Edelhoff (sewage sludge treatment); in France from provision of other public services; in the UK they often originate in construction and public works. So, it is quite common that large firms belong to groups in which the turnover attributable to waste management, though quite large in absolute terms, accounts for a relatively small share of consolidated turnover.

These firms have grown in different ways. Sometimes by winning tenders; sometimes, in Germany, France and Italy (to a lesser extent in the UK) large firms have bought smaller ones, getting their share of the market.

Playing on two chessboards

However, it should be noted that no take-over among large firms has been attempted in the last ten years. In other cases, these firms have 'grown with the market', taking advantage of a new regulation which sets and enforces stringent standards which increase the technical level, and therefore the value added of waste management. Given the ever-increasing demand for environmental quality, the activity and the revenue of the waste management firms increase even while serving the same population. It is worth noting that this is not an easy path to tread for smaller firms: they do not have the necessary technical knowledge. This path of growth is very important in Germany. Finally, these firms have grown by agreement and alliances. In France, Germany and the UK waste management firms have been making alliances with energy producers and distributors in order to build and run big incinerators with energy recovery; in Germany, in order to exploit all the opportunities of the DSD, alliances have been made between waste management firms, energy producers, chemical firms in order to recycle packaging waste.

The analysis of growth paths helps explaining two important phenomena which, in a way, are common to the history of this industry in the countries investigated.

Firstly, their larger scale implies that private firms, contrary to publicly owned ones, would not cater for just one city, but need to manage the waste of more cities. Further, as the industry becomes dominated by large firms, the degree of integration of waste management with the management of other public utilities increases. This phenomenon is especially important in France and the UK.

The other important consequence is technological, and is the shift away from landfilling to more complex disposal techniques.

According to OECD sources, in Germany the share of landfilled waste in 1989 had decreased by 30 per cent since 1970, and a relevant share (22 per cent) is incinerated. German incineration technology, according to industry experts, is among the best in the world.

The incineration rate of waste in France is high (37 per cent), and mostly attributable to large private firms, that, as mentioned above, built several large, efficient plants.

In Italy, on the contrary, the increase in the share of incinerated waste (14 per cent according to OECD; very likely significantly less than that) depends mostly on the strategies of some publicly owned firms in the North, that in the 1970s have built about ten fairly efficient plants. After 1980 neither they, nor private firms, have managed to build any more incinerators, for the opposition of local communities and the environmentalist movements.

In the UK the shift away from landfilling has been least relevant (the 1989 incineration rate is estimated to be about 10 per cent, and again this is probably an overestimate). The main reason for this is that Britain enjoys a relative abundance of nearly ideal landfilling sites (typically spent mines), and this has kept landfilling costs very low. In the UK these costs are about

15—22 ECU per tonne, from one third to one sixth of incineration costs. As a result, anything that is not a landfill makes an economic loss.

The development of recycling has not been so relevant as that of incineration. In spite of many efforts, the share of waste separately collected and recycled is still very small. Table 6.1 shows recycling rates (recycled waste on the total, in weight) in the four countries.

Table 6.1   Overall recycling rate, 1990

Germany	20
France	4
Italy	4
United Kingdom	6

Source: OECD (1991)

To summarize, from 1970 to the mid—1990s the industry has undergone important changes; proprietary, of firm size, of concentration, of integration with other industries, of technological level. This process, which can be interpreted as the birth of the waste management industry from public hygiene, was influenced by several factors. Technical progress certainly played a role, devising new technologies in which economies of scale are more relevant. But the key driver was almost certainly the emergence of a new wave of environmental regulation, which as boosted demand and, simultaneously, changed the rules of the game of competition, basically forcing the adoption of technologies with different scale curves.

3.   THE REGULATORY PROCESS FROM 1970 TO THE MID—1990s: THE NEW INSTITUTIONAL CONFIGURATION AND THE NEW GUIDING PRINCIPLES

3.1   The building of a new institutional configuration

Public hygiene services are network services, and therefore natural (local) monopolies. As such, they pose welfare problems stemming from the impossibility to foster market competition. Since the beginning of the century, this was the reason why European cities had chosen to run these services publicly. In choosing this route, local authorities had followed the prescriptions of state-of-the-art economic theory, agreed on by thinkers of different ideological areas. The basic idea was that the community would best run these services by running them itself. Its direct intervention would set the service standards and costs that best suited it, the workers would enjoy dignified working conditions, and monopoly profits would be avoided. This theoretical framework ruled out efficiency problems, as well as environmental quality ones. The idea was that the local authority would prevent waste of public money, and that citizens would watch over service quality and environmental friendliness. In Germany, the typical Stadtwerke, whose autonomy was well guaranteed by the local authority, is an almost textbook rendition of the model proposed by Pigou (1946), which aimed, among other things, at solving the problem of the possible negative influence of local politics on the management of the service.

So, the local authority was, at the same time, setting environmental and service standards, running the service and watching that the standards were met. This concentration of competencies was challenged by new regulation, aimed at building a new institutional configuration.

The legislative bandwagon was set in motion by Germany, who issued a Waste Disposal Act in 1972. The second mover was the UK, who introduced the Control of Pollution Act (COPA), that, as was noted, introduced WCAs and WDAs. One year later, the first Europe-wide regulation saw the light when the then European Economic Community approved the municipal waste directive of 1975 (442/75). The directive prompted a response from France, which in 1975 issued two decrees: one to set out the general rules for waste management and the other to tackle the technical problems therewith. By a long way the last mover, Italy, only approved its main municipal waste disposal regulation in 1982, with law 915/82.

All these laws have a similar content. To begin with, they lay the foundations of a more rigorous regulation of the industry. Precise definitions of 'waste' and of lawful disposal methods are issued; the principle according to which firms need a permit to be in the public hygiene business is stated; a system of controls over them is devised.

This new wave of regulation takes away from municipalities many of the competencies that, generically defined by the older regulatory framework, they had held almost without interference.

At the European Union level general guidelines are issued (among which the well-known 'ladder principle', which ranks disposal methods according to their environmental friendliness), priorities and environmental objectives are decided, and technical standards for waste disposal plants are fixed. The result of this process is the distribution of competencies summarized in Table 6.2.

Each country's government, following European instructions, sets the industry's main guidelines, as well as priorities and standards. Intermediate layers of government (Departments in France, Länder in Germany, Regions and Provinces in Italy, Counties in the UK) have the responsibility of implementing those guidelines. Given the awareness, by now fairly general, that communes are too small to run waste management efficiently, these same intermediate layers of government are burdened with planning responsibilities, which involve the promotion of consortia of municipalities for the sake of efficiency. Planning competencies, however, are not always clearly traced.

Despite all this, municipalities still enjoy a wide manoeuvring area. It is still them who, ultimately, decide who is going to run the service. The local administration can do the job by itself, or can set up a publicly owned company, or can entrust private firms with waste management. In this last case, the criteria fixed by law on how to choose the firm which wins the tender always leave the municipality some degree of freedom.

Table 6.2   Laws and regulations: administrative levels involved

	France	Germany	Italy	UK
Main guidelines and standard setting	Central Government	Central Government Länder	Central Government	Central Government
Implementation of the guidelines	MoE (a), Departments	Länder	Regions, provinces	Counties
Planning	Departments	Länder	Regions, Provinces	Counties (b)
Responsibility for collecting and disposal (ab)	Municipalities consortia	Municipalities consortia	Municipality	Counties
Control	MoE, Departments	Länder	Province	MoE (b)

Notes: (a) Ministry of Environment
(b) This implies also the responsibility for taking the decision about who will be entrusted with waste management in the municipality area.

The control on service and environmental standards, finally, is assigned to the regional—departmental level.

New regulation leaves ample space for private initiative. In all countries privates can either compete in tenders to supply collection and/or disposal services, or build and run disposal facilities, in order to sell disposal capacity on the market. The building of such a plant is, however, restricted both by environmental regulation and local planning.

To summarize; regulation is issued at the EU and national level, but it is applied, enforced and controlled at the local level. In many cases, control is entrusted to local authorities, or, when it is not, to local agents of central authorities, who are not outside the balance of local politics.

Despite the lack of a serious opposition to the new laws, the activity of waste management planning they prescribed remained a dead letter for years. National laws on local waste management planning were finalized years later, and in most cases the time gap between the approval of a national regulation and the actual implementation of the plans (by local authorities) has been noticeable. However, patterns differ significantly across as well as within the four countries studied.

In Germany, the only country in which planning is now all-pervasive, most plans were finalized only at the end of the 80s.

France is the most remarkable case of delayed implementation. Despite the country's strong planning tradition, French authorities have by and large refused to engage in waste disposal planning. The 1975 law (75/633) did provide for departmental planning for waste management, and the aim was the co-ordination at department level of public and private actors on the field of waste collection and disposal. However, the guidelines for the elaboration of such plans were not given until 1993 (93/139, eighteen years later). The deadline for the presentation of the plans is currently set at February 1996.

In Italy, at the end of the 1980s, about half the regions had finalized their plans. Almost all of them are in northern or central Italy, whereas the south still lacks almost any planning.

As in France, very little action in this direction has been taken in the UK. This, however, is less surprising, given the relatively weak British tradition of planning. A local Waste Regulation Authority (WRA) has been introduced in 1990 to exercise the regulatory responsibility, as administering site licences and drawing up waste disposal plans. WRA functions are carried out at the County level, which is the same of the Waste Disposal Authority. Recall that the very same EPA which introduced WRAs has made planning much more difficult by introducing compulsory tendering, which we discuss below.

The long-standing tradition of independence of European municipalities, and the reluctance of national governments to limit it, is probably one of the explanations for this delay. But there is another hypothesis, namely that it is the consequence of the attempt to protect interests that would be hit by effective planning. We will come back on this matter.

3.2 Enforcement issues

The impact of making laws depends crucially on a (national or local) government's ability to enforce them. It is noteworthy that finding the degree of control and enforcement varies very significantly across and even within the countries examined. We should note that control is not exercised only by the authorities in charge, but also by people, which can report the transgressors to the authority in charge, and can also make pressure on it, denouncing the infringement to the public opinion. Both kinds of control are not homogeneous: stronger in certain areas, much weaker in others. As public control can affect disposal costs, these differences are very important.

Consider a situation in which regulation is enforced with a random mechanism, so that, for a given degree of compliance, each firm can compute the expected value of the fine it is subject to. Of course, the expected value of the fine is a function of the structure of nominal fines and of the chance of getting fined. Clearly, compliance is costly. Firms behaving optimally, then, will trade off compliance costs against expected fine.

Under the hypothesis of risk-neutrality, a situation in which the probability of getting caught is low, but the fines are high, can be made equivalent to one in which enforcement is tough but the fines are low. So, the degree of enforcement *per se* is not a policy variable that firms are interested in: all they care for is the expected value of their compliance costs.

This situation changes if enforcement turns out to be more or less strict according to the type of firm involved. In this case, the group of firms more heavily targeted by the environmental protection agency has an interest towards 100 per cent enforcement and zero or near-zero (expected) fines, which would eliminate the randomness and level out their competitive disadvantage towards their competitors of the other group.

In the waste management industry such a partition into two groups exists. As a consequence of the NIMBY (Not In My BackYard) syndrome and of environmental activism, larger, more visible firms are more closely watched by the public eye then small, local businesses. On the other hand, the unit costs of full compliance with environmental regulation is lower for large firms than for small ones, which suffers from diseconomies of scale and low skill problems.

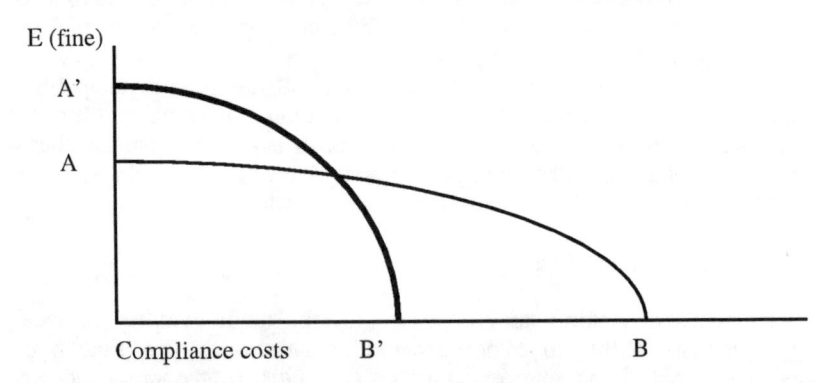

Figure 6.1 Choosing a compliance level

As a consequence of uneven enforcement and economies of scale in compliance, for a given level of regulation stringency and a given structure of nominal fines, the relationship between compliance costs and expected fines is similar to the curve depicted in Figure 6.1 for a large firm (thick line curve) and a small one (thin line curve). The curves are functions mapping from compliance costs per unit of output, represented on the X-axis, to expected value of fines per unit of output, represented on the Y-axis. In order to drive the expected value of the fine to zero, firms must reach full compliance, represented by points B (for a small firm) and B' (for a large firm). Economies of scale in compliance see to it that B' lies to the left of B. The expected value of the fine at low levels of compliance (when compliance costs are low) is, on the other hand, lower for small firms than for large ones; so, at zero compliance, a large firm expects a fine of A' per unit of output, whereas a small firm expects only a unit fine of A.

Notice that increasing the stringency of regulations, but keeping the probabilities for firms in the two groups of being inspected, shifts both curves eastwards, leaving noncompliant small firms greater margins for price competition. On the other hand, 100 per cent enforcement would shift both curves northwards and change the relative position of the two curves so as to make A coincide with A'. At this stage, large firms would enjoy a compliance cost advantage on smaller ones, whatever the level of compliance.

These considerations help understanding the competitive implications of the different countries' enforcement styles.

There seems to be virtually no enforcement problem in Germany. Regulation is usually enforced and controlled in the whole country. Control is made by authorities, as well as by a very environmentally aware population. The other feature of Germany with regard to enforcement issues is the country's readiness to implement European regulation.

By contrast the gap between required standards and the techniques in use today in France by small enterprises and municipalities is quite wide. It is worth remembering that the city of Marseilles is now disposing of its waste in an uncontrolled landfill exactly the same as 20 years ago. Such a landfill, were it run by a multinational, would invite strong local opposition. As noted above, planning is also problematic. However, unlike the other countries studied, France enjoys a relative freedom from NIMBY problems, which clearly enhances its ability to enforce disposal sites location decisions.

Enforcement problems differ substantially across different parts of Italy. Despite exception, in northern Italy regional governments are able to draw their waste management plans, and the degree of enforcement of environmental standards is reasonably high. In the south, on the other hand, hardly any planning is done, and a worryingly high share of waste is disposed of in illegal landfills connected with organized crime. Northern Italians are even more prone to NIMBY than the average European citizen: so it is very difficult to build new disposal sites in this part of the country, for the public authorities and private operators alike. Environmental groups give unconditional support to local protest, a policy seen as trying to make up for their weakness at the national level by demagogy.

In the UK the powers of control assigned to Waste Regulation Authorities are high, but the resources available for control are very scarce. This implies that enforcement is based mainly on informal effort, and that the level of prosecution is fairly low. This, too, results in a disavantage for large firms with respect to small ones.

The uneven level of enforcement and control which has so far been described has very serious consequences both on the competitive and on the regulatory dynamics, as it affects the costs of disposal in the concerned areas, and the structure of the market and industry of waste management. This issue, and its relationship to the regulatory strategies of different groups of firms, is further discussed in section 5.

3.3 The new guiding principles; polluter pays, filière policies, mandatory and voluntary consortia

After the building of the new institutional configuration, under the pressure of green parties and environmental groups (possibly more influential than ever before or since), at the end of the 1980s waste management regulation entered a new phase. Though a preference for source reduction and recycling had been present already in the EU 442/75 directive, with directive 156/91 the commitment to the ladder principle is strongly asserted, and polluter pays becomes operational. In this perspective, environmental policy becomes more targeted, often with initiatives aimed at developing recycling of single waste fractions.

Restless with the relatively slow growth in recycling rates, European governments tackled the issue in a radical way, making compulsory the separate collection and recycling of single fractions of municipal waste. Quantitatively, the most relevant object of these policies is certainly packaging.

The first mover was Italy in 1988. A new law (415/1988) set ambitious recycling targets and set up consortia for the recycling of several waste fractions including glass, paper, plastics, spent car batteries, and waste oil. Participation in consortia was mandatory for these raw materials and intermediate goods producers. Consortia are largely self-financed; for example, the plastics recycling consortium is financed by plastics producers, who levy on themselves a tax on invoices issued for sales of packaging material.

Whereas Italy's recycling targets remained dead letter (except in the case of glass and waste oil), Germany marked a turning point in 1991 by introducing its packaging ordinance, which in turn led to the implementation of the DSD scheme (see Chapter 7).

The change is dramatic: responsibility of packaging waste collection and disposal does not rest with a local authority anymore, but with packaging producers and distributors. The service is ordered by a private company, which may choose its supplier, and no decision is taken at any level by the public authorities. Though the system is far from perfect, and is currently facing revision, it does embody the polluter pays principle to an extent unparalleled in previous municipal waste disposal regulation, as well as accepting that a correct packaging waste management begins with internalizing disposal costs at the design stage. Perhaps the single most important novel element in the packaging ordinance, however, is the idea that the government should set environmental goals, but then leave industry to design the system whereby they can be achieved at the least cost. All three innovations have been embodied in the packaging waste regulation of all the countries examined.

France responded by setting up a similar recycling consortia system (the main consortium is called Eco-Emballage). Just like the German system, the French one assigns responsibility for correct waste management to private firms rather than public bodies, and it works with an upstream collected fee system. However, the French approach to recycling is less radical than the German one: fees are significantly lower, and incineration with energy recovery is allowed to count as recycling.[5]

One principle contained in the German packaging ordinance was embedded in another important piece of British waste disposal regulation, this time an already operational one. The Environmental Protection Act (EPA) had introduced, in 1990, a duty of care on commercial waste producers, handlers and disposers, which aimed to ensure safe and legal management of waste. As already noted in the case of the UK commercial waste (as an example: the waste produced by McDonald's) is collected separately from the normal urban waste produced by households. Local authorities collect the commercial waste only if requested to do so. Commercial waste producers normally buy the private sector disposal services. The provisions of EPA meant that board members of consumer goods retailing firms were personally responsible for polluting the environment if the firm collecting the waste they produce did not obey regulations: they might go to jail. This forces operators to watch over the correct disposal of the waste they have produced. To reduce the risk of being engaged with disposers who violate environmental protection laws, the managers of multi-site firms decided to cut down their number of waste disposal service contractors. Companies wanting to get the contracts with large commercial firms seek therefore to build a nationwide collection network, which is an important competitive advantage, to do business with large, multi-site customers.

This regulation was implemented in April 1992. Further indications to enforce it have been included into the Environmental Protection Regulations 1992 and into the Controlled Waste Regulations 1992. They prescribe some general requirements for the subjects (private and public ones) involved: prevention of illegal disposal of the waste and its getting out of their control, transfer of the waste to authorized companies. But the law says nothing about the methods of control, so the regulation went unenforced — at least up to April 1994.

The system described is similar to the German one. A waste fraction is targeted, polluter pays applies and legal responsibility rests with the producers of the waste instead of a public authority. The main difference with DSD is the absence of recycling targets, which are left to the market. In addition to this system, the UK began in 1994 to engineer a DSD-like system for packaging waste, with centrally set recycling targets.[6]

Since packaging recycling fees are imposed on import goods as well, there is a foreign trade side to this issue. In recognition of this, in 1993 the European Commission drafted a packaging directive which was finalized in December 1994 (94/62). The draft is generic enough to be compatible with both the German and the French system.

The above discussion illustrates how the new regulatory phase beginning in the late 1980s displays four outstanding features: the commitment to source reduction, the implementation of the polluter pays principle, targeted policies and recycling boosting policies. These four features do not necessarily come in a bundle: it is technically and juridically possible to have one without the others (for example, the British commercial waste regulation has polluter pays but no commitment to source reduction or recycling boosting).

The characteristics of the new phase in the European waste policy modified the characteristics of the demand for, and therefore, indirectly, those of the supply of, waste management services, as well as the structure of the waste industry.

Figures 6.2, 6.3 and 6.4 illustrate the point. Figure 6.2 stylizes the waste management market in 1970. Each municipality makes decisions independently from all the others; the demand is very fragmented, sales and marketing economies of scale are nonexistent, and the exploitation of technical ones is difficult.

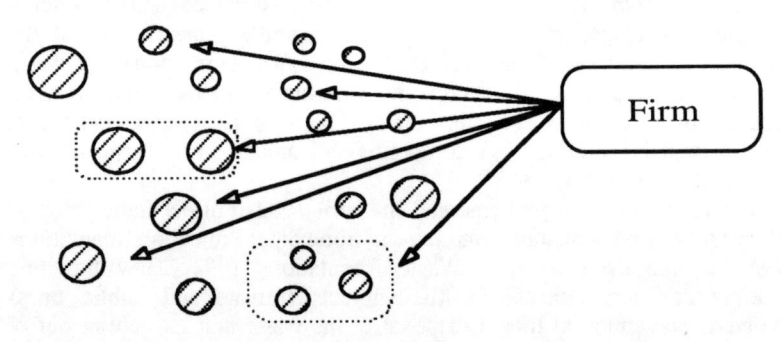

Figure 6.2   Relating to a fragmented market

Figure 6.3 stylizes the situation designed by the body of regulation launched in the early 1970s. Municipalities are grouped in planning units, by initiatives of (regional) planning authorities or of large private firms. This configuration gives a competitive advantages to large firms, and encourages concentration processes. Firms tend to be multi-utility, i.e., to supply planning units with various services besides waste management.

Municipalities and planning unit

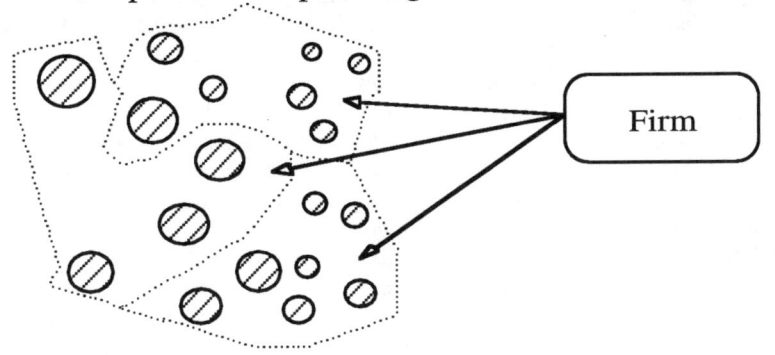

Figure 6.3   Relating to planning units

Figure 6.4 stylizes the model resulting from the new regulatory phase of the late 1980s and 1990s. In this case, the regulation creates new market segments, where specialized firms can find their market space. In fact, segmentation is a likely outcome, since waste fractions tend more and more to be regulated differently.[7]

Municipality

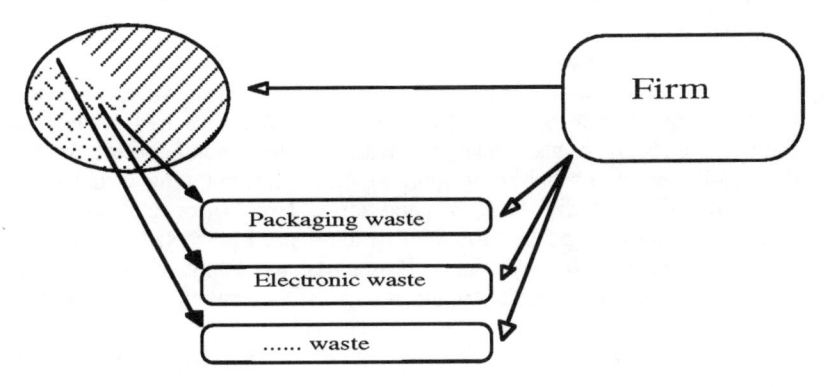

Figure 6.4   Relating to a segmented market

4. SETTING TECHNICAL STANDARDS

4.1 Setting incineration standards

The main regulations on technical standards for waste incineration adopted by the EU are two: directives 89/369 and 89/429.

Drafted and discussed in a political context of growing awareness of environmental issues, the standards on incineration turned out to be much stricter than ever before. The public outcry at the 1976 Seveso dioxine release had a major role in prompting regulators to introduce very strict rules. As we contend elsewhere,[8] the consequence of this move was to make waste incineration technologies more expensive, and more sensitive to economies of scale than they used to be. Interestingly enough, both incineration directives limited themselves to setting emission standards, letting firms find their least-cost technological path towards meeting them.

In the case of incineration, stringent regulation was issued almost effortlessly, without any opposition from industry or from other interested party. Quite the contrary; as far as large firms are concerned, interviewed company spokespersons make no mystery of the fact that stringent regulation means sticking more value added on the service they sell, the bill of which is footed by taxpayers. Typically, large firms have responded to drafts offering their co-operation and expertise to help formulate in a technically precise way the new laws and directives.

It should be noted, however, that regulating waste incineration is not representative of environmental regulation on industry in general. The agents involved were few, in contrast with what happened regulating packaging waste, or landfills, which we discuss below. As Lévêque points out in the introduction to this book, in general new environmental regulation implies a reduction in the demand facing the industry being regulated, even though it can bring advantages to some players and disadvantages to others.

In this case, the 'green' industry with its technology suppliers, which benefit from a more stringent environmental regulation, was the only one affected. So, even though the benefits of the new regulation did accrue more to some players than to others, there was no political clash. It came into force after a relatively short lead and with no great modifications, with a strong support from a public opinion which seemed determined to prevent new environmental disasters. By and large, large firms and industrial associations (dominated by large and medium-sized players) let regulatory agencies have it their way. Small businesses and many publicly owned firms, which did not had the technical expertise to comply with the new regulation and therefore were net losers from its launch, were not present on the regulatory arena, and they had no organizational capacity to react and defend themselves with.

The only problems that could have arisen were those relative to funding more sophisticated (and hence more expensive) waste management systems.

But even 'footing the bill' was unlikely to create much tension. In most cases, waste management is funded not by levying a tariff, covering the cost of the service, but by a tax. The revenue generated by this tax goes into the municipality's budget, and need in no way be linked to waste collection and disposal costs. So, if their disposal costs are on the rise, taxpayers need not perceive it.

4.2 Landfill Regulation

Landfill levy
The idea of a landfill levy first came to the political spotlight in the UK in 1992, consistently with the strategic commitment of the Department of the Environment to economic instruments for environmental policy.[9] The argument for it was that the market equilibrium recycling rate was lower than the socially optimal one, and that this could be corrected for by taxing disposal. This would make recycling more attractive to operators. However, this view was challenged in 1993 by a study commissioned by the DoE to the consultancy company Coopers & Lybrand. They estimated future landfill costs and prices, and forecast that the levy's impact on the recycling rate was likely to be negligible even with a high unit levy: it would take a £20 per tonne levy to achieve a 12 per cent recycling rate.[10] Instead, a landfill levy would favour waste-to-energy (WTE) incinerators, already made more attractive by a government subsidy on electricity produced burning non-fossil fuel. At the same time, the Pearce Report[11] argued that, once external costs are accounted for, WTE was indeed a better option for society than landfilling.

The Pearce Report has come under heavy criticism from British waste disposal firms. British firms have specialized in running landfills, cheaper and safer in the UK than in continental Europe, and they feel that a landfill levy would sharpen the competitive edge of their foreign competitors, who have better expertise at running recycling plants and incinerators. At least two multinationals, Waste Management and Générale des Eaux, operate in Britain. By February 1995 a final decision had not been made yet.

In France, the proposal of a landfill levy was launched by the Ministry of the Environment, but challenged by municipalities, who worried about rising waste disposal costs. The municipalities' position was championed by the Ministry of Finance; in 1993, the levy was introduced, but strongly reduced from 8 to 3 Ecu per tonne. The current level of the levy is estimated to be too low to divert any significant amount of waste from landfills Moreover, smaller municipalities do not pay the levy, on the grounds that they have no weighing device to compute the amount due with: this is of special interest as a sign of the little interest with which this problem is regarded.

Landfill technical standards

The European Commission has been trying to introduce technical prescriptions for landfilling since 1991, when the first draft of a landfill directive was released. In contrast to what had happened with incineration, the directive was meant to set not only emission standards, but the technologies to be employed as well. The discussion on the directive, however, soon became heated on the issue of co-disposal. Co-disposal is the joint disposal of municipal and hazardous waste in the same site. The official position of Member States on the matter is that Germany opposes it strongly, on the grounds that the number of hazardous waste landfills should be kept to a minimum for reclamation purposes, and the UK supports it equally strongly, on the grounds that hazardous waste helps decompose municipal waste faster. In fact, co-disposal is only used in the UK, and British firms have developed a considerable expertise in managing it. It is also a relatively cheap way to dispose of hazardous waste.

As remarked above, the UK is also a sensitive spot from a competitive point of view. In the British competitive arena, the group of the largest British firms (Leigh, Shanks & McEwan, Biffa) confronts the British subsidiaries of waste disposal multinationals (Waste Management, Browning Ferris, Générale des Eaux). The former group controls the co-disposal technology, whereas the latter rejects co-disposal as part of their corporate environmental policy. Clearly, a ban on co-disposal would favour the latter group, damaging British firms. British firms have consistently been lobbying in favour of co-disposal, and have obtained the support of their government. The Department of the Environment has officially taken a stand for co-disposal in September 1993.

At the same time, however, multinationals and the 'greener' Member States were campaigning against it. The second draft of the landfill directive (August 1993) stated that co-disposal would be outlawed in five years. At the beginning of 1995, the landfill directive had not come through the pipeline yet, and was waiting to undergo the second reading in the European Parliament.

5. STRATEGIC INTERACTION BETWEEN REGULATORY AGENCIES AND GROUPS OF FIRMS

5.1 Introduction

In describing the concentration process in the waste management industry and the regulatory process leading to new waste policies, we have mentioned several actors that played a role in one, or both, of these processes. It is useful to list them, describe them, and look at the way they interact, in order to attempt a stylization.

The actors belong to three main classes: regulators, firms and the public.

Regulators operate at various levels of jurisdiction and with different competencies. The European Union issues directives, Member States embody them in their national regulatory bodies or take particular initiatives, local authorities (at an intermediate or municipal level) run the service and control for service quality and environmental friendliness. Each of these actors produces regulation as a result of their interaction with non-governmental actors. There are two headings under which these non-governmental actors may fall: 'firms' and the 'public'.

Firms are very different from each other, ranging from American multinationals to national players, from publicly owned firms and direct management regimes (the latter are assimilated to less structured publicly owned companies for analytical purposes) to small, local private businesses.

The public, too, operates at various levels. Environmental groups, as political parties or pressure groups, make their voices heard, though with uneven degrees of effectiveness and in different ways, at all levels at which regulation is issued.

Firms confront one another on the market, the *competitive arena,* each with its comparative advantages and disadvantages, while new regulation shifts continuously the balance of the relative competitiveness of different types of firms. But the reverse is also true. Each firm's position on the market, on the competitive arena, determines its bargaining and coalition-making strategy in the regulatory process, which, borrowing a concept from political science, may be called the *policy arena.* So, ultimately, firms are really playing the same game, that of competition, on two different chessboards: the competitive arena and the policy arena. In this game, the outcomes on the competitive arena are profit vectors for all players involved; the outcomes of the policy arena are the rules of the game for the competitive arena. A firm's ability to influence the outcomes in the regulatory arena depends on its position in the competitive arenas; symmetrically, its competitive position depends, on the medium and long run, on its ability to secure advantages on the policy arena, so that the two chessboards interact with each other in a complex way. Understanding and describing the role of the actors in each chessboard and the interaction between the two chessboards is the objective of this section.

5.2 The competitive arena

The above discussion points to the existence of different groups of firms, characterized by different behaviour patterns in the competitive arena.

An important group consists of the four multinationals competing on the European market: Waste Management International and Browning Ferries International, American but based in the UK; Compagnie Générale des Eaux (Onyx), and Lyonnaise des Eaux (SITA), based in France. They compete on entry in national markets, in particular, among the countries studied, in the Italian and UK markets.

The four largest German firms are less present on the international market: the current rates of growth of the German market offer them a rich array of growth opportunities.

These eight firms display a wide range of services on offer (often including other network services, such as water management), a high degree of technical skill, a high ability to innovate, considerable financial power, and a high profile environmental policy. Service prices, however, are often low enough to undercut those charged by smaller firms, thanks to the full exploitation of economies of scale. These firms are often connected to technology suppliers that hold important patents.

As regulation imposes more stringent standards, their competitiveness increases. This happens because tougher standards imply a larger minimum efficient scale, unattainable to undercapitalized and underskilled local firms.

Besides being in a position to supply public utilities at a competitive price, large firms have the organizational resources to help cities unite in consortia. Most often in France, but elsewhere as well, these firms forward a scheme for waste management in an area, then strive to get the communes together for the implementation of their plan. A very good asset to gain the necessary consensus, set up the consortium and get the contract is having disposal capacity at a good price. Often these firms make a first agreement with a commune, in order to make the plant, and then start trying to set up the consortium. Only large firms can act likewise: technical knowledge, experience in the field of connection with local authorities, planning and organizational abilities are needed.

The multi-utility nature of these firms is a great advantage in building these consortia. Often firms start by getting the contract for water supply, or public transport, and then use the links established with the local authority to sell it waste management as well.

Up to now, there has been to be surprisingly little direct competition among these large firms. The reason for this is that, throughout Europe, a large share of the market is still in the hands of small and medium-sized local firms and of public local firms. As it has been shown, among the countries examined, large firms are strongest in France and in Germany, where they control circa 40 per cent of the market, and weakest in Italy, where their market share amounts to 15 per cent. There is, clearly, a lot of scope for growing at the expenses of small and medium-sized businesses, avoiding direct competition.

A different group is that of the national and regional medium-sized firms. Firms in this group are smaller than the multinational, and generally more strongly established in the region of origin than in the national market. Most of the British larger firms, such as Shanks and Leigh belong to this group.[12] Some of them are publicly owned.

These firms are characterized by a wide range of services, a medium-high skill level, relatively low innovativeness, and a high profile environmental policy. Service prices are, in general, competitive. They enjoy the best connections with national authorities when (as is the case in Italy and the UK) competitors come from abroad.

A third category is that of specialized firms. They focus on a very narrow range of services, on which they display a high level of technical and innovative skills, a high profile environmental policy and charge competitive prices. Many of these firms were born recently, especially in Germany after the launch of DSD, and operate in activities connected to separate collection and recycling.

Firms in the last group are very different from each other, and they share only their close ties with the cities they cater for. It includes publicly owned firms of all countries. They are relatively few (about 90 in Italy and 40 in the UK, the only two countries for which we have reliable data). Some of them, especially in Germany (but not in Italy and the UK), run not only waste management, but all other public utilities as well. Their size ranges from a few tens of thousands to several million inhabitants served. Their degree of technical skill is also very diverse; some are sadly backwards, others employ state-of-the-art technologies and have even built efficient plants for industrial and hazardous waste. They supply services of different quality levels; the quality level tends to vary with the degree of control exerted by citizens, and to be lowest when they are used as 'vote reservoirs' by local politicians.

Their efficiency level is more homogeneous, and, with exceptions, rather low. This poor performance is largely determined by the lack of separation between political responsibility, management and control; also, publicly owned firms tend to treat their workers more generously than privately owned ones. Finally, undercapitalization (connected with the poor state of public finance) and problems relating to a non-captive (non-local) market also characterize these firms. Note that, in theory, both Italian and British publicly owned firms can pursue a strategy of geographic expansion, even if in practice they tend to think more like local public utilities rather than like companies competing on the national market. But there are exceptions. In the UK, an interesting one is Cambridgeshire East-West, who runs for tenders outside its area of origin, and has even won one in Bedfordshire. In Italy, another one is Modena's AMIU, which has recently won an European tender to organize waste management in Warsaw.

Among these local firms we also count direct management schemes, which survive only in France and Italy, and which, as we noted above, are technically not firms. They display probably the lowest degree of effectiveness and efficiency. Contrary to the predictions of beginning-of-the-century thinkers, European municipalities seem just not capable to manage waste directly without running into clientelism. These schemes are characterized by the highest costs, probably in connection with the need to gather political consent.

Among these firms, unable to expand beyond the borders of the town they work for, there is a large number of privately owned small operators. They cater for a local market, and are characterized by a narrow range of services on offer, low skill and innovative level, low- or no profile environmental policy. Prices are low, often in connection to the lack of compliance with environmental regulation. Low prices and good connection with contracting local authorities are the only competitive advantages of this group of firms. In this market segment the persistency of 'illegal' waste disposal is also worth of note. A good share of waste is still disposed of in illegal landfills in France (7,000 unlicensed landfills) and in Italy (15,000). Unlicensed landfills are owned both by private and by public organizations: in all cases, there is a connivance with local authorities. Also in the United Kingdom, where licensed landfills are available at very low prices, enforcement of environmental standards is far from satisfactory.

As we have seen, at the beginning of the 1970s firms in the last group were basically the only supply structure there was. The ones which are still active are those that, for various reasons, have survived the concentration process of the latest decades. Being systematically inferior to larger, better organized, more productive private firms, they have suffered most from the launch of stricter environmental standards, which they find it difficult and costly to meet. So, the problem is not so much that of understanding why the weight of the private sector has grown so fast, but why so many firms of this last group have survived. The answer to this, as well as other questions lies in the mode of functioning of the policy arena.

5.3 The policy arena

Figure 6.5 stylizes the way in which firms and the public interact with the different administrative levels in the policy arena. Arrows stand for regulatory pressure; a light pressure is represented by a dotted arrow-line.

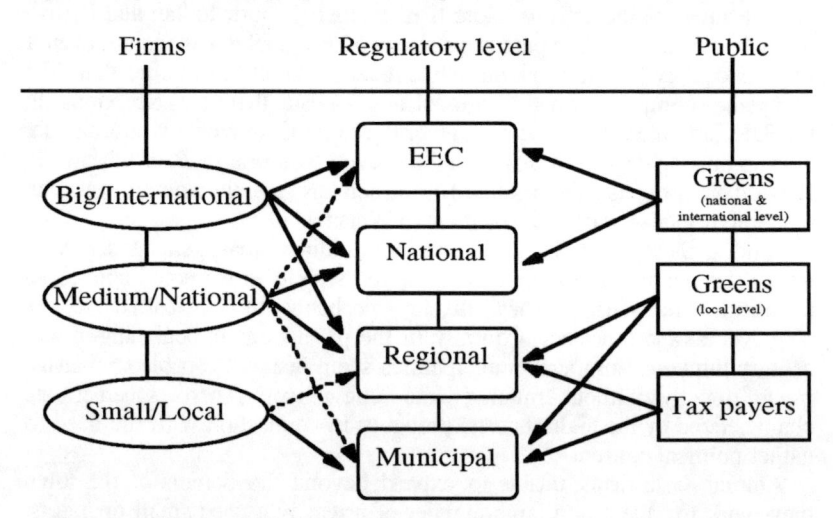

Figure 6.5   Playing in the policy arenas

Large firms competing at the national or European level have a very substantial technical expertise to throw into the debate. Often, this expertise is greater than that of regulating bodies. Quite frequently firms put this expertise at the regulators' service, in order to make regulation as clearly stated and consistent as possible. The role of lobbying for more stringent regulation is, rather, left to the public opinion and the greens.

These firms typically talk to policy makers in two ways. The first one is direct, through their External Affairs departments. This is typically used to talk to national and local governments. However, a very small number of companies (Compagnie Générale des Eaux, Lyonnaise des Eaux, Waste Management Europe, Leigh Inc.) keep a direct line with the Commission as well. The second one, more frequently encountered in relationship with the EU level is through trade associations like the European federation of waste management trade association (FEAD), staffed by External Affairs personnel.

Large firms are quite happy with the stringency of the standards today in place in Europe (although some would welcome a further move towards more stringent regulation and higher value-added collection and disposal methods). And still in certain cases the lobbying action of big firms at EU or national level is made in order to prevent too stringent regulation. As it has been pointed out earlier, a stringent regulation increases the costs of the firm that comply with it. If it is not enforced everywhere, or controlled, it is possible that increase of costs will only concern large, highly visible firms, that cannot sneak through the regulation.

At the country level, the situation is not very different: the major firms act as consultants, and push in order to have regional waste management planning implemented. It is worth noting that, in spite of the fact that recycling is always a good chance for waste management firms, they are not always in favour of it. Not one of them seems to believe in the possibility of recycling a big share of waste, if waste-to-energy incineration is not considered as a recycling technique.

Within the group of large firms, the British ones stand out for a strong dislike of technological prescriptions, which makes them oppose fiercely the ban on co-disposal. This may be interpreted as an effort to make UK technological standards different from the continental ones, therefore raising barriers to the entry of continental conglomerates.

Trade associations make their voices heard only at the national level, and at the EU level they often find a common position between State members associations. An exception to this rule is the British NAWDC, whose members accounts for 60 per cent of the British market, which finds itself at odds with the official position of FEAD (dominated by continental firms). NAWDC has then started to make its points (at the time of writing, mainly opposition to the Landfill Directive and the co-disposal ban) to the Commission leapfrogging FEAD, both directly and through British government officials.

Notice that, in the waste management regulatory process, trade associations have always spoken out in representation of medium-sized, and, above all, large firms. This is a feature shared with most industries; even the Italian craftsmen's associations, which account for more than half the market in the industries they work in, find it difficult to make their voices heard in Brussels. If the regulatory process is command-and-control, this need not be a serious problem, since it is assumed that governments, democratically elected, take into account everybody's interests. If, on the other hand, regulators decide to discuss with the regulated firms the environmental policy agenda, the 'representation unevenness' of trade association can seriously upset competitive equilibria. In other words, it can be contended that, if regulators talk only (or mainly) to trade associations in order to get the feedback they need on the making of new regulations, the control of the associations becomes, itself, a battleground for competition. It could even be conjectured (but not proved, with the evidence we have gathered) that the impossibility to be adequately represented in Brussels forced small firms to turn to other institutions to defend themselves.

Finally, there are locally based firms (publicly owned ones, municipal direct management schemes, small, local private operators). They are not represented in the European regulatory arena nor, generally speaking, in the national ones (a partial exception is Italy, where the association of municipality-owned firms has some visibility at the national level). As we contend above, their influence on trade associations is virtually nonexistent, and they do not have other means to exert pressure. Their influence on the regulatory arena is basically due to the fact that they exist, and that if stringent environmental and technical standards are approved and fully enforced, they are driven out of business. One implication of this is that, since enforcement is in general carried out at the local level and local politicians find it embarrassing to close down publicly owned firms and small, local businesses and to terminate municipal direct management schemes, there is an incentive not to fully enforce regulation.

As well as having its elected representatives serve in regulatory bodies, the general public is a direct actor in waste disposal regulatory processes. This happens in two different ways: via the pressure of environmental groups and green parties and via the representation of taxpayers' interests at the local level.

Organized environmentalists are involved in all debates on municipal waste regulation, and have access to all levels of government. However, their role, weight and priorities differs significantly across administrative levels. At the European level, the 'green lobby' is influential and well organized; its efforts are directed to more stringent environmental standards and recycling targets. Together with the public opinion at large, they are probably the most important drivers of new environmental regulations. This is also true at the national level. At the local level, on the contrary, environmentalists tend to focus on managing NIMBY conflicts.

Taxpayers are not explicitly involved in regulatory processes. On the other hand, their weight is felt at the local level, where governments may refrain from full-fledged enforcement of environmental standards when this may drive out of the market small, local businesses, which have the advantage of costing very little to local taxpayers in terms of waste collection and disposal services.

The above reconstruction of which actors are involved doing what seems to point out that there are, really, *two* policy arenas: one at the European-Member States level and one at the local level.

The European-Member States level policy arena is mainly concerned with institutional regulation, standards and recycling targets setting. This arena has been dominated by a coalition of greens, some national governments (notably the German and, to a lesser extent, the French one) and large non-British firms pushing for stiffer regulation and more ambitious targets, often supported by trade associations. An opponent coalition between British large firms and the British governments has been losing ground to it. Now, however, the drive for further regulation is less clear. Not only has the environmentalist movement been losing some of its political and electoral edge, but large firms are reluctant to push regulation any further for fear of widening the non-compliance area.

The local policy arena is the one where contracts are tendered out and enforcement is administered. Relevant actors are local governments and municipalities, large firms and local firms, local environmentalists and taxpayers.

The only group with a real interest in strict enforcement, as we have contended, is the 'large firms' one. Local firms and taxpayers have an interest in lax enforcement (though not a loudly voiced one).

At this level the co-operation between public, firms and public authorities is stronger — and more complex — than at higher levels. The big firms can make proposals for an integrated management of waste, offering good service and high standard at low price. But private local firms usually have the ability to put pressure on local government, in order to influence regulation: the case of small disposers is typical, who try to get their plant included in plans, or to win the tender to take the waste management contract. In the absence of specific regulation like the British one (but even in the UK, as we tried to argue, communes have some manoeuvring room), publicly run waste management schemes can claim their 'right' to run the service in several ways. They can point to their tradition, defend public provision of services as a principle, defend employment levels that more efficient management would threaten, and, in general, exert a considerable political pressure. The same argument applies to tough enforcement of regulation on locally based firms.

At an intermediate (regional) level, this sort of pressure can hinder and even block all planning activities. Even local greens, paradoxically, sometimes end up defending existing local businesses; while their technical level is low, local committees opposing new plants that large firms would build have a noticeable strength, at least in some countries. They campaign against new plants, and often for fascinating but impossible solutions.

As a result of this situation, industry lobbyists maintain that the quest for enforcement ('a level playing field') has been far more frustrating than that for stringent regulation.

5.4 Conclusions and possible scenarios for the future

The environmental economics textbook approach to waste is to treat it as a pure negative externality. Appropriate environmental policy can and should be designed to internalize it within the budgets of the firms. This may be obtained by setting up a set of taxes and incentives that yields the optimal mix of waste production, disposal and recycling. In general, who carries out the disposal and the recycling, and how he does it, is considered to be important to engineers and civil servants, but of little relevance to economists.

The investigation carried on in this paper showed that this approach is, at best, incomplete. The launch, during the 1970s, of a regulatory framework on waste disposal created, *de facto,* a new European industry: the waste management industry. Waste disposal, which had hitherto been carried out by civil servants working for local authorities, was taken over by private companies which, once on the market place, made their own growth plans and claimed their own say on further developments of regulation. The point it is worth making is that, with regulation, European governments encouraged the birth of a new economic agent in the very market they were trying to regulate; and, in so doing, *they changed both the market itself and their degree of control on it.*

The interaction between the competitive arena and the policy arenas, in some cases, is one of positive feedback. Large firms dominate the field in the Brussels policy arena, and they extract competitive advantages out of it. This improves their performance in the competitive arena, helping them to wipe out smaller competitors and grow larger. As they grow larger, employ more workers and produce more income, they gain influence they can spend in the policy arena, and so forth.

And yet small firms did resist this pressure, exploiting their one asset: a good relationship with local regulators, above all with municipalities. They used this relationship to hold on to their small market share whenever their contracts expired; they managed to get away with a less-than-full compliance, which would not have been tolerated in a large, high profile firm. Certainly, this is partly due to the inadequacy of local authorities, and does not necessarily imply benevolence with respect to small, local firms. Nevertheless, it seems safe to state that ineffective enforcement created a space in which small firms could survive, and that, as we have seen, it eased large firms' pressure for more stringent standards.

In some sense, so, we may conclude that small firms have captured not regulation, but enforcement and control, and in this way they contrasted the growing power of large players.

By now, the latter are beginning to realize that further regulation can be disadvantageous for them unless enforcing mechanisms, at the moment rather feeble, are improved and have stopped asking for more stringent regulation.

There are two ways in which this stalemate may be resolved and both include changing the rules on the local policy arena.

The first one is to move the competencies for control and enforcement to higher administrative levels. This solution is strongly supported by environmentalists, who complain about lax enforcement of waste and environmental regulation in general, and is not an unlikely event in some European countries, notably France and the UK. This solution is advocated by multinationals and large firms, which lobby intensely for national Environmental Protection Agencies endowed with the competencies to enforce waste regulation.

The second one involves altering the ways in which local authorities contract waste management services out. The British approach to this solution is compulsory competitive tendering: since local authorities are compelled to open their markets, there is a serious chance for large firms, financially and technically strong, to occupy them. The continental (French but mainly German) approach, rather different, is to introduce planning. This implies that small, adjacent towns run their waste management system under the same plan, therefore reducing the importance of maintaining good relationships with a single local authority. This scenario, like the 'compulsory competitive tendering' one, is more favourable to large, compliant firms than the business as usual one.

NOTES

1. Sebastiano Brusco, Professor of industrial economics, Department of Political Economics, University of Modena, Via Berengario, 51, 41100 Modena, Italy, tel: 3959417855; fax: 3959417855.
2. Paolo Bertossi, Researcher, Eco&Eco, NOMISMA, Strada Maggiore, 29, 40125 Bologne, Italie, tel: 39516483307/8/9; fax: 3951225352.
3. Alberto Cottica, Researcher, Eco&Eco, NOMISMA, Strada Maggiore, 29, 40125 Bologne, Italie, tel: 39516483307/8/9; fax: 3951225352.
4. The Germans call this regime of relationship between private and public sector *operator scheme* (Reidenbach, 1993).
5. This is a highly controversial point.
6. In fact, there are important differences as well as similarities between the British and the German systems, which we do not develop here (Brusco *et al.*, 1995).
7. Examples already in the regulatory pipeline include end-of-life automobiles, electronic waste and building waste.
8. Brusco *et al.*, 1995.
9. Department of the Environment (1992a).

10. Department of the Environment (1993). It must be noted that the Coopers & Lybrand report defines recycling as 'recycling as material', whereas the British government counts WTE as recycling.
11. Department of the Environment, (1992b).
12. Biffa, with its drive to a nationwide collection network and its presence on the Belgian market, has some of the characteristics of the multinationals without having their size.

REFERENCES

Brusco, S., P. Bertossi and F. Tagliazucchi (1995), *Playing on Two Chessboards — The Municipal Waste Management Industry: Strategic Behaviour in the Market and in the Policy Debate*, ERIC Report for the European Commission (DG XII/D-5), Bologna: NOMISMA.

Cantoni, S. (1992), 'Obiettivi e Risultati della Raccolta Differenziata in Italia', in Conference on *Dalla Riduzione ad una Corretta Gestione dei Rifiuti Solidi Urbani*, Parma, 20—21 February.

Department of the Environment (1992a), *This Common Inheritance — The Second Year Report*, London: HMSO.

Department of the Environment (1992b), *Economic Instruments ans Recovery of Resources from Waste*, London: HMSO.

Department of the Environment (1993), *Landfill Costs and Prices: Correcting Possible Market Distortions'*, London: HMSO.

European Commission (1989), *Strategia Comunitaria per la Gestione dei Rifiuti*, Brussels: European Commission.

OECD (1991), *Environmental Indicators — A Preliminary Set*, Paris: OECD.

Pigou, A.C. (1946), *The Economics of Welfare, fourth edition*, London: Mac Millan.

Reidenbach, M. (1993), 'Privatization of Urban Services in Germany', Conference on *Privatization of Urban Services in Europe*, Poitiers, 3—5th June.

Royal Commission on Environmental Pollution (1993), *Seventeenth Report — Incineration of Waste*, London: HMSO.

7. Voluntary agreements between industry and government — the case of recycling regulations

Thomas Whiston[1] and Matthieu Glachant[2]

1. INTRODUCTION

1.1 A general overview

As outlined in the introductory chapter the prime focus of this chapter in relation to environmental policies is *not* the comparative efficiency of different instruments such as tax or standards, or general competitive, economic or innovatory impact, rather we seek to more fully understand that phase of the *policy process* which *precedes* the adoption of new environmental legislation. In that respect it should be recognized that several dynamic interactions must be kept uppermost in our mind - and demand empirical study. For in that way we can better understand the ways in which the regulatory process can be improved, or subjected to modification due to the informational input from a wide variety of social actors: whether this be the State, intermediate regulatory agencies, evolving consortia, private industry or whatever.

Thus we should note that environmental policies do not just suddenly emerge but rather they demand a phase of preparatory consultation and negotiation between many interested parties. This implies much interplay by different actors. Industry and firms (producers, suppliers or whomever) are often invited by policy-makers to become involved in such preparatory stages. Information exchange, varying perspectives and a process of negotiation can then ensue. Similarly, at the institutional level a range of international or national bodies, governmental ministries, sectoral authorities can and do contribute to the overall policy-dynamics; the formulation, modification and overall steering of the policy formulation process.

As a result of the above interactions — information exchange, lobbying, open debate — there will be tensions, trade-offs, gains and losses of advantage, of the various actors, bureaucratic levels, or individual industrial interests. Such forces and factors may lead to dilution of the initial aims and intentions; a mandatory intention may ultimately become a voluntary agreement and much change in regulatory outlook may result. At the EU level the varying views of individual states may well result in some form of 'lowest common denominator'. Alternatively, open discussion and the wide involvement of numerous actors, may lead to a more rational, realistic, formulation of the environmental objectives and means to be finally adopted.

In this chapter we explore the above issues in relation to recycling regulations. Specifically we examine two areas: that of auto recycling and packaging recycling. The evidence that is considered relates in both instances to the European scene and the related experience of three countries (France, Germany and the United Kingdom).

In relation to both areas the environmental goals and the motivation of the regulatory initiatives was quite similar: namely to reduce the amount of material going to landfill, and simultaneously to increase the amount of material to be recycled or recovered. In both instances, though with important differences of detail, we will note a movement, a negotiation of the regulatory process, leading ultimately to a form of consensus, a co-operation between the administration and the relevant industrial actors. In the case of the automobile sector we will observe a transition from what initially appeared to be a *mandatory intent* toward a much freer *voluntary approach*. In that respect, these two regulatory processes have produced original institutional arrangements that social actors used to name Voluntary Agreements (VA). This is the first original feature of these policy processes.

In general, in environmental policy a voluntary agreement is an agreement between a public authority and a *coalition* of firms whereby industry commits itself to pollution reduction (Glachant, 1994). However the commitments can exhibit various degrees of precision, for example: commitment in setting a reflection process to design a future regulation; commitment in reaching an objective without specifying the means; or a very comprehensive set of commitments specifying an environmental goal and the measures which are required to reach it. These institutional arrangements are subject to a growing interest from policy makers and industrialists as an innovative way to cope with environmental issues. They are seen as a *flexible* instrument adapted to the increasing complexity of environmental policy making. Consequently, at least in Europe, their use is currently increasing. But despite this, they have not yet been subject to a deep analysis by economists especially with respect to their efficiency features and their nature, and many questions remain open. The study of both car and packaging recycling can provide first insights about these questions.

Moreover, with respect to both auto and package recycling, a key point is that the co-operation does not only take place between the private and public side. During development of the regulatory processes, intense activities of a negotiation nature and consensus building have also occurred between the industrial actors — usually in various networks or recycling consortia. This feature is to be linked with the industrial diversity of industrialists concerned with recycling, e.g., material producers, consumer goods industries and post-consumption sectors. This interfirm co-operation led to, and determined, the final form of the regulatory trajectory.

However the *modus operandi* of individual national networks sometimes differed; as did the regulatory perspectives of particular national governments (or their surrogate agencies). In turn these differing national perspectives influenced the wider international perception and policy-dynamics at the European level. These interdependencies between the different institutional levels (European and national) and between different countries is the second interesting feature of these two case studies. Indeed perception of one nation's intent sometimes played a realpolitik role in stimulating another nation's industrial response and reaction. In short it had an energizing effect. Thus, for example, in relation to auto-recycling, Germany's initial intent of requiring auto manufacturers to take back their products free-of-charge from the last owner and to be responsible for setting up dismantling plants and subsequent disposal of residues, stimulated several other nations in particular France (and their respective industries or consortia) to respond in both strategic and analytic terms. The subsequent allocation of the Priority Waste Stream role to France,[3] the history of the voluntary agreement reached in France, the subsequent intentions at a European level, may in turn influence the prevailing ethos in Germany. We can therefore observe an informative evolutionary chain of influence, a process-dynamic, which not only relies upon the relevant social actors, but also requires an understanding within an international framework. Image and mirage were to be as important as hard bargaining and information exchange. Fear may be as strong a stimulus to action and co-ordination, as real intent. In addition the regulator, when confronted with a large industrial coalition, whether the latter be stimulated by unjustified fear or specific regulatory intent, as was the case in the auto sector, rather than competing industry interest groups, is more likely to modify his stance.

The influence of one nation's regulatory agenda upon another nation and the subsequent aim of influencing the regulatory agenda at the European level is also highlighted with respect to packaging recycling. France rapidly attained an agreement between the industry and government as to the global recycling targets because they were considered as a credible counter proposal to the very stringent German objectives in the European policy-making process. In that sense, the French regulation was also designed to be used as a strategic/national weapon in the European arena.

Thus, recycling regulations and their evolution (and continuing uncertainty) demonstrate in both of the areas discussed here an interesting and informative perspective on the policy-making process. Hopefully, they provide some insights into the means of improving the early policy formulation phases.

1.2 The specific societal importance of recycling regulations

Having made the above broad analytic and conceptual points we would note here the considerable societal and environmental importance of State or European initiative to significantly improve the recycling of materials, consumer products or whatever; of which automobiles and waste-packaging are very important constituents of the consumer society. There are several motives in such recycling regulatory initiatives. The aims include retrieval of scarce materials; better use of high value-added components; reduction of environmentally unfriendly landfill; reduction of energy waste and improvement in materials accountancy (viz., reduction in material throughput). In short, less waste products, improved environment and more efficient use of material and energy resources.

The best means of achieving such aims is, however, by no means clear. Thus we may genuinely enquire as to what is the *best* means of achieving an environmental goal? Should one rely on mandatory technical requirements or a voluntary approach? Are specific technological fixes to be encouraged or greater reliance upon open-ended aims? Fiscal or tax approaches or technological mandates? The answers to such questions are not clear (for example, the process as to the choice of policy instruments, and in particular how the regulator can collect the information that is needed). However they are not the specific subject matter that we examine here, except, that is, in as much as such deliberations actually influenced the course of events which we describe.

In this respect, it is recognized by both regulators and industrialists that there is considerable complexity and uncertainty as to how best to achieve certain desirable environmental goals. It is worthy of note with respect to terminology that we should distinguish between uncertainty (i.e., technological uncertainties) and complexity (i.e., strategic uncertainty due to the number and diversity of industrial actors). The latter is no less important than the former. This is true both for packaging and auto-recycling. In turn, therefore, from the perspective of our subject matter here such uncertainty influences both the negotiating techniques and postures adopted by industry. Under such circumstances, under such high levels of uncertainty as to the best practical means of compliance, it is not surprising if ultimately a voluntary agreement, an accord of some form, is realized between regulator and industry. This is because the voluntary agreement permits open-ended evolutionary exploration of alternatives and encourages co-operation across firms and industrial sectors. Thus it is both pragmatic and flexible. This is a clear advantage of voluntary agreements which appears in the analysis of the car and packaging recycling policy process.

At the same time from the perspective of the regulator, the genuine uncertainty as to the most effective means of attainment of environmental recycling goals ensures, or at least favours, that he will be amenable to discussion. In short the regulator is amenable to persuasion and modification. Again this can reinforce the proclivity to arrive at voluntary agreements, open ended potential and partial industrial consensus.

However, industrialists, or even policy makers, are not only motivated by the selection of an *optimal* way to cope with recycling. Hence the evolution of the means and of the environmental objective is subject to modification or development related to political and economic factors. Different industries and countries will experience different forms of loss or gain; in which case we may well expect that potential or perceived changes in economic competitiveness will influence the dynamics and evolution of both the means and objectives (levels) of environmental recycling regulations. This is essentially an economic and political force. As we shall see in the sections which follow it may be expressed at the level of a firm, an industrial sector, or at a more integrative national level.

Thus the two forms of influence — the *political/economic* and the *normative* — can reinforce the nature of the dialogue and subsequent developmental dynamics of regulatory intentions or initiatives. As we shall see both of these forms of influence were at work in the case of the subsequent modifications which characterise auto-recycling and packaging-recycling regulations. Goals were attenuated, voluntary agreements were reached, uncertainties were recognized and faith has been placed in industrial-consensus and co-operation to lead ultimately to compliance.

In the following sections we consider first the case of automobile recycling (Section 2) and then packaging recycling (Section 3). We then indicate our conclusions (Section 4).

2. THE AUTOMOTIVE DISPOSAL AND RECYCLING PROCESS

2.1 Introduction: a complex chain of influence

Across the twentieth century the automobile sector has grown to influence a myriad facets of corporate, economic, social and environmental circumstances. Often the automobile is subject to particular selection as a prime contributor to environmental malaise whether in terms of use of fuel, emissions, use of materials, or whatever. As a consequence the transport sector in general and the automobile in particular has been subjected to much environmental impact analysis, as well as a range of regulatory initiations or enactments (Whiston, 1982; Whiston and Ferguson, 1983).

More recently the legislative framework has extended beyond the design, production and usage of automobiles toward several aspects of their disposal (viz. the later steps of the total life cycle of the product). This new legislative or regulatory concern raises many issues as to the locus of responsibility for disposal, the implications for automobile design, construction and later waste-handling, the overall goals of disposal and recycling, the best means of achievement; the extent to which the existing infrastructure is capable of responding to new challenges and initiatives or whether new forms of organization should be encouraged or explored. In short there is much uncertainty as to what form the regulatory thrust should take; how this might differ from nation to nation; what is implied for the whole manufacturing and disposal chain (viz., material producers, designers, manufacturers, waste treatment and post-use materials handling, etc.); and what new patterns of industrial co-operation might be best able both to respond to contemporary or potential legislation — and be able to develop *new* technological, organizational and innovatory responses to the new recycling agenda.

Unlike other areas of legislation pertaining to the automobile sector (for example vehicle emission controls), the consideration of disposal (and in particular regulatory goals aimed at increasing the amount of material recovered, recycled and not used for landfill), reaches over into a whole area of wider issues of waste disposal, materials recovery and recycling, and thereby intertwines with a complex effluent flow from numerous other consumer streams. Similarly, it reaches back to the necessary consideration of the constituent-source materials used in automobile fabrication (metals, plastics, glass, rubber, paints, textiles, fillers, etc.) and their design, manufacture and use, which in combination play a considerable role in the feasibility of achieving regulatory recycling aims.

Before examining the nature of development of contemporary regulations of impending legislation it is useful to have a general overview of the present materials flowchart for the industry. This is indicated in simplified form in Figures 7.1 and 7.2 below.

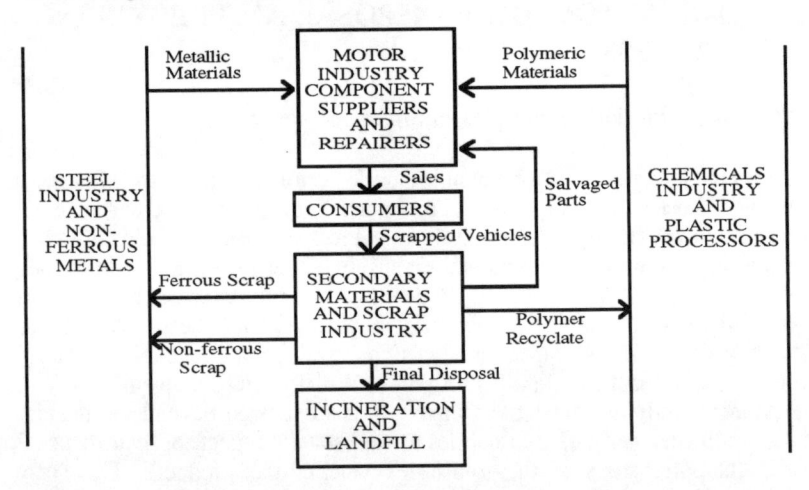

Source: CEST (1991)

Figure 7.1   Simplified materials flowchart for vehicles industry

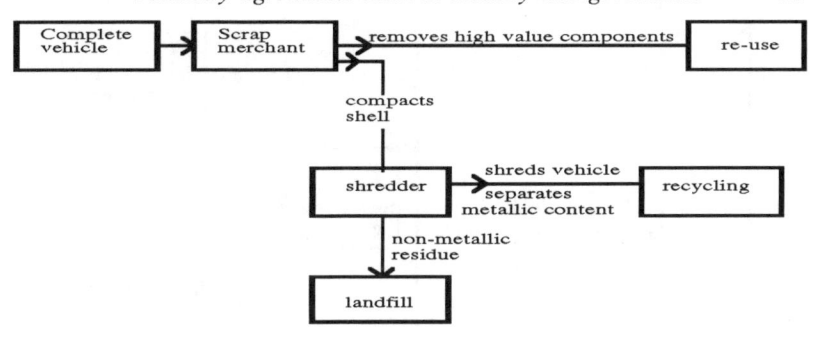

Voluntary agreements between industry and government 149

```
[Complete vehicle] → [Scrap merchant] → removes high value components → [re-use]
                                      ↓ compacts shell
                         [shredder] → shreds vehicle / separates metallic content → [recycling]
                                      ↓ non-metallic residue
                                      [landfill]
```

Source: ACORD (1992)

Figure 7.2   Current disposal process

At present a large percentage of automobile waste is recovered — primarily related to the metallic content. Thus more than 90 per cent of the *metallic* content of automobiles, thereby accounting for 70—80 per cent of a vehicle is recovered in most EU countries (CEST, 1991). In recent years an increased plastic content has been incorporated into vehicles which can result in considerable changes in the economic viability of present techniques of waste handling (viz., revenue loss to the shredder industry — which is further accentuated by increased separating costs, and escalating landfill costs, etc.).

In essence it is the non-metallic components of automobile construction which pose the greatest technological challenge. Thus, as indicated earlier, impending legislation impacts upon materials producers, automobile design and manufacturers, the supply-industry as well as the whole waste-disposal/sorting/shredder/recycling chain indicated in Figures 7.1 and 7.2 above.

Finally before turning to our prime concern, the dynamics of legislative/regulatory change and development, we would note as indicated in Figure 7.3 that the potential form of response for increased recycling and reduced landfill targets can in one sense be reduced to a taxonomy which characterizes different options. As can be seen, the degree of vehicle dismantling and the materials value added constitute the two axes of consideration. Most importantly the choice of strategy then implies an interactive chain of research, development, organizational change and the involvement of numerous industries. *More than that, the technological and organization pathways which are explored or chosen implies different gains and losses in comparative advantage for different actors in the overall productive, design, manufacture, materials-usage and waste handling chain.* It may also imply at the national level significant losses/gains in comparative advantage for certain forms of automobile manufacturer (and related supply industries, etc.). We see here the roots of negotiation, posturing and interaction with the potential legislator.[4]

150 *Environmental policy in Europe*

MATERIALS VALUE ADDED

- Smelting of whole vehicles after crushing
- Enchanced separation of shredded materials
- Partial dismantling before crushing & shredding
- Complete dismantling of vehicles to bare hulks
- National cost of scrap treatment process, increasing rapidly with degree of dismantling

Use existing scrap network ◄──────► Create new dismantling centres

Degree of vehicle dismantling

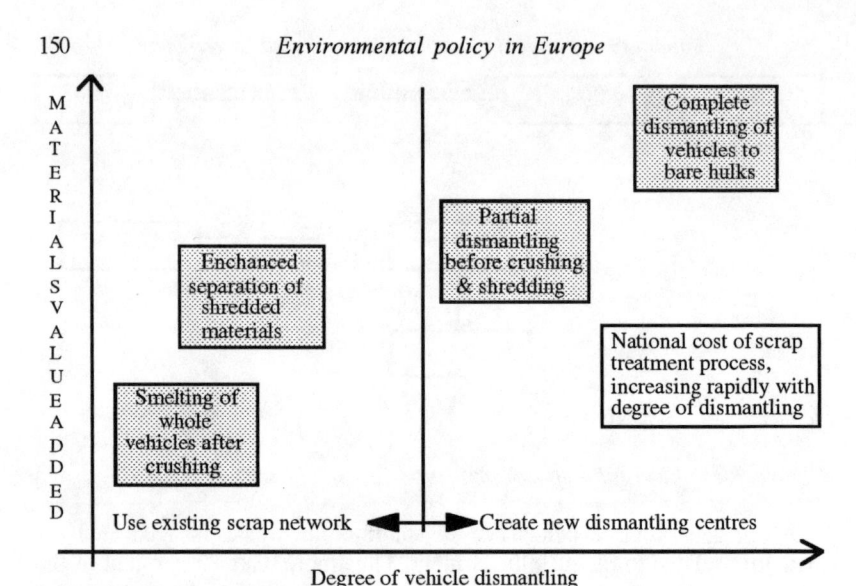

Figure 7.3   Strategic options: variation of materials value added against degree of dismantling

2.2   General context of the regulatory scene

As early as 1989 initiatives from the German environmental ministry indicated a highly stringent approach to the issue of automobile disposal and recycling. The main issues addressed included: the increasingly urgent problem of reducing landfill (of which the residue from car waste which remained after a large proportion of the metallic content of cars had been recovered/recycled was important — as stated earlier 90 per cent of the metallic content is recovered — but overall this still leaves a residual of approximately 25 per cent of the car's body weight); the argument that a greater proportion of a car (after the end of its useful life) should be recycled in any event; and if possible certain components should be recycled. Subsequently (1990) it was indicated by the German government that its prime goal would be to make the automobile manufacturers responsible themselves for taking back automobiles at the end of their useful life (free of charge) and then for the industry to aim at recovery, recycling a greater proportion of the automobiles material content than was at that time the case.

Not surprisingly the German intentions triggered concern and potential legislation at the European level and *inter alia* discussions, analyses and developments in individual nations. We must not forget, however, that a highly organized infrastructure/network exists which includes the collection of old cars end of life vehicles (ELVs), subsequent removal of valuable spare parts, shredding of cars and separation of the metallic content etc., for re-use/recycling. The main problem pertains to the residual — a composite of

Voluntary agreements between industry and government 151

plastics, textiles, etc. Added to this problem is the fact that for many years the plastic/polymer content of automobiles has been increasing, with the consequence, from the standpoint of the automobile waste industry, that this has begun to compromise the economic viability of the shredding-industry (less metallic recovery in relative terms and more to landfill for which they must pay). This economic problem is illustrated in Figure 7.4 below.

Moreover as noted by CEST (1991) 'legislation in Germany focused on specifying levels of contaminants present in shredder residue for it to be landfilled at municipal solid waste sites. Above certain levels of contamination by hydrocarbons and polychlorinated biphenyls (PCBs), the residue will have to be reclassified as hazardous waste, incurring disposal costs of DM 600—1000 per tonne, compared with the already high costs of DM 100—160 for some landfill sites'.

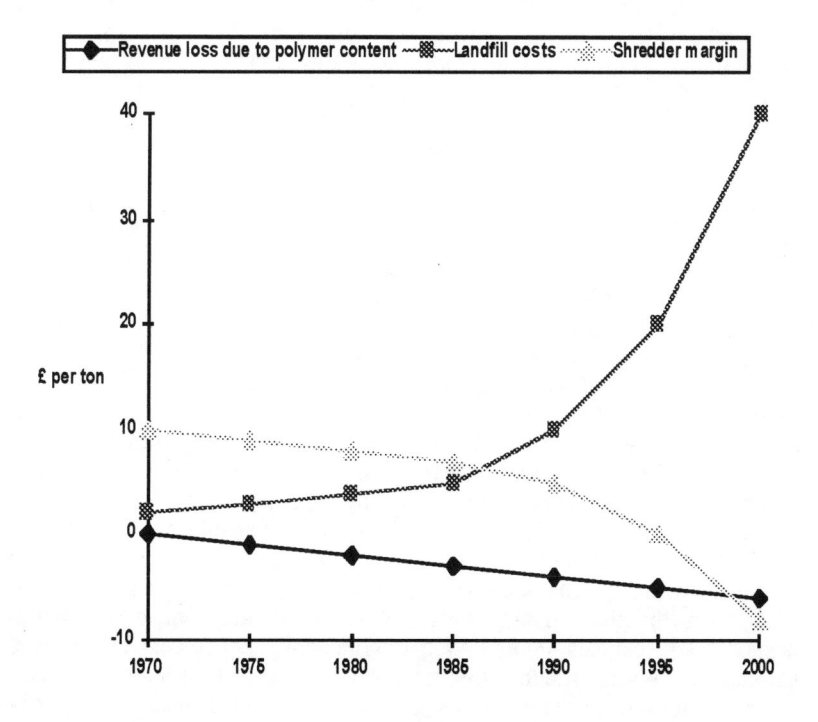

Figure 7.4   Projections of shredder margins and costs

Within this context we begin to see areas of conflict which both legislator and car producer (plus a wide related range of supporting industries) must address. From the legislative perspective there are issues of landfill, types of waste material requiring handling; the need to increase recovery and recycling (and reduction of reliance in incineration); problems of the downside of recovery (viz., shredders, dismantlers, etc.) relating to the increased proportion of polymers. From the manufacturers' and wider industry perspective there are issues of manufacture, design for disassembly of end-of-life vehicles (ELVs), materials identification and separation, materials usage patterns. From the legislative perspective arises the fundamental issue as to whether the whole recovery process can be best handled through mandatory legislation, voluntary approaches, reliance on improved disposal infrastructures or through the automobile manufacturer himself — and at what cost to whom.

2.3 National and European developments and responses

A European perspective
Prior to considering individual nations, it is useful if the broad developments at a European level are considered. In that respect it is important to recognize that developments at the European Union level were occurring in parallel with the unfolding of events at the national level. Over the period 1989—1994 a series of developments and debates developed at both national and European levels. Thus the two levels should not be viewed as separate processes. Following European Community Commission proposals in 1989 the Council of Ministers agreed the need for more efficiently organized treatment of waste of all kinds and of landfill planning. 'Priority Waste Streams' were established and in order to avoid duplication of effort individual member countries were assigned responsibility for analysis of a particular waste stream on a Community rather than a national basis. The 'end-of-life vehicles' waste stream was assigned to France at the instigation of Commission Directorate DG XI in June 1991. By resolution of the ACEA (Association des Constructeurs Européens d'Automobiles), 19 December 1991, full co-operation and support for the project was agreed by the European automobile, metal, polymer, lubricant, shredding and recycling industries.

The final proposed ELV strategy was made available on 23 February 1994. In that document the ELV project group note that 'waste stream management has become a complex issue with many parameters. Therefore a common European strategy for handling end of life vehicles (ELVs) is needed. ELV residues amount to approximately 0.2 per cent of the total Community Waste Stream. 75 per cent by weight of ELVs are recycled today. About 2 million tonnes per year to ELV shredder residue is mostly landfilled'.

In relation to this problem the project group put forward 'a joint short term and long term strategy which attempts to take into account the technical realities and political objectives of both today and tomorrow'. In addition they outline a conditional strategy in the event of industry not meeting the goals required. However they note that 'as prevention/avoidance and recovery are relatively new activities for some materials, logistics and working practices, as well as purely technical considerations, need considerable development and innovation for environmentally acceptable and efficient economic solutions to be found. This is one of the key reasons the solutions need the active co-operation of all concerned partners. Industry must take a reasonable environmental attitude and first of all car manufacturers in vehicle design. In each Member State, national monitoring groups will need to be created and the question of financing any activities will need to be addressed. Monitoring of, and information on progress will be necessary. If insufficient progress is made, some further measures will need to be taken.'

In short, therefore, the ELV project group place the need of compliance across the whole industrial sector (as we shall see not unlike the French Voluntary Agreement and, in the UK, the ACORD viewpoint).

In terms of targets, the ELV project group indicates for all cars, a maximum of 15 per cent disposal per car by weight from 2002 at the latest. For new models from 2002, 10 per cent disposal per car; from 2015, 5 per cent disposal. The targets permit combustion with energy recovery, but materials recovery is a priority. By 1995 every Member State should create a monitoring group who report to the European Commission every two years.

With regard to 'overall strategy [it] is to build upon and improve the existing systems. The short term strategy is to improve the environmental conditions in which ELV treatment takes place and to recover the non-metallic content of ELVs by re-use, recycling and/or energy recovery. The longer term strategy is to promote efficiency in the use of the car and integration in the ELV treatment network and to change the design and material specification for new vehicles' and 'the present system operates without operating subsidies under free market conditions'. The ELV document then outlines improved collection procedures through authorized networks; moves to ensure that ELV shredder residues are *not* categorized as hazardous waste; treatment strategies; the need for design for recycling; and the need for monitoring. Finally, if progress is not satisfactory a conditional strategy is outlined which includes the important point that 'car manufacturers' contribution might be increased by encouraging them to become more involved in the collection, treatment and recycling so that they could then take more direct responsibility for the disposal of their produce.'

What we see in the above, therefore, is close to the 'voluntary agreement' approach with faith in the existing network, but goals that go a little further than present day conditions. Thus each 'actor' in the auto-sector and disposal infrastructure has his part to play — with no fundamental change in the existing structure; rather an encouragement of innovatory developments and an emphasis upon broad industry co-operation. In that sense this is very akin to contemporary developments in most Member States and a compromise between the more stringent potential policy of the German government and the alternative views of industry.

The German perspective

The automotive recycling scene in Germany is perhaps the most difficult one to comment upon with regard to the overall dynamics of interaction between the regulatory body and the numerous representatives of the relevant automobile manufacture and waste handling sector. The reason for this is the as yet unresolved final scene. Thus, on the one hand, Germany has well-developed waste policies relating to numerous sectors; it is probably, together with Sweden, one of the major actors in the European Union of the environmental lobby, viz., it is a leader, whilst other nations are followers. It was the prime initiator in the middle to late 1980s of the need to undertake an urgent appraisal of the automotive disposal and recycling scene; on the other hand at the time of writing no definite legislation has been put in place; industry is exploring numerous technological innovations and continues to contest and negotiate with government as to the final outcome.

For example in 1989 the Bundesministerium für Umwelt, Naturschutz und Reaktorsicherheit announced that the waste from shredding plants would be classified as 'special waste' in the future and would therefore be subject to the proposed 'TA Sonderabfall' (Technical Instructions on Special Waste) implying that plastic which could not be recycled would normally have to be incinerated and not dumped — which would in turn affect the profitability of the shredding business with significant implications for the disposal of automobiles. The Environment Secretary of State saw it as the role of the automobile industry to remedy the problem. In 1990 the German Government announced legislative goals aimed at reducing the vehicle waste programme of which a major requirement would be that car manufacturers or their agents accept used vehicles from the last owner free of charge and subsequently be responsible for disposal with re-use or recycling having precedence over other disposal methods. The deadlines for this agreement have now been delayed. On 18th August 1992 the Environment Ministry presented its draft ordinance on the Disposal of Used Cars which would essentially compel car manufacturers to take old cars back and to ensure that they would be dismantled and as much of the material recycled as possible.

In short over a period of six or so years (1989—1994) the relevant German Environmental Ministries pushed for industry to take back cars at no cost to the consumer and to significantly improve the recycling characteristics.

In response to such calls the German industry undertook a two-pronged strategy. Thus all manufacturers and disposal networks explored numerous technological innovations and changes (e.g., design for dismantling; new incineration techniques; plastic labelling; new sorting techniques, etc.) whilst also negotiating with the government on the issue of cost and means: who is going to pay for the take-back and dismantling of vehicles? Can this be done through the existing infrastructure without the manufacturers themselves being directly responsible?

Over that period as we have noted earlier the EU Priority Waste Stream (ELVs) arrived at a position which whilst setting reasonable recycling targets nevertheless does not endorse the German position regarding direct responsibility for taking back automobiles. Rather the view is to encourage the whole automobile network to explore new ways and means of improving recycling performance. As we shall note later France has arrived at its Voluntary Agreement and Collective Liability approach; Britain through ACORD has encouraged a market approach. Germany would therefore appear to be isolated. Whether or not she will be deterred remains to be seen.

What does appear to be the case is that the initial and ongoing German intentions had several major stimulatory or ripple effects: both within Germany itself, but more widely and seminally across the EU. Thus:

- the legislative intentions stimulated German industry to explore numerous innovatory developments geared to recycling.
- This in turn placed the recycling issue firmly on the EU environmental agenda.
- Individual nations (France, UK) were then forced both through their own automotive networks and in terms of regulatory frameworks to consider in fine detail how they would respond as individual nations *and* how they wished to influence the 'EU agenda'.

The voluntary agreements of France; the market ethos of the UK; the framework suggested by the EU ELV Priority Waste Stream Group, would appear to reflect some form of consensus. To what degree this will give support to the German auto-sector in acting as an 'environmental benchmark' remains to be seen. Germany has certainly affected the other nations' agenda in this area; it remains uncertain as to whether or not the reverse will be true.

The French perspective

The key to the French approach to the ELV issues is the voluntary agreement which was signed in March 1993 between the French Government and all of the various actors of the automobile sector.

The agreement commits the various actors to reach lower levels of landfilling in 2002 (15 per cent for old cars, 10 per cent for new ones). It relies upon the principle of collective liability of all those involved. Why has this voluntary approach evolved? Why the principle of collective liability? Why the reliance upon a free market (similar to the position of the UK)? How and why have these aspects come about?

A fairly detailed analysis has been provided by Aggeri and Hatchuel (1994) who demonstrate that a rigid regulatory approach demands detailed economic knowledge, informed and knowledgeable technical actors — and that at present much of the knowledge is lacking, hence there is a lack of confidence in simplistic, directive, regulations. It is far better to have aims to which all actors are committed where collective learning can ensue.

In 1989 several European nations, the French included, saw the main issues as '(1) the nature and expected levels of landfilling and material recycling; (2) the principle of liability to adopt for the reaching of these levels; and (3) the efficiency of taxes and compensations paying for these additional operations' (Aggeri and Hatchuel, 1994). It should be recalled that at approximately the same time-period Germany had indicated a comparatively stringent regulatory intention with high recycling requirements and manufacturer responsibility. To some degree this influenced the regulatory debate in France although there was already local environmental concern. However different actors (and the State, especially political-economy analysts) saw different dimensions, perceived advantages, varying levels of uncertainty and risk surrounding the whole topic. For example, in France there are approximately 3000 automobile dismantlers who purchase and collect second-hand cars and then repair them or recover spare parts; residual wrecks are sold to approximately 40 shredders. Subsequently scrap-iron is sold for steel-making, or residual waste goes to landfill sites (at the shredders expense). Each of these actors stood to gain or lose in different ways dependent upon the form of legislation that might emerge. For example, if the automobile manufacturers were made totally responsible for ELVs this would radically effect the existing disposal infrastructure; if automobiles were carefully designed in order to optimize dismantling of ELVs this would change the economics of the post-use dismantling, separation and shredding stages; if rationalization of plastic composition of automobiles ensued this would place new demands on the associated supply industry, etc.

Recycling managers, design managers, purchasers of waste material and component manufacturers — each had and still have conflicting views as to the potential losses and gains. French automobile manufacturers were very hostile to the German initiatives and considered there could be competitive loss in the tough world market-place. French public authorities themselves were at variance. Thus the Minister of Environment was very close to German positions while the Minister of Industry was more sensitive to the technical and economic debates about regulation policies. Other analysts (for example environmental economists) reinforced the general uncertainty by pointing out other anomalies, e.g., increased plastics content might improve fuel economy but make recycling more difficult.

Other more technical and pragmatic points were introduced into the general discussion in France regarding uncertainty and problematic factors, for example, the technical complexity of automobile composition and quality problems relating to materials substitution, the economic precariousness of recycling and the doubts regarding experimental dismantling plants.

Against all of this uncertainty and unresolved analytic dilemmas, an increasing recognition developed of the need for continuous, incremental

R&D effort by many agents; new patterns of co-operation and organizational networking; new involvement of designers and analysts. In essence, as pointed out by Aggeri and Hatchuel (1994), the French policy was based on three ideas: (i) several years would be necessary to develop efficient recycling techniques and viable organizations; (ii) regulation should not lock the end-of-life sector in a specific technological path; (iii) the necessary partnerships for recycling would be endangered if only powerful actors, i.e., car manufacturers, were considered as liable for all the costs of this development.

All these arguments convinced the French authorities and firms to sign in March 1993 a voluntary agreement where all partners accepted that the amount of waste from each car ended up in a landfill should be reduced, and this had to be done without any State subsidies (Aggeri and Hatchuel, 1994). The reasons (or at least arguments) for those three policy ideas was that with respect to aspect (i), it was recognized that there exists considerable uncertainty as to the means of complying with the needs of improved ELV recycling. This technological uncertainty plus the complexity of the diverse actors recognized the need for extensive exploration and related organizational as well as technological evolution [hence requirements (ii) and (iii)]. Since this exploration and evolution required numerous actors to participate we see the need of point (iii), new partnerships, information exchange and new patterns of co-operation being required. Thus at the State level the perspective reflects operational requirements — but not hindered by legal regulations; at the inter-firm level there is the need to encourage new design concepts and at the firm level managers need to encourage new strategies and levels of expertise. Indeed during the period under discussion the two major French car manufacturers Peugeot (PSA) and Renault have undertaken numerous initiatives aimed at improved recycling characteristics. Also Fiat and PSA have launched RECAP (Recycling of Automobile Plastics) within the scope of Europe's Eureka research effort. Numerous experiments into improved automobile recycling dismantling projects are being explored (Whiston, 1995). In Renault there are 60 engineers working on ELV projects for example. Peugeot SA commenced a project near Lyon in June 1991 aiming at 'zero' waste after the treatment of scrap cars. This involves removal of hazardous parts, disassembly of parts and non-ferrous materials for recycling, shredding of the empty hulk and treatment of the remaining shredder waste. In the project other partners included Compagnie Française de Ferrailles (CCF), the largest shredder company in France with regard to dismantling and shredding steps. Companies such as ICI and Enichem are partners in the plastic materials recycling and Valerco, a cement producer is examining the use of shredder waste as fuel in cement-ovens (see also Gronewegen and den Hond, 1993). Renault, commencing in September 1992, is experimenting with other car manufacturers in relation to collecting and dismantling cars in the Paris region. Renault also announced in 1992 its intention to use a mobile grinder aimed at transforming waste from old plastic bumpers into granules. In May 1992 PSA published a Plan for the Environment which included sections on 'Inventing the Green Car' and 'Recyclable Cars: The Art of Banishing Waste' which provided an overview of their strategic intentions. Within that strategy is 'building in recycling capability from the ground up means gradually eliminating materials that are hard to recycle or may pose a threat to the environment'. Similarly the RECAP Project (Fiat and PSA) aims to: define separation methods and recycling treatments by family of polymer; design automobile parts that are easy to disassemble and recycle; and find profitable ways to re-use crusher residue, other than as an energy source.

At a wider international level seven manufacturers (BMW, FIAT, PSA, Renault, Rover, Volvo, Daimler-Benz) are involved in the ASP (Automatic Sorting of Plastics Research Programme) which involves four stages: choice of materials; development of prototypes; operating procedures and technological improvement of the latter.

These are only examples of past and ongoing programmes. Each stage: choice of materials, design of components, disassembly techniques, new shredding, sorting and recycling techniques are all being explored within a wide collaborative network.

Finally we should not overlook the fact that France 'hosted' the EU initiative regarding ELV priority waste disposal. The subsequent ELV proposal can be seen, in part, to reflect many of the points made above. Thus France's national perception, or purview, is consistent with the broader EU initiative in relation to auto-recycling.

The UK perspective

The British no longer possess a British owned mass-producer of automobiles though of course there is considerable manufacturing capacity under foreign ownership. In addition — and importantly from the point of view of recycling of automobiles — there is a thriving and extensive supply industry (sub-components, materials, plastics, etc.) as well as a highly developed disposal and recycling sector. Thus there is much vested interest in the form that recycling regulations may take.

Within the UK networking and strategic thinking was undertaken under the auspices of a group referred to as ACORD (Automotive Consortium on Recycling and Disposal). The ACORD Group formed in December 1991 comprises a wide range of participating companies and organizations. It includes vehicle manufacturers, trade associations, major companies in the disposal industry and representatives of government departments (such as the Department of Trade and Industry, the Department of Environment, and the Department of Transport). In one sense whilst the membership is wide it is not quite as extensive as that called for by an earlier study undertaken by the CEST group (CEST, 1991). CEST (Centre for the Exploitation of Science and Technology) was established in 1988 on the recommendation of the UK ACARD (Advisory Council for Applied Research and Development) Study Group. Its role is to improve the exploitation of science and technology by UK industry. It is funded by a consortium comprising the largest 18 UK Companies and linked with Government and Higher Education, though formally independent. The CEST document 'Disposal of vehicles: issues and actions' was an early UK initiative aimed at examining the whole area from a broad national, sectoral and analytic perspective. Those involved in the study included automobile manufacturers, chemical companies, waste handling organizations, university departments and the UK Department of Trade and Industry. One of the main conclusions of the study was the need to create a national Steering Group 'which is charged with the necessary co-ordination and consensus forming responsibilities' to address the whole area of auto-recycling. In part, related to such a concept, the UK ACORD group was formed.

At the time of writing whilst no final agreement between the government and the automobile industry has yet been reached in the UK as to a definitive framework for auto recycling, the ACORD group produced in November 1993 a Preliminary Operating Plan for Review by Government. ACORD suggested that an improvement process relating to auto recycling should be based on the principles of 'using and developing the *existing* disposal infrastructure; *market forces* and maintaining the economic viability of all sectors involved; *joint responsibility* between legislative, affected industry sectors and the last owner; *improved vehicle design; non-marque specific operations'* (our emphasis). Targets include for a car being scrapped in 2002, a maximum of 15 per cent of its initial weight going to landfill (and by 2015, 5 per cent) which are seen to be in line with EU proposals.

In particular the plan involves two key elements: (i) short term improvement of the existing process; and (ii) the longer term development of markets, technologies and vehicle designs to allow further recycling to become economic. In addition it is argued that regulatory authorities will be responsible for enforcing the 'Best Available Technology Not Entailing Excessive Costs' (BATNEEC) standards, and for enforcing the system consistently through the country.

The role of Government (as seen by ACORD) is 'to accelerate development of an improved process through: support for recycling technology and market creation projects; facilitating planning permission for energy recovery projects; fiscal encouragement for energy recovery projects. These in combination should enhance the whole economic framework.' In addition Government could 'promote the principles of this scheme within the EU.'

In several ways the pattern of development of the ACORD group and its wide involvement of numerous actors reflects some of the operational, monitoring and calls for a strategic approach suggested by the EU Priority Waste Stream Group (which made available its views in February 1994). Thus in some ways the work and approach of the ACORD group is both contiguous with the ELV Project Group but also partially pre-dates that initiative. The extent to which representatives of each group (viz., ACORD and the Priority Waste Stream ELV Project Group) influenced each others discourse and final views is not fully apparent. But the resultant general attitudes are not that far apart. The ACORD viewpoint was no doubt an input into the ELV Project Group and played some part in the final EU position but also derived from the wider EU analysis. What we can therefore begin to observe is an international or trans-European level of consensus.

Amongst the various industrial actors in the UK, the extensive supply-industry — component industry and raw materials industry (chemicals, plastics, etc.) has a tremendous vested interest in this area. Also there is a comparatively well-developed dismantling and materials-disposal infrastructure in the UK. All of these actors have much to lose and gain in any final legislation that may emerge. The detailed networking and analysis which the ACORD (and CEST — see above) initiatives reflect therefore seek a balance, a market compromise which still permits discussion of the final enactments pertaining to recycling.

Thus we can conclude that althought unlike in France, a formal Voluntary Agreement on the part of industry has yet to be finalized, the UK is very close to that position, thereby permitting conformity with the needs indicated in any forthcoming European Directive.

2.4 Commentary regarding the regulatory process and the outcomes

What overall pattern can we observe concerning the regulatory process pertaining to automobile recycling which we have just outlined? What future lessons are to be learnt? We would suggest the following: (a) what seems to have occurred is a national and international *chain-reaction*; this is compounded by (b) *genuine uncertainty* regarding the best route to follow; and this has ultimately resulted (c) in an open-ended commitment to further exploration in part built upon *faith and goodwill* and in part upon reliance upon future co-operation and the value of free-market mechanisms.

Thus, with respect to the national and international '*chain-reaction*', the initial stimulus of stringent German legislation which would appear to require automotive producers to be financially and technologically responsible themselves for recycling improvement, the automotive industry has responded in three ways: (i) it has contested the logic and sensibility of such legislation should it reach either the European or national level; (ii) it has formed cooperative networks both to explore innovatory responses and to provide a logistical ballast against such impending legislation; (iii) through negotiation with governments it has arrived at various forms of voluntary agreements. Governments (France in particular and the UK) have combined with their industries to set a legislative agenda or framework which endorses the need for further exploration of the means of compliance through voluntary agreements which in essence place reliance upon industry to comply with the stated goals but without defining the actual techniques or form of compliance. In comparing France and the UK from the standpoint of Voluntary Agreements, France would appear to have made a little more progress. The VA in France is more formalized and focuses upon the evolution of ideas and the related setting of collective objectives. In the case of the UK, the still ongoing ACORD agreement is about the necessity to talk together and to develop learning.

In so doing those governments may have better positioned themselves at a European level against heavy-handed stringent frameworks suggested by the German scene. The recent deliberations of the ELV Waste Priority Stream would seem to confirm that expectation. As to whether or not this chain-reaction will feed back upon the German legislative framework remains to be seen.

In addition, with respect to the *genuine uncertainty*, there is no doubt that due to the complexity associated with both the numerous actors involved and the number of possible economic, organizational and technological trajectories which require to be explored this has legitimated the reliance upon open-ended voluntary agreements. This argument has been most clearly expressed and made explicit in France, but receives reinforcement from the UK ACORD analysis.

Concerning the third aspect viz., *faith and goodwill* much remains to be seen and suggests the need for continuing detailed scrutiny and monitoring of developments over the next few years. The pronouncements of the ELV Waste Priority Working Group rightly indicates such a need. Thus if the desired goals are not attained with sufficient speed or on a sufficient scale then further debate, and further, more stringent legislation, has to be considered.

No doubt as such progress under the aegis of the Voluntary Agreements comes to be more explicitly observable so too will the differential losses and gains of the various 'winners' and 'losers' involved. This may be the supply industry, the materials manufacturer, the automotive manufacturer, the disposal-chain or consumers themselves. Therefore the problem has only been displaced temporally and spatially. Its ultimate resolution will depend upon the form of co-operation (or non-co-operation) which occurs across those numerous actors. The remaining question therefore is how well will industry self-police itself? That in turn raises important questions of both organizational, political and economic interest which again requires monitoring and assessment by both European and national environmental agencies. In that respect the ELV Priority Waste Stream Project Group in its proposed strategy document (ELV Project Group, 1994) indicates that 'in each Member State, national monitoring groups will need to be created. Monitoring of and information on progress will be necessary. If insufficient progress is made, some further measures will need to be taken'. An important pragmatic and operational issue is whether or not such bodies will have the administrative, judicial, manpower and analytic capacity to continually undertake such monitoring.

3. THE PACKAGING RECYCLING PROCESS

3.1 Context

As with automobiles, packaging (and the subsequent landfilling or incineration associated with the waste 'treatment') is a symbol of the consuming society and environmental degradation. Thus there has been, especially over the past five-to-ten years, a political willingness to reduce energy wastage, landfill requirements through an increase in recovery and recycling of packaging materials. However, the determinant of the political willingness was not purely subjective.

More objectively, the context is firstly marked by a continuous growing of domestic waste production. Germany is an exception in the latter respect where it plateaued 20 years ago even though this specificity is partly due to statistical concentions: in Germany recycled waste is not considered in the waste production figures (Table 7.1).

Secondly, in most European countries packaging-waste is the prime component of domestic waste production growth. For example, in France, between 1960 and 1990, domestic waste production rose by 64 per cent whilst packaging-waste has more than doubled (Quirion, 1994). On average packaging waste (for Europe) constitutes 50 per cent of the domestic waste volume and 33 per cent by weight. This continuous growth has led to a contemporary potential saturation of both landfill sites and incinerator capacity. For instance, 50 per cent of the German landfill capacity will be used in the next five years (Staudt, 1993). The potential for near saturation of existing capacity treatment is reinforced by the 'NIMBY' (Not In My BackYard) syndrome whereby local populations are hostile to the siting of new landfills or incinerators. This situation of saturation has been a major driving force for the development of packaging recycling in the face of growing domestic waste production.

Table 7.1   Production of domestic waste in Germany and France

Countries	Germany	France
Domestic waste production (1989)	19,5 Mo t / yr.*	17 Mo t / yr.
Rise from 1975—89 (%)	0%	+ 40%
Domestic waste production per inhabitant in 1989	318 kg / yr.	303 kg / yr.

Note: Mo t stands for million of tons

Source: OECD, 1991

Voluntary agreements between industry and government 163

With respect to the actors involved in the packaging and packaging-waste sectors we should note that, just as in the case of car recycling, they are very diverse (see Figure 7.5).

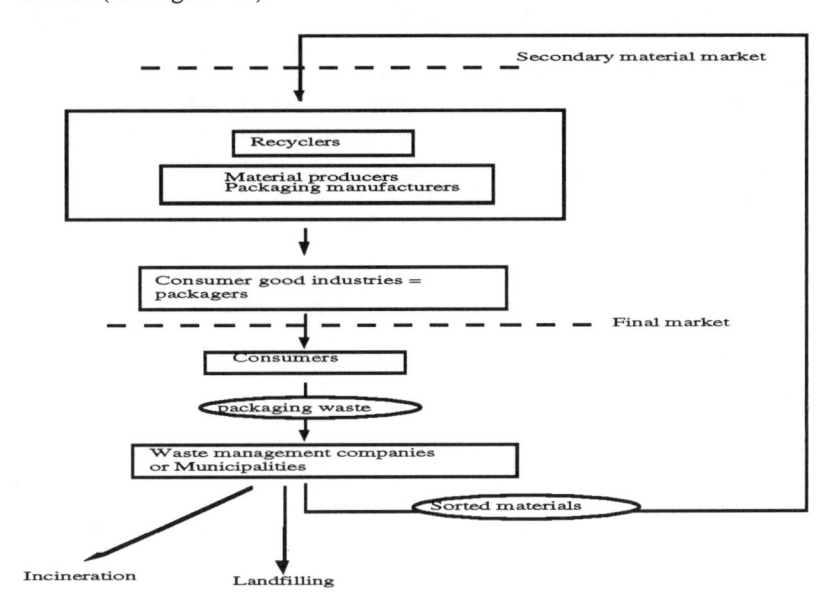

Figure 7.5 The packaging and packaging waste chain

At the upstream level, there are packaging manufacturers and material producers. Concerning these actors, two points should be stressed. First, they are generally vertically integrated. Secondly, whilst the materials used tends to fall into five categories: glass, plastics, tin-plate, paper-cardboards and aluminium, material producers are generally specialized in the production of kind of material. At the intermediate stage, consumer goods industries use the packaging. In this chapter, we will refer to them as 'packagers'. At the post-consumption level legal responsibility for domestic waste management is traditionally given to municipalities who collect and treat waste directly via municipally owned forms or contracted private waste companies. At present incineration and landfilling accounts for approximately 90 per cent of the total waste material handling/treatment (ANRED, 1991).

Concerning the shift of traditional waste management systems towards recycling two points should be made. First, recycling requires a preliminary step of sorting or separate collection of the different materials to be recycled. Second, the recycling ability of the different materials is very heterogeneous. As far as paper/cardboard, glass, steel and aluminium are concerned, recycling technologies are already available and broadly used. But for the moment, recyclers do not use inputs coming from packaging waste. The only exception is packaging glass for which recycling ratios are respectively 41 per cent and 63 per cent in France and Germany (CSVMF, 1993). Nevertheless, the recycling costs of the different materials are very different. As a consequence, the prices on the secondary material market are heterogeneous as shown by Table 7.2. The case of plastics is specific given that its recycling is only emerging. However, one thing is clear: it is the less easily recyclable material. The existence of such differences between materials is crucial to an understanding of the differentiation of the regulatory strategies of industrial actors.

Finally, as in the case of auto recycling, the development of packaging recycling is marked by large uncertainties concerning sorting and separate collection technologies on the one hand and plastic recycling techniques on the other hand. Given the diversity of actors involved e.g. municipalities, waste management companies, material producers and packages, it is also very complex.

Table 7.2   Prices of different secondary materials

Material	Price (June 1993)
Aluminium	from 220 to 230 ECU / t
Glass	from 45 to 55 ECU / t
Tin plate	from 8 to 30 ECU / t
Paper cardboard	from -8 to 0 ECU / t

Source: Recyclage et Récupération (1993)

3.2   Regulatory initiatives

Against the above backdrop regulatory initiatives concerning packaging recycling has taken place, simultaneously, at two levels: (i) at an EU level and (ii) at the national level (France and Germany). At the EU level a formulation of the Directive 94/62/CE commenced in 1990 which aimed to define European recycling and recovery targets to be implemented at the national levels. Whilst at the national level France and Germany have put forward their own regulations. This anticipation may appear surprising since the Directive was not to come into force until 1995. For the two countries the reasons are partly different. For Germany, the regulation is at the beginning a unilateral move. An environmentally aware public has stimulated the German government toward an ambitious policy. This German move is also partly responsible for the EU Commission's decision to design a new Directive. Concerning France, the commencement of the regulatory process was clearly determined by the German regulatory projects, just as in the case of auto recycling. The French strategy was to use its national regulatory activities to thwart German influence in the European process. Concerning the three regulatory processes (viz., the EU level, the German process and the French process) we would note the following:

The EU process
The first draft of the future 94/62/CE Directive was issued in early 1991. It aimed at a stabilization of packaging production at the current level (150 kg/per/year), 90 per cent recovery and 60 per cent material recycling within 5 years which was a considerable advance on earlier EU regulations (e.g., the 85/339 Directive on the recycling of beverages packaging). In particular the 60 per cent materials recycling aim downplayed a reliance on energy recycling.

Over the period 1991—94 intense lobbying by industrialists and a wrestling match between Northern countries (Netherlands, Germany and Denmark) — who were in favour of a very ambitious policy — and others such as France and the UK ensued. This resulted in a diminution in the initial environmental ambitions. The Directive adopted in December 1994 was such that the waste reduction objective was withdrawn, and the recovery objectives are now 50—65 per cent to be reached in 5 years of which a 25—45 per cent recycling component is included.

The German process
The German process initiated in 1989 by the Federal Minister for the Environment constituted a series of consultations with numerous actors concerning an Ordinance which had its foundations in the 1986 law on waste. By 1990 the project included a set of stringent recycling objectives (80—90 per cent recycling by 1995, excluding incineration); a mandatory returnable system for certain kinds of packaging (e.g., beverage packaging); and an obligation for the retailers to take back the packaging placed on the market via a system of containers in the close vicinity of their point of sale. Packagers and retailers must then undertake the recycling of the collected materials.

At this stage, the content of the project have already been very exhaustive since it included precise objectives and a complete set of means to reach them. At the beginning the reaction of the industrialists is both homogeneous and very negative. Through the channels of the BDI, the federation of the employers association and the Chambers of Commerce, they quickly reacted. But motives were rather different. The retail trade industry opposed the responsibility for taking back packaging waste since it would *de facto* lead them to become the leaders of the new waste management systems. Packagers were opposed to the returnable systems: a change in packaging would imply for them heavy marketing and industrial strategy changes. Packaging manufacturers foresaw a decrease in packaging production.

However quickly, industrial regulatory strategies diverged. A pro-active policy on the part of the retailers and packagers ensued. Due to the pro-environmental political and public atmosphere, they considered that the very ambitious recycling objectives could not be challenged. They created a working group, AGVU, which included food producers and supermarket chains aimed at designing counter proposals on the means of achievement of objectives. They aimed at an alternative, avoiding the obligation for retailers to take back packaging waste and limiting the extent of mandatory returnable packaging.

In the meantime, as to packaging manufacturers and material producers their views differed as a function of the nature of the material and its recyclability. On the one hand, producers of the more easily recyclable material were not so reluctant to accept regulatory projects which could lead to an increase in their market share at the expense of other materials. However, they mainly remained passive in the regulatory debate. On the other hand, plastics and paper/cardboard industries were very opposed, focusing their criticisms on the objectives (especially regarding limited incineration).

In January 1991 an AGVU counterproposal emerged: the so-called Duales System which exempted the distributors from their obligation to take back packaging waste, relying on a fee-system paid to a consortium who would take charge of reaching recycling targets. Concerning this counter-proposal, two points should be underlined. First, the Duales System was clearly a unilateral initiative by industry resulting from the wrestling match with the administration; the government not being involved in the reflections of the AGVU. Secondly, it was not designed and proposed by all the industrialists. Material producers played only a marginal role or no role at all. As a matter of fact, the initiative was supported by the glass industry and only supported by the plastics industry at the final stage (recognizing no means of avoiding new regulations and the importance of public opinion); the paper/cardboard industry remained opposed.

The Federal Government reacted positively and quickly to this counter-proposal in the Ordinance which was adopted in 1991.

The French process

In France, the policy process was deeply influenced by the German Ordinance. As already noted, this interdependency is due to the simultaneous designing of the Directive 94/62 aiming at setting common recycling goals. The French officials knew that the implementation of the Directive would oblige them to design a regulation to reach the objectives of the Directive. In 1991, France was opposed to the very ambitious German stances which proposed to include the objective of the ordinance into the Directive. An anticipating strategy allowed them to increase the credibility of their proposals.

Just before the adoption of the above German Ordinance the French Minister for the Environment announced a target of 'a recovery rate of 75 per cent by 2002' for packaging recycling — and asked the Chairman of the BSN food group to set up a process of reflection. Major guidelines and methods of application were drawn up by another industrial consultative committee. It should be noticed that the process was more co-operative than in Germany. In the process the leaders were clearly the consumer goods industries and retailers but packaging manufacturers and material producers were also consulted. Moreover, public authorities have initiated and taken part in the collective reflection

In essence the outcome can be characterized by two points. First, it kept the objectives of 75 per cent of recovery, initially announced by Lalonde. Given that incineration with energy recovery was possible, we should notice that the French objectives were less stringent than the German ones. Concerning the means, the proposal was inspired by the German process being based on the obligation for packagers to take part in a consortium responsible for recycling targets. The final French system, the so-called Lalonde Decree was issued in April 1992.[5]

3.3 The nature of the system

For France and Germany the regulatory outcome in terms of means is similar. Both regulations are based on a transfer of responsibilities for waste management from municipalities to industrialists: the packagers in France and the retailers in Germany. The overall process which operates depends upon a system of two kinds of organization, the *consortium* and the *guarantors* as shown in Figure 7.6.

The consortia finance the collection and sorting of packaging waste through a series of contracts with domestic waste collectors and sorters in Germany or with municipalities in France. They are financed by contracting firms (generally packagers). The fee is based on the nature of the packing material and the volume of packaging aided by the 'green-dot' system printed on the packaging.[6]

Nevertheless, there are some differences between the German and French consortia. For example, in France Eco-Emballages is responsible for financing only sorting costs and not collection costs. Furthermore, the strategic decisions concerning Eco-Emballages (fees, contracts) have to be agreed by the public administration. In Germany the fees to be paid by packagers are differentiated according to the nature of the material and take into account the differential sorting and recycling costs. In Germany the consortium DSD is strictly monopolistic whereas in France there are three consortia, but dominated by Eco-Emballages which is a quasi-monopoly.

Ultimately, consortia use a system of subsidies towards municipalities or domestic waste collectors and sorters to promote recycling, finance being collected from packagers. Thus, to reach the objective, the sytem is in fact based on economic incentives towards municipalities or collecters/sorters. At the level of the packager, the fee provides an additional incentive to lower the quantity of material used for packaging leading to the completion of secondary environmental goals of the regulation, i.e., source reduction. The incentives scheme is not very original. But an originality lies in the fact that it is managed by a consortium. Traditionally, these schemes are managed by public fiscal agencies. *In one sense the consortia are very strange fiscal agencies in that they are private instead of being public and are owned by a co-operation of firms which are in fact its tax payers.*

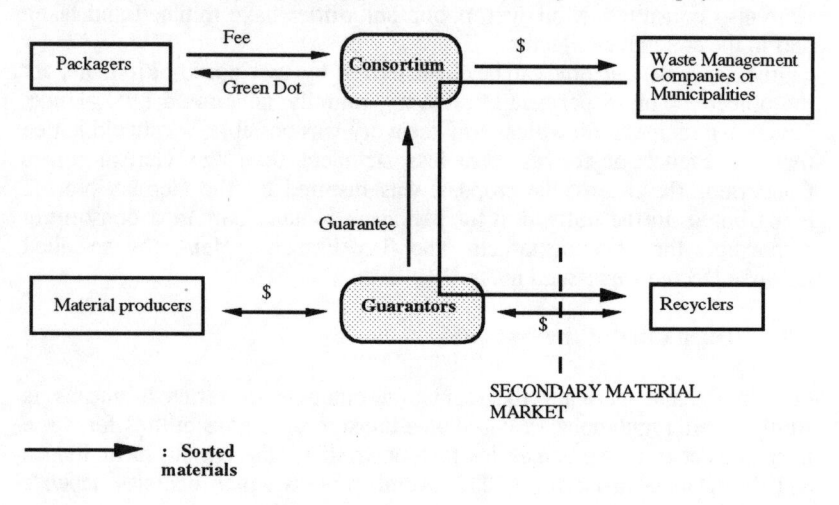

Figure 7.6 General organization of the Duales System

The *guarantors* on the other hand guarantee to receive any sorted material from the consortium at a fixed price and to arrange recycling. The guarantors do not have a significant financial role other than stabilizing the very fluctuating secondary material market prices. It facilitates subsequent investment plans of the recyclers and sorters.

3.4 Commentary and analysis of the regulatory processes and their outcomes

The packaging recycling regulations adopted in France and Germany are seen as very original by policy-makers and industrialists for two main reasons: (i) their evolution has been marked by a large voluntarism of the firms given the fact that the means were in fact defined by the industrialists themselves; and, (ii) the adopted means, i.e., the consortium based solution, is viewed as very original and potentially useful for a large spectrum of waste problems. The originality lies in the fact that they are characterized by fiscal agencies owned by a co-operation of the financing firms. What is the underlying logic of these two features?

Concerning the first feature, the voluntarism of the industry can be surprising. In the case of auto recycling, two factors were pushing towards the voluntarism of the car industry. First, they produce consumer goods and a good public image was thus crucial for them. Second, the compliance costs to reach the global car recycling targets was expected to be very low or even nil. If the former argument can be used in the case of packaging recycling, the latter is no longer valid. Packaging recycling is expected to be very costly.

However, an attentive analysis can bypass this difficulty. For this, we have to distinguish between *regulatory goals* (i.e., the stringency of abatement imposed by the regulation) and *means* to reach these goals. In relation to these two elements, the logic of negotiations between the industry and a public authority is different (Glachant, 1994). If we consider that a regulatory goal has been previously selected, with regard to *means* both regulator and industry want the cheapest routes of compliance. Hence, at this stage, consensus between the administration and industry is possible — as was observed for this packaging-recycling study both in France and Germany. However, regarding the regulatory goals, the economic motives of regulators and firms will differ. As compliance is costly for the industry, firms want an objective as low as possible whereas the regulator wants to set the socially efficient objectives.

This analysis about the asymmetry between the means and the objective fits well with the German case. The objectives were accepted by the packagers, but with reluctancy because public opinion prevented a challenge to them. This reluctancy remained until the end in the case of paper/carboard producers. On the contrary, the Duales System proposed by the industry was very quickly accepted by the public authorities. In France, if the same is true with the means, our analysis seems contradictory with the fact that the objectives proposed by Lalonde, the Minister for the Environment were spontaneously accepted by French firms. The reason for this is that the status of the objectives was to be (can be seen) as a counter proposal to the German objectives in the European policy-making process. In that sense the French regulatory goals were not negotiated but used as a strategic/national weapon. Thus to a certain degree it can be said that the collusion between the French government and its industry at the European level has stimulated/permitted co-operation at the national level.

However, as already mentioned the voluntarism did not concern all the industrialists to the same degree. We can note that in both France and Germany the regulatory strategies of the packagers and/or retailers on the one hand and that of the material producers on the other have been slightly (in France) or very (in Germany) different. 'Voluntarism' mainly concerned the former. Two arguments can be presented. First, the packagers are close to final markets and the public image argument is more true for them. Second, the incurred costs can be easily recaptured in the price of final goods. Indeed the pattern of material use/costs is similar for most packagers and retailers, hence little inter-company competitive changes will occur. On the contrary, for the materials producers recycling costs vary as a function of the particular material. Hence, there is clearly a competitive differential and a less unified response pattern. There are winners and losers (the former being producers of more easily recycled materials, e.g., glass, aluminium). We therefore observed that potential losers (paper/cardboard and plastics industry) were more recalcitrant, as was the case in Germany, and more obstructive.

The second essential feature of these policy process is the selected means: the consortium based solution. It is not an original policy instrument since basically, it is a system of subsidies. What is original is that the subsidies scheme is managed by an organization which is in fact a co-operation of firms. And this feature is relevant since the consortia was seen as an evolving system aiming at carrying on a collective learning. We then find exactly the logic in progress concerning the voluntary agreements in auto recycling. Inter-firm negotiations and networking can go some way to resolving the competitive complexities. The consortia referred to earlier provide a framework for inter-firm bargaining in order to reconcile individual strategies and permit a continuing effort on a shared basis. We therefore see the strength and potential of 'voluntarism' which in itself demands the emergence of co-operation between firms. If co-operation is not to become collusion, however, the mechanisms of interaction between government, regulatory agency and the wider industrial network have to be submitted to constant inspection, monitoring and vigilance (Whiston, 1982).

4. OVERALL CONCLUSIONS

A remarkably similar pattern concerning the development and dynamics of regulations in the 'recycling arena' can be observed, and should be stressed, when we compare the packaging and automobile recycling details which we have provided in this chapter.

1) At the European level the initial stringent intentions have, through a series of challenges or discussions with the relevant industrial and commercial sectors, come to be modified towards goals of more modest attainment.
2) The overall regulatory reliance has moved away from mandatory towards voluntary approaches. This does not imply regulatory capture. On the contrary, because of the considerable complexity and uncertainty which pertains to such areas — for example, the context is complex (because of the number of actors involved) and uncertain (the development of recycling entails in both cases considerable technical, economic and organizational uncertainties) — such a development is understandable and logical.
3) With respect to the interaction between the national and the European level: in both cases the regulatory processes have taken place simultaneously at the European and national level, each informing the

other. It has produced interesting dynamics whereby a collusion between industrialists and government in the European process has structured their interaction at the national level. This is one explanation of the voluntarism in the two case studies.
4) More specifically a mechanism or dynamic might be posited on the following lines: Germany has initially sought, at the national level, to seek out and enact stringent environmental (recycling) regulations. Inter alia this has set an initial agenda for stringent regulations at the European level. Subsequently, following numerous interactions, analyses and interactive dynamics between industry and government at the national level (e.g., in France, the UK or wherever) a modified more modest environmental goal has resulted. And usually this has been in the form of an institutionalized voluntary approach. In turn such legislation has informed the European level. Thus, in summary, Germany has led (and stimulated) debate but not set the subsequent agenda at the European Union level. France and the UK have in different ways 'followed' but through voluntary, attenuated regulatory goals.
5) As part of the above dynamics especially with respect to France, there would appear to be evidence that the French, having been stimulated by German intentions, have rapidly achieved their own level and forms of regulatory frameworks in order to more speedily counter German influence at the European level. We see here both pragmatism and defence mechanisms.
6) The complexity of the industrial and commercial actors involved (producers, recyclers, materials handlers, material manufacturers, distributors and the like) suggests that one must be careful in making any simple generalization regarding their mode of interaction with regulatory bodies. However we can observe the influence of (a) national and international networking on a considerable scale of activity and involvement; and (b) the importance, in a 'perceptual sense' of events in one country — stimulating pro-active and re-active organization in another country — thereby reinforcing the pattern indicated in (4) above.[7] Thus the initial environmental concerns relating to recycling which developed in Germany have triggered responses in both France and the UK; and influenced the subsequent regulatory agenda at an EU level. The irony is that the issue has not been (as yet) specifically resolved in Germany!
7) Finally we would note that one of the major developments in relation to the area under discussion in this chapter has been the contemporary reliance upon Voluntary Agreements. It will be remembered that Voluntary Agreements are made between a public authority and a coalition of firms and that the content of the agreement can exhibit various degrees of precision. Thus, in the case of the UK, the ACORD agreement (still ongoing) is about the necessity to talk together and to develop learning. The Voluntary Agreement in France

concerning automobile recycling focuses upon the evolution of ideas and the setting of collective objectives. With respect to packaging regulations in France and Germany the Voluntary Agreement reflects an agreement concerned with learning, collective objectives and the means of undertaking.

The common points of all Voluntary Agreements are that it organizes and encourages a collective answer at the implementation stage. The emergence of co-operation between firms is as important as the co-operation between the public authority and the industries concerned. However, it should be noted that there are both advantages and disadvantages related to Voluntary Agreements.

With regard to the advantages, the Voluntary Agreement allows a collective learning in order to reduce genuine uncertainty. Through the establishment of organizational links (e.g., consortia) it stabilizes the interaction between actors (firms, municipalities) and in so doing reduces another dimension of uncertainty due to complexity (viz., the diversity of the involved actors). It is especially useful for recycling regulations given that an intrinsic feature of the development of recycling is to put in contact actors who do not have the habit of working or interacting together, viz., the post-consumption actors on the one hand (shredders, dismantlers, municipalities, waste management companies) and on the other hand industrial actors such as car manufacturers and consumer goods industries.

Finally, since the agreement concerned not only the content of a contract but also revision procedures (given that the contract is unavoidably incomplete) this provides the Voluntary Agreement with evolutionary features which fits well with a very uncertain and complex environment.

Concerning the disadvantages of the Voluntary Agreement it must be recognized that it favours collusion between firms that may be to the detriment of intense competition. For instance, in the case of Eco-Emballages, fees to be paid by packagers are not differentiated according to the nature of the material. Thus the impacts of the development of recycling on the market shares of the different materials are frozen.

In addition, as Voluntary Agreements are well adapted to an uncertain environment, they are of a transitory form given that uncertainties will (hopefully) tend to disappear. Finally there is always the danger that united monolithic consortia may have an intimidating effect upon the regulatory authority. Indeed the uniformity of the consortia's position and views perhaps compromise the speed, form, scale and perceived potential of regulatory compliance. This last aspect raises important questions relating to the competence and political or environmental 'will' of regulatory agencies and public authorities in general.

NOTES

1. Thomas Whiston, Senior Fellow, Director of Studies (Technology and Innovation Management), SPRU, University of Sussex, Falmer, Brighton, East Sussex BN1 9RF, UK, tel: 441273686758; fax: 441273685865.
2. Matthieu Glachant, Researcher, Centre of Industrial Economics, CERNA, Ecole Nationale Supérieure des Mines de Paris, 60, bld St Michel, 75272 Paris Cedex 06, France, tel: 33140519091/9071; fax: 33144071046.
3. The EU Council of Ministers agreed proposals in 1989 on the need for improved treatment of waste of all kinds and of landfill planning. Various Priority Waste Stream groups were set up in order to overcome duplication of effort. The assignation of the 'End-of-Life Vehicle' waste stream was made to France in June 1991. The Proposed Strategy emanating from the ELV Project Group was made available in February 1994 (ELV, 1994).
4. For example the interactions and discourse between the ACORD group formed in the UK with UK Regulatory Agencies.
5. Quantified general objectives are prohibited by the French Constitution, the objectives, however, are included in the Administrative Agreement of Eco-Emballages issued November 1992.
6. Manufacturers are permitted to place a 'green dot' on their product so long as they pay into the system.
7. More detailed discussion of the findings and conclusions indicated in this chapter are given in Whiston, 1995 and Glachant, 1995.

REFERENCES

ACORD [Automotive Consortium on Recycling and Disposal] (1992), *End of Life Vehicle Disposal: Preliminary Concept*, London: ACORD.

ACORD (1993), *Preliminary Operating Plan*, London: ACORD.

Aggeri, F., A. Hatchuel and P. Lefebvre (1994), 'Waste Car Policy: Shared Uncertainty In The Regulatory Process' in Sorensen, K.H. (ed.), *The car and its environments: the past, the present and future of the motorcar in Europe*, Brussels: European Commission, Social Sciences, pp. 256—272.

ANRED (1991), *Guide pour leTraitement des Déchets Solides Municipaux*, Brussels: European Commission, DGXVII.

CEST [Centre of Exploitation of Science and Technology] (1991), *Disposal of Vehicles: Issues and Actions*, London: CEST.

CSVMF (1993), *Note d'information*, Paris: Chambre Syndicale des Verreries Mécaniques de France.

ELV Project Group (1994), *Proposed strategy of the ELV Project Group for the treatment of 'End of Life' Vehicles*, Paris: ELV.

Glachant, M. (1994), 'The Setting of Voluntary Agreements between Industry and Government: Bargaining and Efficiency', *Business Strategy and the Environment*, **3**(2), pp. 43—49.

Glachant, M. (1995), *The Regulatory Processes in Packaging Recycling: Co-operation between Industry and Regulatory Authorities*, ERIC Report for the European Commission (DG XII/D-5), CERNA: Paris.

Gronewegen, P. and F. de Hond (1993), 'Product Waste in the Automotive Industry: Technology and Environmental Management' *Business Strategy and the Environment,* **2**(1).

OECD (1991), *OECD Environmental Data,* Paris: OECD.

Quirion, P. (1994), *La Gestion des Déchets d'Emballages Ménagers en France et en Allemagne: Eléments d'Evaluation Economique,* Université de Paris 1: UER Economique 2.

Recyclage et Récuperation (1993), Mercuriales des Cours des Matières Secondaires, Juin.

Staudt, E. (1993), *A Comparison of the Cost Structure and Fees for Domestic Waste Disposal and Recycling,* University of Bochum: DSD.

Whiston, T.G. (1982), *Environmental Regulations and the European Automobile Industry: Compliance costs, Corporate Consequences and Productivity Issues,* Paris: OECD (Environment Directorate).

Whiston, T.G. (1995), *Disposal and Recycling of Motor Vehicles: An International Perspective,* ERIC Report for the European Commission (DG XII/D-5), SPRU, University of Sussex UK.

Whiston, T.G. and E.T. Ferguson (1983), *Product Life and the Automobile: a Policy Perspective for the Netherlands,* The Hague, Netherlands: TNO.

8. Voluntary initiatives and public intervention — the regulation of eco-auditing

Jürgen F. Franke[1] and Frank Wätzold[2]

1. INTRODUCTION

The present chapter focuses on the involvement of the chemical industry in the regulatory process associated with the Eco-Management and Audit Scheme (EMAS, Council Regulation 1836/93).[3]

The Eco-Management and Audit Scheme was first presented by European Communities Commission in 1990 as a mandatory scheme. The chemical industry responded homogeneously and rejected the compulsory nature. When the Commission decided to change the Scheme into a voluntary one, the response of industry became diverse. Three interesting features could then be observed:

Firstly, apart from Germany, the chemical industry in general welcomed EMAS and chose a strategy of co-operation. A number of severe accidents which had occurred in the course of the 1970s and 1980s such as those in Seveso (Italy) or Basel (Switzerland) had left the chemical industry with a bad image. As a response the chemical firms had themselves started a number of initiatives aimed at regaining trust from their clients, the public and the regulatory authorities. The most important initiative was the Responsible Care Programme (RC). RC was partially successful, as it helped to improve the image of the chemical industry. However, one of its problems was that it lacked credibility. EMAS was therefore seen as a useful complement to RC as it is validated by an independent party.

Secondly, Germany, having a reputation as a first mover in European environmental policy continued to oppose the regulation. It was perceived as being unfair that companies in Germany which have to comply with comparatively high environmental standards would receive the same 'Statement of Participation' as companies in other countries. Furthermore, the more technology oriented approach by German companies to environmental problems does not correspond well with the management oriented Scheme.

Thirdly, the UK was an active advocate of EMAS. UK industry is much more management oriented than German. Moreover, as it had taken the lead in environmental management systems and environmental auditing it was keen that these concepts be adopted throughout the European Union (EU). It viewed its experience in this area as a competitive advantage at a time when green issues are gaining importance.

This chapter is divided into four sections. The regulatory background is presented in Section 2. The main features of the chemical industry and its environmental impact are described. The reactions of the public and the authorities to pollution caused by the chemical industry are also presented. The chapter goes on to examine the Responsible Care Programme. Finally, the concept of environmental auditing is introduced. To familiarize the reader with the regulation, an overview of EMAS is given at the beginning of Section 3. Then, the regulatory process, which may be divided into three phases, is presented. The first phase is characterized by industry's strong rejection of EMAS as a reaction to the mandatory nature of the Scheme as first intended by the Commission. The second phase started with the publication of a voluntary EMAS as a Commission proposal and ended with the adoption of the regulation (93/1836) by the Environment Council. This phase is characterized by a mixed response from industry and a large number of slight modifications to the Scheme. The third phase of the process involves the implementation of the Scheme in the various countries. This is still continuing at the time of writing. Section 4 analyses the interests and strategies of the main players of the EMAS devising process. Section 5 summarizes the main findings of the EMAS case study and gives a forecast on the number of companies that will participate in EMAS and an opinion as to whether EMAS will replace RC.

2. THE BACKGROUND OF THE REGULATION

2.1 The chemical industry and the environment

The impact on the environment by the chemical industry may be classified as follows. Firstly, emissions arise as a by-product in the production process. This may happen in a continuous way in a normal production process, but also in a sporadic manner in the form of accidents. The emissions diffuse into air, soil and water and some of them cause harm to plants, animals or human beings. Among the most important emissions are CO_2, SO_2, NO_x, CO, dust, organic and inorganic volatile compounds, heavy metals, nitrogen and phosphorus. Another problem is the amount of waste generated by the production process. Typically a chemical process has by-products which preferably may be used as raw materials in other processes but often have to be treated as waste. It is also important to note that parts of the chemical industry are very energy-intensive. Secondly, an impact on the environment may also arise when chemical products are used or discharged by other industrial branches or by the consumer. An example in which the usage of chemical products is harmful to the environment is the damage caused to the ground water by the use of fertilizers. An example in which the discharges of chemical products are detrimental to the environment are the emissions from incineration plants.[4] As the Eco-Management and Audit Scheme focuses on pollution from production sites, environmental damage arising from production processes is considered only.

The public's perception of the chemical industry and its relation to environmental problems has changed since the Second World War. A general trend can be identified in all the four countries under review. In the 1950s, the chemical industry was regarded by the public as a contributor of wealth and a guarantor to progress. This attitude changed gradually in the 1960s. The public became more aware of environmental problems caused by the chemical industry. The negative aspects of insecticides like DDT were the content of most public debates. A milestone in this context was the publication of Rachel Carson's book 'Silent Spring' in 1962. In the 1970s, the general discussion on environmental problems intensified for many reasons such as the growing environmental disruption brought about by rapid growth in the industrialized countries, a desire for an increasing quality of life, etc. However, the general public and green groups paid little attention to the chemical industry in this period. This changed when a number of accidents occurred in the mid—1970s (e.g., a cyclohexan vapour explosion caused 28 deaths in Fixborough, England in 1974, a dioxin release caused injuries to hundreds in Seveso, Italy in 1976) which drew special attention to the chemical industry. In the 1980s, further accidents (e.g., Bhopal, India with more than 2000 deaths in 1984, a spill of pesticides into the Rhine in Basel, Switzerland in 1986) and an ever growing public awareness of environmental problems in general, but also of those caused by the chemical industry, led to increasing public pressure on the chemical industry. Some chemical factories such as one of the Montecatini factories in Italy, Chemiefabrik Marktredwitz and Boehringer Ingelheim (Hamburg) in Germany were forced to close down by a combination of pressure from the public and the regulatory authorities.

The impact of the chemical industry on the environment and the rapidly worsening public image drew reactions from both governments and industry.

National governments as well as the European Commission responded with the introduction of environmental policies and legislation. In this context, the chemical industry has been affected not only by general environmental legislation, but also by legislation especially targeted at it. The regulations which affect the chemical industry are numerous. For example, the German chemical industry is now confronted with 2000 different laws. In the course of the 1970s and 1980s, environmental legislation was introduced in many countries. Today, in all the four countries under review, water pollution, emissions into the air and waste are covered by legislation. Over the past twenty years, the previous four EU

Action Programmes on the Environment have given rise to over 200 pieces of environmental legislation on the European level (cf. Chapter 2).

Though much has been achieved for the environment by legislation, the Commission recognized the limits of this so-called command and control (CC) approach. It is very costly to monitor, inspect and, when necessary, punish those organizations subjected to traditional environmental legislation. As the financial means are limited, controls are not comprehensive and consequently many companies do not comply with the legislation. Moreover, it is often that only minimum environmental standards can be imposed and it is difficult to cover all environmental effects by legislation. For example, in the chemical industry many new chemicals are invented and introduced into the market every year. Given the limited financial means, it is difficult for regulatory bodies to monitor and control the effects of these new chemicals and their production processes. Furthermore, the traditional CC approach does not stimulate creativity and expansion of knowledge in companies in relation to environmentally friendly technologies. Under the CC approach, companies have no incentive to do more for the environment than required by the existing legislation. The 5th Action Programme on the Environment which started in 1993 tries to take these deficiencies of the CC approach into account (cf. Chapter 2). One way to do so is to rely more on market based tools. It is hoped that they stimulate the creative energies of companies and direct these towards improving the environmental performance in a way which could not be achieved with the CC approach. It is in this context that the Eco-Management and Audit Scheme was developed.[5]

The attitude of the chemical industry towards the environmental problems which it caused has changed over time. In the 1970s, the approach of the chemical industry may be described as defensive. In general, industry considered mere compliance with environmental legislation as sufficient. When chemical firms infringed the law, they considered such acts as trivial offences and hoped for the sympathy of the authorities. Environmental problems were played down and demands for improving environmental performance were answered by pointing at possible increases in costs and corresponding job losses.

It is interesting to look at the example of Boehringer Ingelheim in Hamburg to illustrate the defensive approach and the reasons why it failed. Boehringer was involved in the production of herbicides in Hamburg since 1951. In the 1950s, Boehringer discovered that the so-called dioxin (2,3,7,8-tetrachloridbenzodioxin) was released as a by-product from the production process. The company developed a process to reduce its release but could not eliminate it completely. In the 1960s and 1970s, waste contaminated with dioxin was dumped into waste disposal sites around the factory. After the Seveso incident, pressure from green groups, the media and also the regulatory authorities on the company increased. The company responded by playing down the danger of dioxin. In 1983, the conflict aggravated and demonstrators demanded the closure of the plant. The factory management responded by saying that the production process which caused dioxin had been discontinued and that there was no old waste containing dioxin. An investigation by the authorities in 1984 discovered that dioxin was still released in the production process. The huge public outcry and anger at the misrepresentation led the local authorities to impose very strict environmental rules. As a result of these strict rules, the company was forced to close down the site in July 1984.

The chemical industry did learn from experiences like the Boehringer Ingelheim case. It realized that it could not ignore the growing public concerns and that its image had to be improved. The Boehringer Ingelheim example may be generalized to show that the major reason which prompted the chemical industry to change its mind was the growing public pressure in the 1980s, particularly, the pressure from the local and the regional public which in some cases was supported by a nation wide media coverage. The growing public awareness also encouraged the authorities to impose and enforce stricter rules. The significance of the combination of public pressure and more action from the regulatory authorities became very obvious when in cases such as the Boehringer Ingelheim example, factories primarily had to close down for environmental reasons.

The growing pressure on the chemical industry for environmental reasons in the 1980s led the chemical industry in most of the industrialized countries to retreat from the defensive approach and to be more proactive. The core elements of the new approach are:

- intention to practice environmental protection on its own initiative and assume more responsibility,
- responsibility for the safe manufacturing, handling, use, and disposal of products,
- open dialogue with the public on environmental issues.

The Responsible Care initiative and the management instrument of environmental auditing will be considered in more detail now. These two concepts played an important role within this new approach and also influenced the EMAS devising process.

2.2 Responsible Care

The new proactive approach was not only exercised by individual firms but also by national chemical associations. The reason for the total involvement was that the bad public image was shared by the whole chemical industry and was not limited to individual firms. The national chemical associations promoted the new policy in the different countries in different ways. The most prominent of these initiatives was the 'Responsible Care' (RC) programme initiated in Canada by the Canadian Chemical Producer's Association in 1984. Since then, it has been taken up by a large number of national chemical industry associations all over the world. The aims of RC are described as follows:

'Under the Responsible Care concept, Chemical Companies are committed, in all aspects of safety, health and protection of the environment, to seek continuous improvement in performance, to educate all staff, and work with customers and communities regarding product use and overall operation.' (CEFIC, 1991, p. 3).

The International Council of Chemical Associations (ICCA) has developed a set of principles which national chemical associations are supposed to adopt when they intend to implement RC. These principles include:

- 'a formal commitment on behalf of each company to a set of Guiding Principles signed, in the majority of cases, by the chief executive officer,
- a series of codes, guidance notes and checklists to assist companies to implement the commitment,
- the progressive development of indicators against which improvements in performance can be measured,
- an ongoing process of communication on health, safety and environmental matters with interested parties outside the industry,
- provision of fora in which companies can share views and exchange experience on implementation of the commitment,
- adoption of a title and a logo which clearly identify national programmes as being consistent with and part of the concept of RC,
- consideration of how best to encourage all member companies to commit to and participate in RC' (CEFIC, 1993, p. 5).

The European chemical industry association CEFIC started the promotion of RC in Europe in the late 1980s. All the chemical associations in the four countries under review have signed the RC programme although some differences, especially between the UK and Germany, can be observed.

In the beginning, the German 'Verband der Chemischen Industrie' (VCI) was reluctant to join the programme. However, as more and more countries joined the RC initiative the VCI felt compelled to be part of it. The board of directors of the VCI adopted the 'VCI Responsible Care Concept' in 1991. The 'VCI-Umweltleitlinien' (VCI-Environmental Guidelines), developed in 1986, were declared as the VCI Responsible Care Guiding Principles. The lack of interest in the RC initiative may be seen from the fact that the individual companies did not commit themselves to the principles but that the VCI signed on behalf of all its members. The uninterested attitude of the German industry may be explained as such. The chemical industry had already developed the 'Chemie im Dialog' initiative to improve its relationship with the public in 1986. The guiding principles of the Chemie im Dialog initiative were similar to those described above as the core elements of the proactive approach. Because of the Chemie im Dialog initiative the chemical industry considered RC as unnecessary.

Another reason why RC has not been popular in Germany is that the German approach towards environmental problems is different from the approach of RC. RC is based on the idea that the top management expresses its commitment to the environment by signing the RC declaration. Then, the ideas behind RC diffuse throughout the company and influence its policies. By changing the policies of the company, the environmental performance is finally improved. The German approach may be described as more 'engineer driven' or 'performance oriented'.[6] The typical German company does not establish a policy first but starts from a problem (i.e., an emission is considered as too high). It tries to solve this problem in most of the cases by developing a new technology. The success is measured in terms of whether the targeted reduction is achieved or not.

In the UK, RC has been adopted much more positively than in Germany. The UK Chemical Industry Association (CIA) launched the programme in 1989 and has been very active in promoting it among its members. Today, all of its members (over 200 companies) have given signatory commitment to the Responsible Care Guiding Principles. One reason for the positive attitude is that until 1989, the CIA did not have a programme to respond to the public pressure. Moreover, the approach of UK companies towards the environment is closer to the ideas of RC than the approach of German companies. The approach of typical UK companies can be described as more 'management driven'. The typical UK company starts with developing an environmental policy and establishing an environmental management system. Then it audits the system and thereafter it looks at the benefits for the environment. This does not mean that environmental technologies are not used and the environmental performance is not important, but, in the first place, an environmental management system is established.

In the assessment of RC as a mean of self-regulation, it is interesting to ask two questions. Firstly, what are the incentives and disincentives for companies to join the RC initiative, and secondly, how is free-riding overcome among the participants? The first question is relevant because the initiative provides not only benefits for the participants but also for non-participants. RC leads to a general image improvement of the chemical industry which is a positive externality for all firms in the industry. Therefore, companies can decide not to participate and still hope that they may benefit from an overall image improvement. However, those firms run the risk of being labelled as 'black sheep'. The risk increases with the size of the company and its degree of fame. Answering the second question, one should bear in mind that RC does not imply a binding commitment to reduce specific emissions to a specific extent. Once a company decides to apply RC seriously it will certainly improve its environmental performance. However, it is also possible that a company might claim to follow the RC principles, but does not do anything to improve its environmental performance. Although this form of free-riding cannot be avoided it may also turn the tables on some companies. Firstly, the interested public will not be satisfied with a simple statement that the company is a participant but will be interested in knowing what the company has done to improve its environmental performance. Most of the big companies have already anticipated this and have given performance indicators in their environmental reports. Secondly, if a company signs its commitment to the RC principles and the company does not practise these principles, it runs the risk of loosing its credibility when its incompliance is discovered (Gunningham, 1995).

The concept of RC allows companies different ways to improve their environmental performance. One of the instruments which has frequently been used in the context of RC and which has also influenced the EMAS-Regulation is environmental auditing.

2.3   Environmental auditing

Environmental audits were developed in the United States by the chemical industry and the oil industry in the beginning of the 1970s. Several companies began independently to establish an environmental audit system to inform their shareholders that the companies were complying with environmental laws and that accidents with liability consequences were not likely to occur. In the course of the 1970s, the environmental audits were quickly adopted by other companies as a result of a general increase in environmental concerns, stricter environmental laws, higher penalties and the promotion of the Environmental Protection Agency. It was also developed further from a pure 'compliance-audit' designed to check the compliance of a company with the law to a management instrument meant to control and improve the environmental management system of a company and to detect potential risks. In the course of the 1980s, American multinational companies brought environmental audits into Europe. Since then most of the big companies in the chemical sector have carried out environmental audits, mainly aimed at protecting themselves against liability claims. Smaller companies have also carried out audits, but to a much lesser extent than big companies. Today many consultancy firms such as A.D. Little, KPMG and Ernst & Young carry out environmental audits for companies.

A milestone in the history of environmental auditing were the 'Guidelines for environmental auditing' published in 1989 by the International Chamber of Commerce (ICC). The guidelines were developed with the help of many experts in environmental auditing, amongst them members of CEFIC, and were very successful in promoting environmental audits. According to the ICC guidelines, environmental auditing is defined as 'a management tool comprising a systematic, documented, periodic and objective evaluation of how well environmental organisation, management and equipment are performing with the aim of helping to safeguard the environment by (i) facilitating management control of environmental practices and (ii) assessing compliance with company policies, which would include meeting regulatory requirements' (ICC, 1989).

3. THE ECO-MANAGEMENT AND AUDIT SCHEME REGULATORY PROCESS

To introduce the reader to the Regulation 93/1836, an overview of EMAS is given first. Then the EMAS devising process is described in detail. The section ends with a presentation of the implementation phase.

3.1 The Eco-Management and Audit Scheme explained

The Eco-Management and Audit Scheme was published as Council Regulation (EU) No. 93/1836 of 29th of June 1993 in the official journal of the European Communities dated July 10th, 1993. The participation in the Scheme is voluntary and restricted to companies performing industrial activities. A company may register one or several sites. To register in the Scheme, a company must:

- adopt a company environmental policy, which must not only provide for the compliance with all relevant environmental regulatory requirements but also include commitments aimed at the reasonable continuous improvement on environmental performance with the intention to reduce environmental impacts to levels not exceeding those corresponding to economically viable application of best available technology. The objectives of the company environmental policy in terms of detailed goals are set by the company itself;
- conduct an environmental review of the site, i.e., an initial comprehensive analysis of the environmental issues, impact and performance which are related to activities at the site;
- introduce in the light of the results of the environmental review, an environmental programme for the site and an environmental management system which is applicable to all activities at the site. The environmental programme is aimed at achieving the commitments contained in the company environmental policy towards a continuous improvement of environmental performance;
- conduct environmental audits at all the sites concerned;
- prepare an environmental statement which is specific to each audited site. This statement must include an assessment of all the significant environmental issues which are relevant to the company's activities at the site concerned, a summary of the figures on pollutant emissions, waste generation, consumption of raw material, energy and water, noise and other significant environmental aspects and a presentation of the company's environmental policy, programme and management system implemented at the site under consideration;
- have the environmental policy, programme, management system, review or audit procedure and environmental statement or statements examined to verify that they meet the relevant requirements of the regulation and

the environmental statements validated. This must be done by an accredited environmental verifier;
- forward the validated environmental statement to a competent body of the Member State where the site is located and disseminate it as appropriate to the public in that State after registration of the site in question.

Once a site is registered, the company has the right to use a statement of participation which is embodied in a logo. The company may use this statement of participation to publicize its involvement in the Scheme by including it in company's environmental statements, brochures, reports, head paper and advertisement.

Member States have to establish an independent and neutral body for the accreditation of independent environmental verifiers and for the supervision of their activities by the 10th April, 1995. EMAS and its effectiveness are to be reviewed in five years' time and if the Scheme does not work appropriately, the Commission may modify it.

The implicit assumption behind EMAS is that market pressure will compel companies to join the Scheme.[7] The first few companies which are awarded the EMAS logo will be considered as especially environmentally friendly. The statement of participation will improve the participant's image in the eyes of its clients, suppliers, the relevant authorities and the general public. When more companies join the Scheme, the advantage of having the EMAS logo will diminish as it will become normal for companies to have it. However, the incentive to join EMAS will remain because those companies without the EMAS logo will have an increasing disadvantage of not possessing the logo as they will be considered as being particularly environmentally unfriendly. Besides reputation incentives the Commission has established another incentive to join EMAS. The Regulation 93/1836 requires that, in the context of company environmental policy, the environmental performance of contractors, subcontractors and suppliers shall also be considered. There will consequently be pressure on these companies to demonstate an awarenesS of environmental issues. A straightforward way of doing this is themselves to register with EMAS.

There is a need for governmental interference because one of the conditions that competition on environmental grounds works is that the environmental performance of a company can be assessed by those who are interested in it. If there is no governmental interference, the problem of asymmetric information arises. A company itself is more capable of assessing its environmental policy and performance than anybody else, likewise, it is able to hold back unfavourable information about its environmental policy and performance. Therefore, interested parties may not trust the information given by a company itself. With EMAS, the government provides a framework in which credible validation of the information given by companies is possible. A company may choose to implement an environmental policy, to have it audited and to have its audit and its environmental performance validated by an independent party. It is this independent validation which gives credibility to the information from the company. Nevertheless, it should be borne in mind that the verifier has only limited time and means to check the correctness of the information given by the company. Therefore, asymmetric information may still exist under EMAS, but to a lesser extent than in the absence of it. In the assessment of EMAS, one should also bear in mind that two firms which have very different environmental performances, but are otherwise comparable, may both get the logo. This is because the logo will be rewarded to a company when it follows the procedures explained above and not when it complies with a certain environmental standard.

3.2 The first phase of the devising process

The first phase began when the idea of an Eco-Management and Audit Scheme emerged in the Commission. This was followed by the publication of a consultation document. This period is characterized by a strategy of obstruction from industry. This phase ended when the Commission responded to industry's criticism by adopting a voluntary approach. The first phase of the regulatory process took place in Brussels. The main player was the Commission which had initiated the proposal and submitted it to discussion.

EMAS was first developed in the Commission. It is difficult to state the sources of the Scheme, but, a number of events may be identified which could have played an important role. Firstly, the EU's 5th Action Programme on the Environment was significant in that it initiated the search for suitable market based tools to supplement the Command and Control approach. Secondly, the ICC position paper on environmental auditing gave credit to this instrument. Thirdly, the RC initiative by the chemical industry may be seen as a successful promotion of a scheme similar to EMAS by an industrial sector. There are indeed some similarities between the RC programme and EMAS. Both approaches are voluntary and emphasize the responsibility of the company. In both approaches, communication with the public also plays an important role. Furthermore, some companies carried out environmental audits in the context of RC. Fourthly, the US experience with the 'Superfund Amendment and Reauthorisation Act' which was introduced in 1986 was also important. Section Three of the Act provides that companies must declare their emissions to the authorities. The Act listed approximately 300 different emissions which must be reported when they exceed more than 12t per year. The duty to declare emissions had a positive effect in that companies became very concerned with their public image and some even reduced their emissions voluntarily.

The first paper introducing the Scheme was released by the Commission as a consultation document in December 1990. Subsequent discussions of the consultation document brought about a number of modifications. The most important alteration was to change company participation from voluntary to mandatory. Industry was very surprised when the Commission publicized the consultation document. Even the ICC did not expect that the instrument which it had promoted a year ago was now taken up by the Commission. However, industry responded quickly, strongly and homogeneously. It did not criticize the approach in detail but focused its criticism on the mandatory nature of the Scheme. It felt that it was an interference on the part of the government to prescribe which management tool a company should use. Confronted with industry's strong resistance, the Commission agreed to adopt the voluntary approach.

3.3 The second phase of the devising process

The second phase began with the publication of EMAS as a Commission proposal in the EU's Official Journal on the 27th March, 1992 and ended with the adoption of the Regulation by the Environment Council on the 29th June, 1993. Compared to the first phase of the devising process, the response of industry changed in two ways. Firstly, while industry on the whole kept a lower profile on the matter than it did at the first stage of the regulatory process, lobbying by the UK and especially the German industry was still considerable. Secondly, the united and homogeneous response of industry disappeared. While the German government and industry continued with their strategy of obstruction, the general attitude of governments and industry was now cooperative with the UK being the most active supporter. The cooperative strategy of the industry led to numerous small modifications to the Scheme which were intended to make it more attractive for industry to join EMAS. Besides the German and the UK industry, CEFIC and the Commission were the main players in this period.

In order to observe what practical difficulties companies would face if they complied with EMAS, a pilot study was carried out from May 1992 to June 1993. It included 17 enterprises in six countries of which 5 are chemical firms. The experience of the pilot study and other criticisms from industry led to a number of changes in the proposal and the publication of a revised proposal as an internal paper on the 18th December, 1992. The nature of modifications which were adopted in this period are as follows. Firstly, they were minor changes. The aim was to modify the regulation but not to alter it completely. Secondly, many of the changes were aimed at making the Scheme clearer and more precise and the requirements more workable and practical. Thirdly, most of the changes were made with the intention of making participation in the Scheme easier and were, therefore, orientated by the interest of industry. One alteration to the scheme which is typical for the alterations made in this period was the separation of the environmental audit and the external environmental statement. According to Article 5 of the initial proposal, the external environmental statement should include the results of the environmental audit. However, industry was anxious that environmental audits would be devalued as an instrument for the detection of internal deficiencies. Participants might try to hide information if the results of the audit were to be published. In the revised proposal, the public statement need not include the results of the environmental audit. The pilot study also showed that companies felt that the regulation was not prescriptive enough. For example, companies complained that the definitions of 'environmental management system' and 'environmental programme' were not very clear. In general, the criteria and procedures in the proposal were made more specific and precise to avoid interpretation problems. The regulation also orientated itself closer to the British Standard (BS) 7750, an environmental management system which was developed in the UK. There were very few changes made which were against the will of industry. One example for such a change is that unlike in the initial proposal it was made clear in the revised proposal that the auditor and the verifier must be independent. The Commission had carried through this change as it feared that it could lead to less stricter control if the auditor and the verifier were not independent. Industry had opposed the change to save costs.

CEFIC was the main player which acted in the common interest of the chemical industry in this phase of the project. It saw its role mainly in lobbying for a short, uncomplicated and inexpensive EMAS. CEFIC established two groups looking at the likely effects of EMAS. One task force was especially concerned with environmental auditing, the other was concerned with environmental management system standards. There were many informal talks between the working groups from CEFIC and the Commission and some seminars were even conducted together.

The German industry did not only oppose the proposal but suggested two alternatives to EMAS. The first was the introduction of the German 'Betriebsbeauftragtenwesen' on a European level. According to various German environmental laws, German companies must appoint a person, a 'Beauftragten', inside the company when certain levels of waste or emissions into the water and into the air are exceeded (Wasser, Abfall- und Emissionsbeauftragter). Companies also have to appoint a special 'Beauftragten' when they are involved in the transport of dangerous materials (Gefahrgutbeauftragter) and when there is a risk of dangerous accidents (Störfallbeauftragter). The 'Beauftragte' is responsible for the corresponding areas (e.g., for compliance with relevant environmental laws) and it is hoped that he/she acts as the 'conscience' of the company. Secondly, the German industry pressed for a harmonization of environmental standards in the EU at a high level. As in many areas the German environmental standards are the highest in the EU, most of the other standards would have to be raised to the German benchmark.

The opinion of the Social and Economic Committee and of the European Parliament was sought according to the Treaty of Rome, Article 130(s), as modified by the Single European Act (1987). The Economic and Social Committee gave a positive opinion on the Scheme on the 20th October, 1992. The European Parliament voted in favour of the proposal on the 19th

January, 1993. The EMAS proposal appeared on the agenda for the Environment Council Meeting on the 22nd and 23rd March, 1993. Eleven Member States were in favour of the regulation with Germany being the only country against it. As unanimity was required for the Scheme, it could not be adopted by the Environment Council. However, Germany knew that it could only delay, but not prevent, the regulation. With the final ratification of the Maastricht Treaty by all 12 Member States, legislation framed under Article 130(s) does not require unanimity. Consequently, the EMAS review by the Environment Council could be ratified by majority voting and a single country could not oppose it. Therefore, Germany finally gave in to the strong pressure from the other 11 Member States. Before giving in, Germany tried to modify the Scheme and introduced a clause which states that companies must use best available technology. At the insistence of the other Member States, this clause was modified to the use of best available technology only if it is economically viable. Having reached this compromise, the adoption of the proposal on the Environmental Council meeting on the 29th of June was a mere formality.[8]

3.4 The beginning of the implementation phase

The implementation process of EMAS in the four countries under review differs considerably. The focus of the debate is the accreditation system for verifiers which must be established in the different Member States. While in the UK, and to a lesser extent in France, industry and government have agreed quickly on the accreditation system, industry and government in Germany and Italy are divided over the issue.

In Germany, the Ministry of the Environment suggested in its proposal for an accreditation system that the responsibility should be divided between industry and government. According to the proposal, a body from industry is responsible for the examination of the professional skills of the verifier. The Umweltbundesamt (the German Environmental Protection Agency) then investigates whether the applicant is free from potential conflicts of interest and finally decides on the accreditation. The supervision of the verifier is to be done jointly by industry and government with duties identical to those in the selection process. A committee is to be implemented to help the industrial body and the Umweltbundesamt. The committee consists of members from concerned NGO's, representatives from verifiers and the government. The most important task of the committee is to develop guidelines for the examination and supervision of verifiers.

However, industry fears that the influence of the Umweltbundesamt would lead the verifier to investigate too deeply and thoroughly to ensure the compliance of the company with the law. Therefore, two German business organizations, the Bundesverband der Deutschen Industrie and the Deutsche Industrie und Handelstag, have proposed another accreditation system. The proposal suggested that the Trägergemeinschaft für Akkreditierung (the German accreditation body for quality auditors which is run by industry) establishes an environment committee which is responsible for the examination of the professional skills of the verifiers. It also establishes guidelines for the examination and supervision of the verifiers. The accreditation itself is done by a joint body from two other German business organizations, the Industrie- und Handelskammern and the Handwerkskammern.

There was a declaration of support for the proposal of the Ministry of the Environment by different green groups, research institutes, trade unions, two environmentally oriented industrial organizations (Bundesdeutscher Arbeitskreis für umweltbewußtes Management and Unternehmensgrün) and the Bundesverband Junger Unternehmer, an organization of young entrepreneurs. The declaration brought forward two arguments in favour of the proposal from the Ministry of the Environment. Firstly, industry already has a large influence on the behaviour of verifiers as it is free to appoint the verifier of its choice. As verifiers have an interest to be appointed again, it is likely that they act in the interest of their clients. Therefore some counterbalance is needed which is only ensured when the verifiers are monitored by the Umweltbundesamt. Secondly, it is emphasized that only the reputation of the Umweltbundesamt can ensure the credibility of EMAS in the eyes of the public.

In Italy the debate resembles the debate in Germany. Industry wants a private body with only some state control whereas the government wants a more state controlled body. Industry suggested a system similar to the accreditation of the quality management auditor. This system is to be organized by a private agency and state influence is only existent in the form of a controlling body. The reason behind the conflict is basically the same as in Germany. There is a suspicion that the group which controls the accreditation system also has a strong influence in the way the verifier inspects the company.

In France, the government has mandated the Comité Français d'Accréditation (COFRAC) as the agency to accredit verifiers. So far, the responsibilities of COFRAC consists mainly of accrediting quality management auditors. COFRAC itself is an independent body founded by the Ministry of Industry. The administrative council of COFRAC includes representatives from the Ministry of Industry, Ministry of Finance and Ministry of Agriculture. There has been no big debate on this issue in France. Government and industry are satisfied with the solution, however the Ministry of the Environment would have preferred to be more influential in the matter.

Among the four countries under review, the UK has made the most progress in the implementation process. The government gave the mandate to accredit the verifiers to the National Accreditation Council for Certification Bodies (NACCB) at the end of 1993. The NACCB has been working under the guidance of the British Standard Institute, but it is intended that it becomes an independent organization with its own board of management. The board members will come from industry but also — to give it a higher credibility — from other fields such as regulation and environmental control agencies. The NACCB has been accrediting certifiers for the BS 5750 — the British quality management standard — and they were also mandated to do the same for the BS 7750 — the British environmental management standard. When the government proposed the NACCB as the accreditation body, it was unanimously accepted by all relevant groups, including green groups.

4. ANALYSIS OF THE REGULATORY PROCESS

This part analyses the interests and strategies of the main different players which were involved in the regulatory process.

4.1 The Commission

The main regulatory body in the first and second phase of the regulatory process was the Commission. Embedded in the context of the 5th Action Programme, the aim of the Commission was to develop market-based tools to protect the environment. Throughout the regulatory process, the Commission adopted a strategy of co-operation. It sought contacts with industry and accepted many suggestions from industry to change the EMAS proposal.

The first important point when the Commission accepted the demands of industry was when it changed the Scheme to a voluntary one. Nevertheless, the Commission may have not adopted the voluntary approach because of the pressure of industry alone. It might have also considered that a mandatory approach has disadvantages compared to a voluntary approach. Unlike a voluntary approach, a mandatory approach has no image and first mover advantages for companies. Further, audits may be carried out effectively as well as ineffectively. The reason is that there is asymmetric information between the audit team and the employees concerning the environmental performance of a company. An effective audit is one in which the employees provide all the necessary information to the audit team. This is likely to happen when the interest to improve the environmental performance of a company among the participants is present. An ineffective audit is one in which the employees try to hide information from the audit team. This is likely to be the case when the participants have little interest in the audit and want it completed as soon as possible. The interest of the participants is likely to be high when there is management commitment, a genuine interest on the side of the company to carry out an audit and it is carried out voluntarily.[9] However, the Commission did not close the possibility for a mandatory Scheme totally. The clause in the Regulation which states that EMAS shall be reviewed in a few years' time was mainly introduced to give the Commission the discretion to make the Scheme mandatory if it does not work the way the Commission hopes.

The general reasons for a co-operative strategy of the Commission were twofold. Firstly, there were informational asymmetries. As mentioned above, the instrument of environmental auditing had been developed inside companies as a response to various external and internal demands. Those companies with experience in environmental auditing had accumulated knowledge on the most economical ways to carry out efficient audits. The Commission did not possess this knowledge although it was important for the device of the Scheme. A strategy of co-operation would be the best way to obtain this information. Secondly, once the Commission had decided to drop the mandatory approach, the voluntary character of the Scheme made co-operation with industry even more necessary. If the Commission had chosen to introduce elements into the Scheme which were totally against the interest of industry, it would have run the risk of low participation in EMAS.

4.2 Common interest of the chemical industry and role of CEFIC

Despite the differences which will be explained in-depth later, the chemical industry was influenced by some common factors and shared some common interests. Industry in general was influenced by the fact that environmental audits and environmental management systems were well established management tools in the beginning of the 1990s. Especially the promotion by the ICC had given credence to environmental auditing. There were also many companies with experience in quality management systems and quality management audits. Therefore, EMAS did not introduce something which was wholly new but a concept which companies were already used to, and, in most of the cases, with positive results. Depending on the company and the way it conducted its audits, most of the existing environmental audits do not require much modifications before they are in compliance with the EMAS-Regulation 93/1836. Therefore, it is not very costly for companies with experience in environmental audits to join EMAS. Another important factor which influenced the attitude of the chemical industry was that the philosophy of EMAS was similar to that of RC. As most companies had positive experiences with RC, they were more inclined to look at a similar approach favourably. Furthermore, many companies had already implemented parts of EMAS in the context of RC. The pilot study observed that the chemical sector was the most experienced industry with environmental management and environmental audit systems. This was attributed largely to the widespread promotion and use of RC in the chemical industry. Nevertheless, the main advantage EMAS has over RC is, as felt by many companies, the third party validation in EMAS which makes it more credible. These factors might have influenced some companies to be in favour of EMAS and others to be less opposed to EMAS.

During the first phase of the regulatory devising process, the chemical industry chose a strategy of obstruction. Its aim was to change the Scheme from mandatory to voluntary. The reasons for this strategy were twofold. Firstly, the voluntary nature of the Scheme enables those companies for which participation is too costly, or which expect little gains in terms of reputation, to save costs by not participating in EMAS. Secondly, a mandatory scheme destroys potential first mover advantages for those companies which already have an environmental management system in place and experience with environmental auditing. If EMAS were mandatory, they would be just one out of many other companies which comply with EMAS. On the contrary, if EMAS is voluntary, they will be able to be among the first companies which join EMAS and, therefore, they will be considered particularly environmental friendly companies and enjoy reputation gains.

In the second phase of the process, the chemical industry changed the intensity of lobbying and its strategy. Altogether, it kept a rather low profile and turned from an obstructive to a co-operative approach. Apart from the UK and Germany, EMAS was neither promoted by industry nor strongly objected. The reason was that industry expected advantages as well as disadvantages from the Scheme, both of which were not so significant. As mentioned above the potential gains industry receives from the Scheme are mainly credibility and a better image. But, as the chemical industry had already adopted RC to improve its image, it was not so interested in the Scheme as it might have been without RC. The potential losses for industry are the costs of complying with EMAS. However, the costs to join EMAS are relatively low even for those companies which have no experience with RC nor environmental auditing.[10] An additional reason why there was relatively little lobbying may be the voluntary nature of the Scheme. Companies which were against the Scheme and would have opposed it otherwise simply did not do so because they thought that they need not join the Scheme if they do not wish to.

The reason why industry chose a co-operative approach in the second phase of the devising process was that it had achieved its main objective — a voluntary EMAS — in the first phase, and that the discussion focused now on the details of the regulation proposal. Industry hoped that in such a situation co-operation with the regulatory authorities would provide the best opportunity to influence the Scheme in its interest.

4.3 The main opponent: Germany

By contrast to the other countries German industry continued its strategy of obstruction in the second phase of the regulatory process. The reasons given by the German industry as to why it opposed the Regulation were many. EMAS does not take into account different emission standards required by different countries. The German industry perceived it as unfair that a German company which has to comply with the high environmental standards in Germany would receive the same EMAS logo as a company in another country with lower standards. The German companies also felt that it would be difficult for them to show continual improvement when they already have very good environmental technologies. Moreover, the German industry approaches environmental problems differently from the approach in EMAS. EMAS is management oriented. The idea is to improve a company's environmental performance by establishing a good environmental management system and then auditing it. As explained earlier, German industry is more engineer driven. In order to improve their environmental performance, German companies prefer to invent or install a new technology. Therefore, EMAS is alien to the culture of German companies. In this context, it is interesting to note that this does not only apply to environmental management but also to quality management. Quality management systems are much less popular in Germany than, for example, in the UK. German companies also felt that, compared to the companies in other countries, they have little to gain in terms of direct benefits such as saving energy and water from the Scheme. They claimed that they have already implemented all costs-saving environmentally friendly innovations as a result of the high awareness on environmental problems in Germany. German companies also expected to be compelled by the market to participate in the Scheme. They said that, therefore, the Scheme is *de facto* not voluntary, but mandatory. Furthermore, companies have, in general, a negative attitude towards any new development which consequences are unforeseeable and which involves uncertainty. As it will be further elaborated below, German companies were in this respect particularly worried about the verification process.

The strategy adopted by the German industry in the regulatory process was not limited to rejecting EMAS, but also to lobbying the German government to push, on a European level, for environmental measures which are present in Germany. Obviously, the aim of this strategy was to gain competitive advantages over other European firms. Whereas German companies had already implemented these measures, they would be costly for their European counterparts. The German suggestion to choose the Betriebsbeauftragtenwesen instead of EMAS and the bid by the German industry to increase the severity of environmental laws in Europe so as to harmonize EU law with German laws can all be interpreted in this context. Last, but not least, the German pressure to introduce the best available technology clause in EMAS was also an attempt to introduce more 'German' elements into the proposal. Firstly, the best available technology clause is in line with the German engineering approach and, secondly, German environmental laws require German companies to introduce the best available technology anyway.

The German government was divided on the EMAS issue. Urged by industry, the Ministry of Economics was opposed to the Regulation. Apart from a general tendency to support the interest of industry the Ministry also raised some conceptual concerns. In the context of the German 'Ordnungspolitik', it was felt that the state should only provide a framework, but should not intervene into areas regarded as the original matters of business. This means in the context of environmental policy that it is sufficient to set the right prices according to social costs and to introduce liability rules. The Ministry of the Environment adopted a positive approach towards EMAS and considered it as a useful supplement to the existing environmental policy instruments. However, as EMAS was not one of its priorities it kept a low profile in the beginning of the debate and became only more involved in the later stages (beginning 1993) during the implementation phase.

The German industry continues a strategy of obstruction in the third phase. At first glance, the reasons behind the conflict between German government and German industry are easy to understand. Industry wants to minimize the state influence, whereas the state wants to gain control. More precisely, industry and government believe that the body which controls the accreditation of the verifier can also influence the depths of the inspection whether a company fulfils all the requirements demanded by EMAS. Industry fears that the inspection supervised by a state controlled body would result in an inspection which would be too deep. On the other hand, government fears that with a pure industry controlled body the inspection would be too lax. However, it should be borne in mind that certain state influence is in the interest of industry because it provides credibility to the Scheme. Furthermore, state influence even through a state controlled accreditation body would be rather small. The state can hardly control the actual work of the verifier inside the company, i.e., the depth of the inspection. Moreover as mentioned above companies have the choice to appoint the verifier. Therefore, if a verifier controls in the eyes of a company too deeply the company has the possibility to choose another verifier the next time. In addition to that, the longer the delay in the implementation of the accreditation system, the more competitive advantages the UK environmental management and auditing consultants would have in the European auditing market.

4.4 The main supporter: the UK

The industry in the UK was in favour of EMAS and adopted a strategy of co-operation after the Scheme became voluntary. Generally speaking, the reason was that industry hoped to gain a competitive advantage. The UK was the first country to develop an environmental management system standard — the BS 7750. The BS 7750 was developed on the initiative of the UK industry by the British Standard Institute. It was drafted a few years ago and around 230 companies were involved in a pilot testing in 1992/93. The experience of the pilot testing was good and it showed that companies which participated could actually save a lot of money by saving water, raw materials, energy and waste. Now it is estimated that approximately 1000 companies are working towards implementing the BS 7750. The introduction of an environmental management standard was facilitated by the established culture of management systems in the UK. The BS 5750 and ultimately the ISO 9000 series — the international quality management standard — were very successful received by the UK companies. There are more companies in the UK registered with the ISO 9000 series than in all other countries in the world put together. As the UK industry has taken the lead on environmental management systems, it was quite keen to push it throughout Europe. The UK companies regard their experience in this sector as a competitive advantage for the UK industry in the light of the rising importance of green issues. As the experience with BS 7750 has influenced the requirements of EMAS for a management system,[11] those UK companies having experience with the BS 7750 will find it very easy to comply with EMAS.

Although the UK industry was very supportive in general, it was quite opposed to the late German amendment on best available technology. The reason was that the focus on best available technology was not in line with the UK approach which, as explained earlier, is more management driven. According to the 1990 Environmental Protection Act, UK companies must only use best available technology when its use does not entail excessive costs. Therefore, British companies regarded the best available technology clause as an additional burden which would make it potentially more expensive for them to join the Scheme.

There has been a close co-operation between industry and the government on EMAS along the whole regulatory process as the government was also in favour of the regulation. Apart from the intention to give the UK industry general support, the government felt that the idea of giving the public access to environmental information was in line with the policy of open government. Furthermore, EMAS is a market-based tool and this is also in line with the UK governmental policy. Another reason why the government supported the regulation was the advantages which the UK environmental management consultants and auditors may gain from EMAS. As an environmental management system has been developed in the UK earlier than in the other European countries, environmental management consultants and auditors in the UK are expected to have a competitive advantage in the newly developing European market of environmental management and audit consultancy. The co-operation of government and industry is shown by the fact that Her Majesty's Inspectorate of Pollution and the local authorities are now considering whether to reduce inspection of those companies participating in EMAS. This is an important incentive as companies must pay for the inspections and, therefore, less inspections mean lower costs for the companies. At the European level, the UK government has been giving EMAS considerable support since it was first released as a Consultation Document. Consequently, under its Council Presidency from July to December 1992, the government listed it as one of its priorities and made great efforts to push for its adoption.

The close co-operation between the UK government and industry continues into the implementation phase. One can identify two reasons why the implementation process is very smooth. Firstly, the UK government and industry have the most experience with environmental management systems and environmental auditing among the countries under review. Therefore, there are less doubts, fears and uncertainties which usually hinder a quick implementation process. The presence of well established and widely recognized procedures as in the case of BS 7750 also reduces potential conflicts and mistrust. Secondly, the UK wants to secure its lead in environmental management and audit consultancy. Therefore, the UK is eager to implement an accreditation system quickly.

5. SUMMARY AND OUTLOOK

The main and, as we think, most interesting features which characterize the EMAS regulatory process are the overall co-operative approach of the chemical industry once EMAS became voluntary and the differences between the UK and Germany.

The positive attitude of the chemical industry in the second phase of the devising process can only be explained in the light of the several developments which occurred in the 1980s and early 1990s. The image of the chemical industry was at a low and the chemical industry realized that a switch from a defensive to a more pro-active approach was necessary. It implemented a scheme with some similarities to EMAS, the RC initiative, and achieved, on average, positive results. Furthermore, environmental auditing was a well established management tool in the beginning of the 1990s. Without these developments, the attitude of the chemical industry towards the regulatory process would, most likely, have been much more negative.

One of the most striking aspects of the regulatory process is the contrast between Germany and the UK. Those features which made the Scheme attractive to the UK were exactly the same which made it unattractive to Germany. EMAS is management oriented. This is very much in line with the UK approach towards environmental problems but not with the German more engineer driven approach. Furthermore, EMAS does not set precise targets in terms of reduction of emissions. This is good for UK companies which tend to have higher emissions than their German counterparts. It is rather bad for German companies because their previous efforts to reduce emissions will not be appreciated. In the light of these features the attempts made by the German and the UK industry to influence the regulatory process may be interpreted as a battle to bring European environmental legislation on a path which the national industry intends to, or has to, follow anyway. As German and UK companies had either chosen or were forced by national legislation to take different approaches in handling environmental problems both tried to influence the regulation so that it would fit their respective approach. The German suggestion to choose the Betriebsbeauftragtenwesen instead of EMAS, the German attempt to introduce the best-available-technology clause, and the bid by the German industry to increase the severity of environmental laws in Europe so as to harmonize EU law with German law can all be interpreted in this context.

The extent to which companies are expected to participate in EMAS depends on the size of the companies (small companies are less likely to join the Scheme) and varies from country to country. It is expected that many companies will join the Scheme in the UK. As mentioned above, EMAS is in line with UK company culture and many companies already have experience with BS 7750. It is interesting to note that despite the resistance of German industry to EMAS, it is expected that many companies in Germany will join the Scheme. This is mainly because the compulsion in Germany for companies to have a green image is higher than in other countries. The growing popularity of the Scheme (or the increasing market pressure) may be illustrated by the demand of the Deutsche Bundesbahn to the Minister of the Environment to allow it to join the Scheme. It needs a special permission as it is not a production company but a service industry. It is expected that a medium number of companies in Italy will join the Scheme. Many companies hope that their image will be improved when they join EMAS. Compared to the other countries, not many companies in France are expected to join the Scheme. Most companies adopt a wait and see attitude as the pressure for them to join EMAS is less than in the other countries. For all countries, a snowball effect may be expected. Once a certain number of companies have joined the Scheme other companies will be forced to join it, too. The first driving force is the firm's interest to maintain a good image. The second driving force is the demand by the regulation that, in the context of company environmental policy, the environmental performances and practices of contractors, subcontractors and suppliers shall also be addressed. This will lead to a demand from those companies which are participants of the Scheme to their suppliers, contractors and subcontractors to also register with EMAS.

If EMAS becomes more popular, the question is whether the chemical industry will replace RC — a form of self-regulation — with EMAS — a form of co-regulation. As explained above, there are similarities between the two Schemes, but EMAS is more credible as it is validated by a third party. It is our opinion that, in the short run, EMAS will most probably not replace RC, but the two systems will exist together. There are two reasons to justify this belief. Firstly, RC is specific to the chemical industry, whereas EMAS covers all industrial activities. Therefore, people identify the RC as a particular effort by the chemical industry. This linkage may be regarded as an image advantage. Secondly, RC covers more activities than EMAS such as, for example, product stewardship. Therefore, not all activities of RC are replaced by EMAS. In the long run, RC might disappear. In our opinion, there are two preconditions for this to happen. The first is that the image of the chemical industry improves and therefore there is less necessity to pay particular attention to it. The second is that the state provides alternative methods for dealing with areas which are ignored by EMAS but taken into account by RC.

NOTES

1. Jürgen F. Franke, Professor of industrial economics, Institüt für Volkswirtschaftslehre, Technical University of Berlin, Sekr. WW 18, Uhlandstrasse 4-5, 10623 Berlin, Germany, tel: 493031424969; fax: 493031423708/23247.
2. Frank Wätzold, Researcher, Institüt für Volkswirtschaftslehre, Technical University of Berlin, Sekr. WW 18, Uhlandstrasse 4-5, 10623 Berlin, Germany, tel-fax: 493031423247.
3. A homogeneous terminology for the Eco-Management and Audit Scheme has not been developed yet. Throughout this chapter, it is referred to as the Scheme, the Regulation or the EMAS which is the term used by the British Standard Institute.
4. For more details see, for example, Pohle (1991).
5. See also Hillary (1994).
6. The description of the 'typical' German engineer approach and the 'typical' British management approach in the following paragraph characterizes only a tendency. In reality, of course, some form of management system and some form of environmental technology exist in UK as well as in German companies.
7. See also Hillary (1994, p.6).
8. For a more detailed description, see Hillary (1994).
9. The preconditions of effective environmental auditing are discussed in more detail in ICC (1989).
10. This is different for small companies. The role of small companies is elaborated in more detail in Franke and Wätzold (1995).
11. BS7750 and the description of an environmental management system in the Annex of the EMAS-regulation are nearly identical.

REFERENCES

CEFIC (1991), *Proceedings of the First International Workshop on Responsible Care in the Chemical Industry*, Brussels: CEFIC.
CEFIC (1993), *Responsible Care — A Chemical Industry Commitment to Improve Performance in Health, Safety and the Environment*, Brussels: CEFIC.
Franke, J.F. and F. Wätzold (1995), *The Chemical Industry and the Eco-Management and Audit Scheme*, ERIC Report for the European Commission (DG XII/D-5), TU Berlin.
Grant, W., A. Martinelli and W. Paterson (1989), 'Large Firms as Political Actors: A Comparative Analysis of the Chemical Industry in the UK, Italy and West Germany', *West European Politics*, **12**, April, pp. 72—90.

Gunningham, N. (1995), *Environment, Self-regulation and the Chemical Industry: Assessing Responsible Care*, Australian Center for Environmental Law: Environmental Law and Policy Papers.

Hillary, R. (1994), *The Eco-Management and Audit Scheme: A Practical Guide*, Oxford: Stanley Thornes Pub.

ICC (1989), *Environmental Auditing*, Paris: ICC.

European Commission (1993), *Panorama der EG-Industrie*, Brussels: European Commission.

Pohle, H. (1991), *Chemische Industrie: Umweltschutz, Arbeitsschutz, Anlagensicherheit*, Weinheim.

9. Conclusion

François Lévêque[1]

The purpose of this book has been to describe and explain the regulatory process and its outcome in the case of eleven recent pieces of EU environmental legislation. 'How is new environmental policy formed and what is the influence of industry?' is the question which we attempted to answer. Thus, the book's perspective has primarily been positive. The investigation has focused on the actual behaviour of firms and public authorities, not on the designing of optimal mechanisms to regulate. Nevertheless, the observed patterns raise interesting normative issues to be discussed.

The economic analysis of the genesis of European environmental regulations has put evidence on three main patterns.

Inter-firm competition in the market influences competition on regulation and vice versa. As a rule, the introduction of a new environmental regulation is divisive and raises conflicts between firms. The devising process of environmental regulations thus offers a new arena of competition to firms. Throughout the book the strategic use of the regulation-devising process by firms has been observed as a pervasive phenomenon. Inter-firm competition on regulation reflects competition in the market in two ways. The access to the regulatory arena depends on market structure, in particular large firms' presence prevails whereas small and medium-sized enterprises stay outside — they are pure regulation-takers. Besides, a firm's stake and preference for the outcome of the regulatory process, and subsequently its regulatory strategy, are determined by its position on the market (e.g., advantages in reputation, technology, cost). Reciprocally, inter-firm competition on regulation influences the competition in the market. The rivalry between the industry interest groups influences the outcome of the process, which in turn will influence the firms' position in the market. Environmental regulations modify technology performance, market growth in different market segments, location advantages, competitive balance between large and small firms, and so forth.

Member states compete on the future European environmental legislation. Environmental policy is not purposely set by EU countries to gain a competitive advantage. Germany is not implementing a very ambitious environmental programme primarily to boost its exportations in green technology, nor is Italy failing to enforce environmental legislation to attract foreign investments. However, during the negotiation of future EU legislation, the position of Member States at the Council conspicuously reflects their national economic interests. An alignment of interest between national authorities and industry is observed at the Brussels arena. The former have frequently appeared as the spokesmen of the latter, and conflicts between member state regulators as reflecting conflicts between national industries. When the regulated area is new (e.g., car or packaging waste recycling), and thus neither the Commission, nor the Member States have previous experience, the member state which moves first, will learn first, and its proposal is likely to strongly influence the European stage. The setting of European environmental policy triggers a race for its pre-emption.

Very significant changes, in particular a lowering of the environmental objective, are noticeable between the contents of the initial proposal and final directive. The revisions concern both the objectives of the regulation and the measures to achieve it. As a rule of thumb, the environmental objective as stated in the first draft is more stringent and ambitious than the objective that is finally retained. Moreover, one observes an enlargement of the regulatory goal to include non-environmental objectives such as employment or economic competitiveness. The revisions of the measures concern several aspects (date of compliance, means of enforcement, choice of liability, etc.), but, as a major trend, a move from mandatory towards voluntary approaches has been observed. These important changes are documented to be progressively caused by the entry and strategy of new industry interest groups and public authorities into the regulation devising process.

Such regularities raise two obvious normative concerns: Are environmental regulations captured by industry? Does environmental policy result in restriction of competition?

The transition from a positive to a normative perspective is uneasy. Our economic analysis departs from the conditions which allow assessment whether the resource allocation is efficient or not. The players of the regulatory game have been studied by considering that they are confronted with imperfect information and make their decision according to a bounded rationality. They are not purely rational economic agents who choose between a complete set of alternative options and can calculate *ex ante* the consequences of their choice. Possible outcomes are numerous and there is no reason why they would be Pareto-optimal. Assessing allocative efficiency would have required a specific investigation. The empiric test of statements such as that the final environmental objective and measures are more efficient (or inefficient) than the ones in the initial draft of the environmental directive, or that regulatory failures outweigh market failures (or the reverse) was not the purpose.

In such circumstances, there is a tendency to fall back upon *a priori* reasoning. A Chicagoan would assume that the outcome is likely to be efficient whereas environmental economists will see in our observations a confirmation that environmental policy is persistently undermined by industrialists and politics. According to the Chicago school, regulation is primarily a redistributive process where interest groups choose to influence government at the level where marginal benefit is equal to marginal cost. In essence, regulations are captured by private interests, and an efficient policy equilibrium is achieved on the regulatory market-place (see Chapter 3). On the contrary, environmental economists would view the devising process of regulation as primarily a negative phenomenon. The closest content to their prescriptions is observed for the initial proposal rather than for the final proposal. Besides, there is a widespread inclination amongst them to view policy-makers as poorly equipped in economic understanding not to say stupid bureaucrats. Our aim in the discussion below is not to impede the reader from jumping to his own conclusion according to his preferred theories but to provide him with some qualitative and pragmatic insights before jumping. We will attempt, in particular, to see how some potential regulatory failures can be limited.

It would be wrong to infer from the observed revisions of environmental regulatory proposals that environmental policy is captured by industry.

In common language, the term regulatory capture means that regulation benefits one player or pressure group. It is derived from the vision of Stigler (1971) who argued that regulation primarily serves the interest of industry. This conjecture has been falsified by the wave of deregulation of public utilities and by the growth in environmental policy. One cannot advance that environmental policy (or deregulation) primarily serves the interest of regulated firms since they strongly obstruct it. Furthermore, it must be noticed that not all claims from industry are taken into account by public authorities. One basic demand which is most often expressed by business at the beginning of the devising process is simply the dropping of the regulatory project. This complete obstruction has only been successful in one case, the European carbon/energy tax. Moreover, we demonstrated that under the generic term of industry participation and interest there are competing industrial interest groups. The acknowledgment by the regulator of a demand from a group of firms is a success for this group, but a defeat for another one. There is a large difference of appreciation when one looks only at the beginning and the end of the process, or when one observes the entire evolution of the process.

A second argument is to say that the contents of the initial proposal define, or is a good approximation of, an optimal policy and that the subsequent play of industry interest groups would transform it into an inefficient one. To put it in a caricatural picture, the devising process would be interpreted as a deformation of a theoretically sound model to a final proposal *entachée* with bureaucratic red tape and special interests unrelated to environment issues. The evolution of the carbon/energy taxation would be a typical illustration. As mentioned above the standards of proof to validate or invalidate such a statement are difficult to grasp, not to say impossible. The initial environmental objective is more stringent that the one that is finally adopted, but there is no reason to believe that the former one is closer to the optimum of pollution than the latter. The initial pollution reduction target is not fixed on the basis of a cost-benefit analysis as recommended by textbooks in environmental economics. The benefits of pollution abatement whose valuation raises the problem of non-market value, are not known. Even a second-best perspective assessment is unachievable. The cost of the measures as included in the first proposal and in the final one cannot be compared for they correspond to different environmental objectives.

A more optimistic view can be proposed about these revisions in proposals. Before the beginning of the devising process, a pollution concern has raised a public interest. The first regulatory proposal is the reification of this interest. At the end of the process the objective is lowered and mixed with other public goals. It may be conjectured that the devising process reveals the respective weight of the environment in comparison to other legitimate public concerns such as competitiveness, employment, trade liberalization, etc. The process would ensure a sort of compatibility between different public goals as an alternative to an *ex ante* economic valuation where job losses of fishermen and benefits of preserving blue whales would be aggregated in monetary terms.

A less radical vision of capture is provided by Laffont and Tirole (1991 and 1993) and by Foster (1992). It argues that the potential for capture is pervasive but is generally mitigated by institutional arrangements. Collusion is only the tip of the iceberg. The bigger part is the organizational response to prevent regulatory abuse. The capture of regulator by regulated is rooted in informational asymmetries. The devising phase of regulation is aimed at clearing the asymmetries. Within this theoretical perspective the revisions of the proposal would materialize the increase in the information of the regulator and counterparts provided to firms to encourage their participation and communication. The relevant issue is therefore to identify a possible solution to limit the potential of capture, and regulatory failures in general, rather than to demonstrate whether a firm's involvement in the regulatory process distorts the allocative efficiency of environmental policy.

Two policy relevant implications may be addressed. Public authorities, in particular the European Commission, must ensure the access to regulation of all industrial interests and promote competition between industry interest groups. A pattern of under-representation of certain groups of firms has been observed and explained throughout the book. It concerns mainly small and medium-sized enterprises and potential winners. Public authorities may encourage the entry of these participants by providing them with financial incentives. Promoting rivalry between interest groups is critical. It reduces the obstruction of industry as a whole and increases the information of the regulator.

The potential risk of competition distortion due to environmental policy is high. If policy-makers do not care, an environmental gain in pollution reduction might be easily associated with a loss in inter-firm competition.

Several examples have been documented by case studies. For instance, an extention of innovation protection in the new pesticide regulation allows an increase in environmental performances of products but also strengthens the monopolistic positions of major agro-chemical producers. Similarly, the proximity principle in limiting traffic of hazardous waste reduces the risk of environmental damage but increases the local monopoly on waste facilities. The risk of distortion is rooted in the behaviour of the players in the regulatory game. Firms enter the game to reduce the absolute abatement cost but also to obtain a relative competitive advantage on parties which are outside the game. Moreover, national representatives act frequently in the Brussels arena as spokesmen of national industry. Finally, the environmental regulator has incentives to offer a gain in the market arena as a counterpart provided to firms to communicate their information and stop their obstruction to the project.

Limitation of the potential competition distortion is not uneasy to achieve in public regulation when the regulator ensures the access to regulation of all industrial interest groups and promotes rivalry between industry interest groups as required for limiting potential capture. It is more difficult to achieve in the case of voluntary approaches. In self-regulation (e.g., the Responsible Care Programme exemplified in Chapter 8) and co-regulation (e.g., car and packaging waste regulation documented in Chapter 7), the measures to achieve the environmental objective are set by firms themselves. The regulator is confronted with a single industry interest group, eventually a regulatory network grouping several industries (e.g., suppliers, car manufacturers, shredders, recyclers). In this case, promoting rivalry between firms endangers the collective action of firms and poses a threat to the public good that it supplies (e.g., collective learning in abatement technology, network economies in waste collection, or reputation in environmental performances labelling). The risk of limitation of potential competition is high and has to be monitored.

The allocation of liability is critical. A policy-relevant conclusion is that the liable industry must be preferably selected as the one whose competitive stakes are the lowest on the issue. In France, packaging waste liability has been put on the shoulders of conditioners. In Germany liability has been put on the shoulders of retailers. Conditioners prefer a *status quo* with respect to relative prices of different materials. Their investments in using specific materials are partly sunk. On the contrary, food retailers are neutral *vis-à-vis* material substitution. As a result, in France, unlike Germany, the recovery and recycling scheme, in particular the fee system, is organized to prevent an intense competition in environmental performance of materials; it is likely that market shares between materials would not significantly change owing to the new regulation. A second recommendation is that specialized authorities in charge of competition policy, like DG IV at the European stage, would be more involved in horizontal discussions of environmental policies.

Environmental policies are growing in number worldwide. This pattern is associated with a regulatory reform. Regulatory methods and instruments are changing. More emphasis is being put on dialogue and consultation with concerned parties, on industry participation in defining the measures to reduce pollution and on market-based instruments.

The environmental regulatory reform is rooted in the recognition of some limitations in the command-and-control approach and shortcomings in implementation and enforcement. The European Union has been amongst the first to experiment with this new regulatory regime. However, it is a recent, on-going process. New, unexpected difficulties are likely to occur in the future as, for instance, the monitoring of potential competition distortion related to voluntary approaches. Whether the reform will succeed in overcoming the limitations of the old regulatory regime and implementing more cost-effective environmental policies remains an open question. A historical perspective is lacking.

In analytical terms, it is recognized that limiting potential regulatory failures is a necessary complementary strand of correcting the environmental externalities caused by market failures. Public intervention is not without cost and is restrained by informational and institutional constraints. Environmental economics has specialized in comparing policy instruments and valuating environmental non marketed goods. It improves the first draft of environmental policy. Reflecting and suggesting methods to improve the interactive process of devising regulation which transforms the draft to a final version has became as important. To paraphrase A. Kahn,[2] one would say that the regulating of pollution is not just a marginal environmental benefit to calculate.

NOTES

1. François Lévêque, Professor of economics, Deputy Director of CERNA, Centre of Industrial Economics, Ecole Nationale Supérieure des Mines de Paris, 60, bld St Michel, 75272 Paris Cedex 06, France, tel: 33140519091/9071; fax: 33144071046.
2. A. Kahn is a former chairman of the Civil Aeronautics Board. He championed deregulation in the US airlines and used to say that airplanes are not just marginal cost with wings.

REFERENCES

Foster, C.D. (1992), *Privatization, Public Ownership and the Regulation of Natural Monopoly*, Oxford: Basil Blackwell.

Laffont, J.J. and J. Tirole (1991), 'The Politics of Government Decision-Making: A Theory of Regulatory Capture', *The Quarterly Journal of Economics*, **LVI**(4), pp. 1089—1127.

Laffont, J.J. and J. Tirole (1993), *A Theory of Incentives in Procurement and regulation,* Cambridge Mass.: MIT Press.
Stigler, G.J. (1971), 'The Theory of Economic Regulation', *Bell Journal of Economic and Management Science,* **2**, pp. 3—21.

Index

ACEA (Association des Constructeurs Européens d'Automobiles) 152
acid rain 76, 84, 89
ACORD (Automotive Consortium on Recycling and Disposal) 153, 155, 158–9, 161, 171
Aggeri, F. 48, 155, 156, 157
agrochemical industry
   competition in 54–9
     and environment 57–9
     features 54–7
   cost of compliance 68–9
   leading companies 55
Agrow 65
Aimeri (firm) 117
Air Quality Directives (80/779, 85/203) 6
air quality policies 26–7
   public regulation in 44–5
aluminium: price of 164
American Cyanamid (firm) 55
ANRED 163
Association des Constructeurs Européens d'Automobiles (ACEA) 152
Association Française des Entreprises pour l'Environment 47
Audit scheme Regulation (93/1836) 6, 10, 28–9
Australia 18
automobiles *see* motor-vehicles
Automotive Consortium on Recycling and Disposal (ACORD) 153, 155, 158–9, 161, 171

Barnett, A. 81
Basel (Switzerland) incident (1984) 45, 177
BASF (firm) 55, 87
Baumol, W.J. 33, 34
Bayer (firm) 25, 40–1, 55

BDI (Federation of German Industry) 22, 102, 165
Becker, G.S. 38
Belgium: carbon/energy tax proposal 98
Bertossi, Paolo 113–42
Beverage recycling directive (85/339) 11, 13
Bhopal (India) incident (1984) 45, 177
Biffa (firm) 118
BMW (firm) 158
Boehmer-Christiansen, S.A. 86
Boehringer Ingelheim case 178–9
Bonazzi, C. 56
Bouygues-Saur (firm) 116
BP (firm) 81, 82
British Standard 7750 on environmental management 187, 194–5
Browning Ferries International (firm) 117, 118
Brusco, Sebastiano 113–42

Canadian Chemical Producer's Association 179
carbon emission regulations 26–7, 76
   and carbon/energy tax 95–6, 100–1
   and EMAS 176
   public regulation 44–5
   in regulatory game 33, 43
carbon/energy tax proposal 94–104
   and climatic change 95–6
   development of 96–9
     Commission's role 95, 96–8
     Council of Ministers' role 95, 98–9
   impact on business 99
   lessons learned 103–4
   overview 94–5
   in regulatory game 20–1, 22
   regulatory process 100–3
     business on 100–2
     industry on 100–3
Carson, Rachel 177

CBI (Confederation of British Industry) 22, 102
CEFIC *see* European chemical industry association
Central Electricity Generating Board (CEGB, UK) 88–9, 90–1, 93
Centre of Exploitation of Science and Technology (CEST) 149, 151, 158
CFF (firm) 27
chemical industry: and EMAS 176–9
    role of 192
Chemical Industry Associations (CIA, UK) 181
chlorothalonil (pesticide) 56–7
Christian Democratic Union (Germany) 86
Christian Social Union (Germany) 86
Chrysalis Environmental Consulting 45
Ciba-Geigy (firm) 55
climatic change
    and carbon/energy tax proposal 95–6
    and combustion emission regulations 104–5
Coase, R. 34, 36
co-disposal in landfilling 132, 137
COFRAC (Comité Français d'Accréditation) 189
Cohesion Funds 98–9
combined cycle gas turbines (CCGT) 80, 83, 84, 92
combustion emission regulations 12–13, 75–111
    carbon/energy tax *see* carbon/energy tax proposal
    and climatic change 104–5
    electricity generation 78–81
    integration pollution prevention and control 105–6
    large combustion plants *see* Large Combustion Plant Directive
    nitrogen 12, 23, 27, 28
    oil refining 81–4
    sulphur 12, 16, 23, 27, 28
        in liquid fuels 106–7
    trends in 104
Comité Français d'Accréditation (COFRAC) 189
command and control regulations 18, 33
    and EMAS 178

commodity manufacturers in pesticide registration (1994–) 66–8
    entry barriers to 56–7
    issues 66–8
    outcomes 68
Common Agricultural Policy 61
Compagnie Française de Ferrailles (CCF) 157
competition
    in agrochemical industry 54–9
    and environment 57–9
    features 54–7
    distortion and environmental policy 204–5
    and future legislation 201–2
    inter-firm, and regulation 24–6, 201
    in landfilling 25
    in waste policies 24–6
compliance costs
    agrochemical industry 68–9
    waste disposal 124–5
    in waste industry regulation 123–6
Confederation of British Industry (CBI) 22, 102
Control of Pollution Act (UK, 1970) 115, 121
Controlled Waste Regulations (UK, 1992) 127
co-regulation 48–50
Cottica, Alberto 113–42
Council of Ministers 9, 11, 20–1
    and carbon/energy tax proposal 95, 98–9
    and LCP directive 77, 84–5
credibility problem in self-regulation 46

Daimler-Benz (firm) 158
de Hond, F. 157
Denmark
    carbon/energy tax proposal 98
    and Large Combustion Plant Directive 13
    in pesticide registration 61, 62
DowElanco (firm) 55
Drinking Water Directive (COM 80/778) 60, 64
Dual System Deutschland (waste disposal) 24, 48–9, 126, 128, 135, 167–8

Index

DuPont de Nemours (firm) 40–1, 44, 55, 57

ECCA (European Crop Care association) 66, 67, 68
Eco Emballage SA 24, 127, 167
Eco-management and audit scheme Regulation (93/1836) 6, 10, 28–9, 175–99
  background to 176–82
  and chemical industry 176–9
  environmental auditing 182
  registration in 183–4
  regulatory process 183–90
    analysis of 190–6
      CEFIC and chemical industry 191–2
      European Commission 190–1
      German opposition to 192–4
      UK support for 194–6
    devising
      consultation 185–6
      proposals 186–8
    implementation 188–90
  and Responsible Care 179–82
  scheme explained 183–5
Economic and Financial Affairs Council (ECOFIN) 95, 98
Economic and Social Committee of European Parliament 187
Eco-tax Proposal (92/226) 6, 17, 20, 26
ECPA (European Crop Protection association) 58–9, 65–6, 67, 69
Edelhoff (firm) 116, 118
Electricité de France (EdF) 79, 116
electricity generation, Europe 78–81
  national differences 79–80
  role of supply industry 78–9
  technology in 80–1
EMAS *see* Eco-management and audit scheme Regulation
End of life (ELV) of motor-vehicles Proposal 6, 21, 24
  and recycling 150, 152–3, 155
End of life (ELV) of motor-vehicles Project Group 161
ENEL (Italy) 79, 92
enforcement issues in waste industry regulation 123–6
ENI (firm) 81, 82, 92

Enichem (firm) 157
Environment Council of European Parliament 95, 188
environmental auditing in EMAS 182
environmental economics 33–4
environmental legislation, future 201–2
Environmental Protection Act (UK, 1990) 117, 127
Environmental Protection Agency (USA) 182
Environmental Protection Regulations (UK, 1992) 127
environmental regulations
  ante-Maastricht 10–13
    and economic policy 12
    technical standards 12–13
    unanimity requirements 13
  changing methods 1–2
  consultation and negotiation 1
  European fabric of 9–30
  failures in 2–3
  firms involved in 2
  genesis of 19–29
    firms, entry into process 26–8
    initial and final proposals 28–9
    inter-firm competition 24–6
    players in 19–22
    rivalry 22–4
  and market structure 3
  new regulatory framework 16–19
    command and control regulation 18, 33
    conduct regulation 17
    externalities in 16–17
    stakeholder consultation procedures 17–18
  post-Maastricht 13–15
  and textbook examples 2
European chemical industry association (CEFIC) 102–3
  and EMAS 180, 182, 186
  role of in environmental auditing 191–2
European Commission
  and access to regulation 204
  and carbon/energy tax proposal 44–5, 95, 96–8, 105
  and EMAS 177–8, 184, 190–1
    devising process 185–6
  and landfilling standards 132

and LCP directive 84–5, 87–8, 93, 94
on motor-vehicle recycling 152–3
on packaging waste recycling regulations 165
and pesticide regulation 60–1, 64–5, 67
and regulatory regimes 9, 11, 15, 16, 20
European Court of Justice 11
European Crop Care association (ECCA) 66, 67, 68
European Crop Protection association (ECPA) 58–9, 65–6, 67, 69
European federation of waste management (FEAD) 137
European Industrial and Employers' Federation (UNICE) 22, 100
European Parliament 11
and EMAS 187–8
and LCP directive 77
European Union, Treaty on 16–19
externalities
in environmental economics 34–5, 36
in environmental regulations 16–17
Exxon (firm) 81

FEAD (European federation of waste management) 137
Federal Economics Ministry (Germany) 86–7
Federal Environment Office (UBA, Germany) 86
Federation of German Industry (BDI) 22, 102, 165
Ferguson, E.T. 147
Fiat (firm) 157, 158
firms
entry into regulatory process 26–8
involved in regulatory process 2
large, in waste industry 25, 119, 133–5, 136, 137
regulation, involvement in 39–44
and distribution of regulatory stakes 41, 42
gain and losses 42
and level of regulatory stakes 41, 42
objectives of 40–1
strategies 43–4
and uncertainty 41–2

small and medium-sized
as players in regulatory game 19–20
in waste industry 25, 136
in waste industry 118–19
competition in 133–6
future of 140–1
and policy 136–40
and regulatory agencies 132–41
Fisia (firm) 117
Flixborough (UK) incident (1974) 177
flue gas desulphurization (FGD) 80, 86, 91, 92–3
forest dieback 76, 84, 85, 86
Foster, C.D. 37, 204
Framework Convention on Climate Change (FCCC) 85, 104
France
carbon/energy tax proposal 99
domestic waste production 162
electricity supply industry 80, 81
EMAS, implementation of 189
landfills in 131, 136
and Large Combustion Plant Directive 87, 92
motor-vehicles
disposal policies 21–2, 24, 27
end of life (ELV) of 155–7
recycling regulations
developments in 155–8
voluntary agreements 145
voluntary agreements in recycling 157, 160–1
oil refining industry 82
and packaging waste policies 24, 26, 205
recycling regulations 166–7
in pesticide registration 62
self-regulation in industrial wastes 47
sulphur emission regulations 91
waste industry
1970s 114–15
mid-1990s 116–17
firms in 118–19, 134
laws and regulations 122–3
recycling 120, 127, 128
Franke, Jürgen 175–99
Free Democratic Party (Germany) 86
free-rider problem in self-regulation 46

Index

Gabel, H. 44
Gas Oil directives (75/716, 87/219) 12
gas oils, sulphur in 12, 28
Générale des Eaux (firm) 116, 118, 131, 133, 137
German Society of Engineers (VDI) 86
Germany
  air quality policies 27
  carbon/energy tax proposal 98
  combustion emission regulation process 85–7
  domestic waste production 162
  electricity supply industry 79, 80, 81
    and Large Combustion Plant Directive 86
  and EMAS 175, 186–7
    implementation of 188–9
    opposition to 192–4
  gas oil legislation 12
  and Large Combustion Plant Directive 13, 23, 86, 87, 92
  liability allocation 205
  motor-vehicles
    disposal policies 21, 24, 27, 150
    end of life (ELV) of 155
    recycling regulations
      developments in 154–5
      voluntary agreements 145
    voluntary agreements in recycling 155, 160–1
  oil refining industry 82
  and packaging waste policies 24, 28
    co-regulation in 48, 49
    recycling regulations 165–6
  pesticide registration in 61, 62
  in Responsible Care programme 180–1
  sulphur emission regulations 86, 91
  waste industry
    1970s 114
    mid-1990s 116
    firms in 118–19, 134
    laws and regulations 122–3
    recycling 120, 126–7, 128
GIFAP (Groupement International des Associations Nationales de Fabricants de Produits Agrochimiques) 60, 61
Glachant, Matthieu 33, 143–74
glass: price of 164

Greece: carbon/energy tax proposal 98–9
Green Parties 11, 61
Gronewegen, P. 157
Groupement International des Associations Nationales de Fabricants de Produits Agrochimiques (GIFAP) 60, 61
Gunningham, N. 45, 46, 47, 182

Hannequart, J.P. 11
Hatchuel, A. 155, 156, 157
Hoechst (firm) 55
Hourcade, J.C. 44

ICI (firm) 157
Ikwue, Antony 75–111
incineration 119
  technical standards for 130–1
  waste-to-energy (WTE) 131, 137
  see also Municipal waste facilities directives; waste industry
Industrial Federation of Intensive Energy Consumers (IFIEC) 22
industrial interest groups 22
information
  asymmetry of
    in market failures 35, 36
    in pesticide regulation 59
  costs, in self-regulation 47
Institute for European Environmental Policy (IEEP) 10, 18
integrated gasification combined cycle (IGCC) 80, 83, 92
Integrated Pollution Prevention and Control (IPPC) 105–6
International Chamber of Commerce (ICC) 22, 102, 182
  and EMAS 182, 185–6
International Council of Chemical Associations (ICCA) 180
International Standards Organization 9000 quality management standards 195
Ireland
  carbon/energy tax proposal 98–9
  and Large Combustion Plant Directive 13
  in pesticide registration 62
ISK (firm) 56–7

Italy
  carbon/energy tax proposal 98
  electricity supply industry 79, 81
  EMAS, implementation of 189
  and Large Combustion Plant Directive 13, 87, 92
  oil refining industry 81–3
  sulphur emission regulations 91
  waste industry
    1970s 115
    mid-1990s 117
    firms in 118–19, 135
    laws and regulations 122–3
    recycling 120, 126

Kahn, A. 206
Kahneman, O. 42
Kay, J. 17
Keeler, T.E. 38

Laffont, J.J. 204
landfilling 119
  competition in 25, 136
  levy on 131
  and packaging waste 162
  technical standards for 132
  see also Municipal waste facilities directives
Large Combustion Plant Directive (88/609) 6, 12–13, 23–4
  and EU regulation process 76–7, 87–91
    1984–85 88–90
    1986–87 90
    agreement on 90–1
  German regulation process 85–7
  lessons from 93–4
  overview 84–5
  regulation process, member states 91–3
  revisions to 106
Leigh (firm) 118, 137
Lévêque, François 1–8, 59, 201–7
  on environmental regulations 9–30
  on regulatory game 31–51
Little, A.D. 83, 182
Local Authority Waste Disposal Companies (LAWDCs, UK) 118
Local Government Act (UK, 1988) 118
Luxembourg: carbon/energy tax proposal 98

Lyonnaise des Eaux (firm) 116, 118, 133, 137

Maastricht, Treaty of
  environmental regulations after 13–15
    co-decision procedures 14
    subsidiarity in 14
  environmental regulations before 10–13
    and economic policy 12
    technical standards 12–13
    unanimity requirements 13
Manutencoop (firm) 117
market failures in regulatory economics 34–7
market incentives in self-regulation 46
Marshall, Lord Walter 88, 89
Mobil (firm) 81
monopolies
  natural in market failures 35
  in self-regulation 47
Monsanto (firm) 55, 57
motor-vehicles
  disposal and recycling of 21, 24, 28
    co-regulation in 48–9
    current processes 149
    dismantling, degree of 150
    regulations 147–61
      chain of influence 147–50
      developments and responses 152–60
      outcomes 160–1
      regulatory scene 150–2
      shredder margins and costs 151
  End of life (ELV) of
    Proposal 6, 21, 24
    and recycling 150, 152–3
    materials flowchart 148
municipal waste disposal regulation (Italy, 1982) 121
Municipal waste facilities directives (89/369, 89/429) 6, 23
  SMEs in 19
  technical standards in 130–1

NACCB (National Accreditation Council for Certification Bodies) 189–90
Nadaï, A. 47, 53–73

National Accreditation Council for Certification Bodies (NACCB) 189–90
National Association of Waste Disposal Authorities (NAWDA, UK) 137
National Power (UK) 79, 92–3
Netherlands
  carbon/energy tax proposal 98
  and Large Combustion Plant Directive 13
  in pesticide registration 62
nitrogen emission regulations 12, 23, 27, 76
  and EMAS 176
Noll, R.G. 41
'Not In My Back Yard' (NIMBY) syndrome 124, 125, 138
Nuclear Electric (UK) 79

Oates, W.E. 33, 34
oil refining, Europe 81–4
  energy policy 83–4
  national differences 82
  technology in 82–3
Olson, M. 38, 41
Organization for Economic Cooperation and Development (OECD) 105, 119, 120
Oster, S. 40
Otto (firm) 116
Owen, B.M. 41

packaging waste
  co-regulation in 48, 49
  domestic waste production 162
  policies 24, 26, 28
  recycling regulations 162–70
    analysis of 168–70
    context of 162–4
    organization and outcome 167–8
    regulatory initiatives 164–7
  secondary materials, prices 164
  SMEs in 19–20
  waste chain 163
Packaging waste directive (94/62) 6, 164–5, 166
paper & cardboard: price of 164
Paper recycling recommendation (81/972) 10

Pareto optimality in resource allocation 35, 36, 202
patent protection in agrochemical industry 55–6
  duration of 69–70
  end of patent 56
  protecting 57, 70
  extension of 65
Pearce Report (UK) 131
pesticide registration 53–73
  competition in agrochemical industry 54–9
  and environment 57–9
  features 54–7
  regulatory process in EU 60–70
    commodity manufacturers in (1994–) 66–8, 69
      issues 66–8
      outcomes 68
      dynamics of 68–70
    features 60–70
    regulatory compromise (1976–1991) 61–3, 69
    speciality manufacturers in (1991–1994) 64–6, 69
      issues at stake 64–5
      outcomes 65–6
    review process, task forces for 67
Pesticide Registration directives (91/414, 94/43) 6
  in regulatory compromise 61–3
    aspects 62–3
  in regulatory process 60, 66
pesticides 28–9
  life-cycle of 56
  profile of 58
  public regulation 44
Peugot (firm) 27, 157
Pigou, A.C. 34, 36
Political Union, Treaty on 13, 15
polluter pays principle in waste disposal 126–7, 128
Portugal
  carbon/energy tax proposal 98–9
  and Large Combustion Plant Directive 13
PowerGen (UK) 79, 92–3
pressurized fluidized bed combustion 80
pressurized water reactors 80

Priority Waste Stream groups 145, 152, 155, 160
privatization: electricity supply industry 78–9, 90–1
Programme of Action (fifth) 10–12, 14, 17
  carbon/energy tax proposal 96
  and EMAS 185
  and Large Combustion Plant Directive 93–4
PSA (firm) 157, 158
public authorities
  as players in regulatory game 20
  policy instruments of 33
public intervention in self-regulation 46–7
public regulation 44–5

Quirion, P. 162

recycling law (Italy, 415/1988) 126
recycling regulations 143–74
  automotive disposal process 147–61
    chain of influence 147–50
    developments and responses 152–60
    outcomes 160–1
    regulatory scene 150–2
  packaging 162–70
    analysis of 168–70
    context of 162–4
    organization and outcome 167–8
    regulatory initiatives 164–7
  societal importance of 146–7
  in waste industry 120, 126
regulation
  combustion emission *see* combustion emission regulations
  economics of 35, 38–9
  and inter-firm competition 24–6, 201
  lower environmental objectives in 202–4
  modes of 44–50
    co-regulation 48–50
    public 44–5
    self-regulation 45–8
  pesticides *see* pesticide polices; pesticide registration
  waste industry *see* waste industry regulation

regulators
  and competition distortion 205
  in environmental economics 34
  incentives systems 36–7
  own agenda of 37
  pesticide, expectations of 58–9
  and regulatory capture 37–8
  and regulatory failures 36–7
regulatory capture 37–8, 203–4
regulatory game 31–51, 202
  firm's involvement 39–44
    industry's involvement 41–4
    objectives of 40–1
  in pesticide registration 68–9
  theory 33–9
regulatory stakes
  and regulation, involvement in distribution of 41, 42
    gain and losses 42
    level of 41, 42
    uncertainty of 41–2
Renault (firm) 157, 158
research and development 25
  in agrochemical industry 54, 56, 57–8
Responsible Care programme 45–6
  and EMAS 179–82, 192
Rethmann (firm) 116
Rhône-Poulenc (firm) 25, 55
Rome, Treaty of 10, 187
Rover (firm) 158
RWE Entsorgung (firm) 80, 116

Sandoz (firm) 55
Schering (firm) 55
self-regulation 45–8, 205
Seveso (Italy) incident (1976) 12, 177
Shanks & McEwan (firm) 118
Shell (firm) 81, 82
Single European Act (1986) 10–11, 187
Skea, J. 16, 75–111
Social Democratic Party (Germany) 86
Sorain Cecchini (firm) 117
Spain
  carbon/energy tax proposal 98–9
  and Large Combustion Plant Directive 13
speciality manufacturers
  in agrochemical industry 55
  in pesticide registration process (1991–1994) 64–6

issues at stake 64–5
  outcomes 65–6
stakeholders consultation procedures
    17–18
Staudt, E. 162
Stigler, G. 37–8, 203
STOA 104
Stockholm Conference on the Human
    Environment (1972) 10
strategic game *see* regulatory game
sulphur emission regulations 12, 16, 23,
    27, 28, 76
  and EMAS 176
  in Germany 86, 91
  in large combustion plant directive
    88–91
  in liquid fuels 82–3, 106–7
Supplementary Protection Certificate
    (SPC, on patents) 65, 66, 68

Telster, L.G. 47
Thatcher, Margaret 88
tin plate: price of 164
Tirole, J. 39, 204
'Towards Sustainability' Programme
    14–15
Traffic of Waste regulation (93/259) 10

UNICE (European Industrial and
    Employers' Federation) 22, 100
Uniform Principles (EC) 64
Union of Industrial and Employers'
    Confederations of Europe (UNICE)
    100
United Kingdom
  carbon/energy tax proposal 99
  electricity supply industry 79, 80, 81
  and EMAS 176, 187
    implementation of 189–90
    support for 194–6
  and Large Combustion Plant Directive
    13, 23, 88–9, 90–3, 94
  motor-vehicles
    voluntary agreements in waste
      recycling 159, 160–1
  motor-vehicles recycling regulations
    developments in 158–60
    end of life (ELV) 155–7
  oil refining industry 82, 83–4
  in pesticide registration 62

  in Responsible Care programme 181
  sulphur emission regulations 88–9,
    91
  waste industry
    1970s 115
    mid-1990s 117–18
    firms in 118–19, 133, 134
    landfill levy 131
    landfill standards 132
    laws and regulations 122–3
    recycling 120, 127
United Nations Conference on Environ-
    ment and Development (UNCED)
    95, 100

Valerco (firm) 157
VDEW (German electricity trade
    association) 86
Verband der Chemischen Industrie
    (VCI) 180
Vickers, J. 17
voluntary agreements in waste recycling
    144–5, 147, 171–2
  motor-vehicles 153, 155, 157, 159,
    160–1
  packaging waste recycling regulations
    169
Volvo (firm) 158

Waste Collection Authority (WCA, UK)
    115, 118, 121
waste directives (75/442, 91/156) 11, 13,
    126
Waste Disposal Act (Germany, 1972)
    121
Waste Disposal Authority (WDA, UK)
    115, 118, 121, 123
waste industry regulation 113–42
  1970s 114–15
  mid-1990s 116–18
  firms in 118–19, 132–41
    competition in 133–6
    future of 140–1
    and policy 136–40
  incineration 119
  landfilling 119, 136
  policies 24–6
    competition in 24–6
    self-regulation in 47
  recycling in 120, 126

regulatory agencies in 132–41
    and competition 133–6
    future of 140–1
    and policy 136–40
regulatory process 120–9
    changing markets 128–9
    enforcement issues 123–6
    laws and regulations 122
    new configuration 120–3
    new principles 126–9
technical standards 130–2

Waste Management (firm) 117, 118, 131, 133, 137
Waste Regulation Authorities (WRA, UK) 123, 126
waste-to-energy incineration 131, 137
Wätzold, Frank 175–99
Weitzman, M.L. 34
welfare economics 34
Whiston, Thomas 143–74

Zeneca (firm) 55

DATE DUE

NOV 0 6 2011			

Demco, Inc. 38-293